The Poetry of Petrarch

TRANSLATED BY DAVID YOUNG

PETRARCH *(Francesco Petrarca, 1304–74) is widely considered the first modern poet; his lyric works, especially the sonnet, established Italian as a literary language and inspired Chaucer, Shakespeare, and Spenser.*

DAVID YOUNG *is Emeritus Longman Professor of English at Oberlin College. He is the author of nine volumes of poetry, most recently* At the White Window, *and has translated Rainer Maria Rilke, Miroslav Holub, and numerous Tang Dynasty poets.*

The Poetry of Petrarch

The Poetry

of Petrarch

Translated and with

an introduction by

David Young

Farrar, Straus and Giroux

New York

FARRAR, STRAUS AND GIROUX

19 Union Square West, New York 10003

Translation and introduction
copyright © 2004 by David Young
Distributed in Canada by Douglas & McIntyre Ltd.
Printed in the United States of America
Published in 2004 by Farrar, Straus and Giroux
First paperback edition, 2005

The Library of Congress has cataloged
the hardcover edition as follows:

Petrarca, Francesco, 1304–1374
[Rime. English. Selections]
The poetry of Petrarch / translated by David Young.— 1st ed.
p. cm.
Includes index.
ISBN 0-374-23532-5 (alk. paper)
I. Young, David, 1936– II. Title.

PQ4496.E23 2004
851'.1—dc22

2003060844

Paperback ISBN-13: 978-0-374-52961-1
Paperback ISBN-10: 0-374-52961-2

Designed by Quemadura

www.fsgbooks.com

1 3 5 7 9 10 8 6 4 2

Contents

Petrarch: An Introduction

Time is our delight and our prison. It binds all human beings together, since we all share the pleasures and burdens of memory, and we all know the anticipation of cherished goals and the dark prospect of personal mortality. While the problem of living in time is a long-standing preoccupation among philosophers, theologians, and storytellers, in some respects the exploration of temporality might be seen as the special province of lyric poetry, which records moments of heightened awareness in the temporal process and can accumulate a rich and moving record of an individual's lifelong engagement with time. Lyric poetry both submits to temporality and resists it. Individual poems draw themselves away from the temporal flow, and collections of lyric poems, while they may reflect experience and composition over time, also tend to resist the demands of story, history, and biography.

Francesco Petrarca, known simply as Petrarch, who lived from 1304 to 1374, stands out as a powerful and original lyric poet, particularly for his ability to portray the individual consciousness, examining its subjection to time and inventing strategies to overcome that subjection. Petrarch's *rime sparse*, "scattered rhymes," as he calls them in the opening sonnet of his great collection, revived a practice from the classical world (for instance, the odes of Horace) and fashioned an important paradigm for the modern world. The body of his work, written in the vernacular language of his native Italy and carefully arranged to reflect the chronology and psychology of his own life, became a powerful example of the way that incomplete and even contradictory particles of experience— his own nickname for his collection was *Rerum vulgarium fragmenta,* "fragments of matters in common speech"—could accumulate to sketch out a powerful story without following the conventions of narrative.

He made this the work of a lifetime, adding to the manuscript and revising its contents over some forty-seven years. The earliest poems date from around the time he fell in love with Laura, in 1327, and the latest were composed in the last year of his life, 1374. Many readers may have a passing acquaintance with the poet, based on a few anthology pieces or the famous versions of Wyatt and Surrey, while being quite unaware of the scope and intricacy of the finished sequence. It is a formidable work for a reader, given its length and its emotional and moral complexity, but it ranks with other literary masterpieces in terms of the concomitant rewards it offers, rewards that have been obscured by its spectacular success, both in its own time and place and as a model to poets of the centuries that followed.

While long interested in the literature of the Middle Ages and the Renaissance, I ignored Petrarch for many years for two reasons that I suspect are widely shared: the difficulty of the medieval Italian, which is just different enough to isolate Petrarch even from modern readers of his own language; and the impression that what was attractive in the sonnet sequences of subsequent practitioners was their introduction of non-Petrarchan and even anti-Petrarchan elements. That last opinion has been especially harmful, so it is worth stating here, boldly and emphatically, that what we love in the sonnets of Shakespeare and Sidney and Spenser, among others, is in large part a reflection of their having absorbed and continued Petrarch's powerful example. They may occasionally repudiate some aspects of stale Petrarchan rhetoric ("My mistress' eyes are nothing like the sun"), but their subjects and structures, their thoughtful portrayals of the self, immersed in love and time, all owe their considerable power to the master's originating example. As that recognition dawned for me, I knew I had no choice but to try to produce a modern version of this neglected masterpiece.

I feel as though I am recovering a lost treasure, partly because Ezra Pound and T. S. Eliot, who had such a hand in shaping twentieth-century tastes in poetry, embraced Dante and repudiated Petrarch, when in fact a better acquaintance with the latter would probably have benefited the work of both. Trying to produce a clone of the *Divine Comedy* in our world makes very little sense, really. Understanding the structural and stylistic lessons of the *rime sparse*, by contrast, is still very much worth a poet's while. If the high modernists did not quite know how to value Petrarch, their heirs, the postmodernists, ought to be quick to recognize his relevance. Like them, he is distracted, playful, eclectic, and many-minded.

The body of poetry he organized is essentially a love story, one marked by failure and frustration in life and an expectation of something better after death. It reflects the originating example of St. Augustine, in his

Confessions, documenting the moral and spiritual growth of an individual through the painful lessons of experience, a process of maturing and aging by means of frustration, error, and loss. But Petrarch was not simply reiterating the Augustinian experience, nor was he tied to Dante's example, in the *Vita Nuova,* of conversion, through love of a woman, to a knowledge of and union with God. Dante's account is securely didactic and spiritual, partly because he arranged his sonnets in a useful order and then connected them with prose commentary that both narrates their circumstances and expounds their meanings. By dropping the prose passages between poems, Petrarch, as several commentators have pointed out, opened his sequence to more meanings and less interpretive constraint.*

Furthermore, while his story shapes itself to a Christian conclusion, its world is far more secular, more richly ambivalent, than that of any predecessor. It both celebrates and condemns eroticism, making the beauty of this earthly life an enticing alternative to the heavenly realm. Eventually, of course, as old age ripens and death approaches, that worldly alternative is rejected. While Petrarch never achieves a union with Laura in the course of the sequence, he does find, after her death, that he is learning to master his desire and take in the importance of focusing on the afterlife. There is a crescendo of wonder, confidence, and reconciliation in the last third of the sequence, culminating in the final tribute to another woman, the Virgin Mary.

Petrarch succeeded, we might say, in portraying what theologians call the double motion of the soul, its simultaneous attraction to the earthly and to the heavenly. In doing so, he complicated the schematics of medieval Christianity and confirmed what we all know from our own experience: to live in time is to experience continually contradictory impulses and responses, gusts and vagaries of emotion and thought. He demonstrated that a lifetime of such experience, accurately recorded, can perform what looks like a graceful arc from a distance and reveals a turmoil

---

* C. S. Lewis, for example, points out that "the difference between the *Vita Nuova* and Petrarch's *Rime* is that Petrarch abandoned the prose links, and it was they that carried the narrative" (327). Teodolinda Barolini adds, "In other words, Petrarch takes the idea from Dante of transcribing previously written lyrics into a new order where the order generates significance, but he does not take Dante's means of controlling significance, namely the prose" (2).

of conflicting possibilities up close. It can, in other words, constitute a whole that is more than the sum of its parts.°

For that reason, as well as for its size, power, and eloquence, Petrarch's documentation of his emotional growth, the shape of his life and love, proved so persuasive that it spawned an excess of imitators and imitations. The adulation eventually obscured the remarkable freshness and originality of his achievement. What looked easy to imitate is in fact inimitable. Its balance is too delicate and exact, its stylistic mix too carefully calculated. Thus, Petrarch needs to be rescued from Petrarchism in the same way that original thinkers such as Aristotle, Freud, Marx, and Nietzsche may need to be rescued from their own subsequent disciples and adulterators. The disreputable formulas of Petrarchan style that held European poets in thrall for two centuries have little to do with this poet or his work. Petrarch's imitators mistook the surface rhetoric of contrary emotions—the cold heat, the bitter sweetness, the healing wounding, and so forth—for the experience that underlies them. They tended to ape the rhetoric without really sustaining the vision of existence that tells us how complicated our emotional lives can be. Our emotions seldom exist unalloyed, without their opposites, and the texture of our life is a rich compound of loss and gain, pleasure and pain, interesting at every moment for its mixed and contrary features.†

As soon as the rhetoric loses its emotional underpinning, it sounds silly. But in Petrarch's hands it is the instrument of a vision that implicitly questions the account of our life proposed by the Christian theology he espoused and embraced.

° David Kalstone, in a study of Sidney's poetry, makes the useful point that Petrarch's appeal is finally based on the ability of his poems, both individually and as a sequence, to hold contrary emotions in an equilibrium. What makes this possible is the concentration on memory. Pain and sweetness, recollected, reveal their paradoxical joint existence, even perhaps their interdependence. The memory of Laura, which is also the memory of Petrarch's failure to persuade her to return his love, persists as an inspiration, a token from the past that clarifies and illuminates the present and the future. Morris Bishop, in his biography, sounds a similar note: "In the chemistry of the spirit the emotions do not neutralize each other" (247).

† Bishop quotes Edgar Quinet, a nineteenth-century French critic: "Petrarch's originality consists in having realized, for the first time, that every moment in our existence contains in itself the substance of a poem, that every hour encloses an immortality" (253).

＋

Probably the best way for English-speaking readers to approach the meaning and nature of Petrarch's achievement is through comparison with his most adept reader in English, William Shakespeare. The fact that our own culture has a lively and extensive appreciation of Shakespeare's sonnet sequence gives us an excellent gateway to an appreciation of Petrarch. In Shakespeare's sequence we find a shorter but remarkably comparable example of the cumulative power a sonnet cycle can develop. Centered on the problem of Eros, and documenting the blisses and frustrations of trying to realize and sustain human love through time, both sequences show us a development not only in the remarkable mastery of a highly expressive form through repeated experiment but also, as I suggested earlier, a development in the poet's moral and spiritual understanding. A thoughtful poet can make excellent use of the repeated engagement with a compact poetic instrument, the sonnet, that is partly a formal and musical challenge and partly an opportunity for introspection, address to the beloved, and even a sort of journal keeping. Over time (the traditional enemy here being gradually turned to the prisoner's advantage) the sonnet becomes an instrument of meditation and a measure of accumulating insight.

Pleasure grows out of pain in such circumstances, partly for the artist and more surely for the reader, who can sample powerful erotic currents and witness the obsessions that develop around deprivation and disappointment from a vantage of relative safety. It is as though the sonnet sequences give us gloves for the safe handling of hot or radioactive materials. The gloves lift messy emotions up and reconfigure them in bright formal patterns, musical and elegant. As we read, enjoying the pleasures of form, the graceful dance of language, we also grow in self-knowledge and understanding.

"All right," my reader may say at this point. "I see the value of the analogy between Shakespeare's sonnets and those of Petrarch. But the difficulties I may have with the former—the sonnet form, the love conventions, the way in which the moral and spiritual growth is interlaced with clever comparisons and extravagant wordplay—are greatly compounded in the latter. For one thing, there is the matter of sheer size. Petrarch's poetic sequence contains three hundred and sixty-six lyrics! How am I to find my way around in this gigantic collection?"

The point is well taken. This is a life's work, and it does not present us with a simple, engrossing story. Dante, for one comparison, and the *Beowulf* poet, for another, belong to equally foreign worlds and distant cultures, but they hold us as readers or listeners by the power of their tales, the desire to learn what happens next. What will guide us through the labyrinth that Petrarch constructed? What will help us both to appreciate individual poems and to remain oriented to the work's larger concerns?

There is no simple answer to these questions other than my confident assertion that Petrarch grows on you and that the freedom of movement he gives us to explore his labyrinth is an interesting alternative to the seductions and constraints of narrative. If he took forty-seven years to assemble it, we certainly may—and should—take our time in getting fully acquainted with it. For the purposes of this introduction I have selected three groups of poems from different phases of the sequence. I will use these samplings to demonstrate how the sequence moves steadily forward while always both anticipating and looking back. I can also show how the poems carry on a kind of conversation among themselves, maintaining their discreteness and completeness while contributing, always, to the growth of the whole.

+

Take, for the first cross section, poems 11 through 18. They illustrate, as a group, the reigning aesthetic of the sequence, which delights in variation and elaboration while using a single point of reference to tether so much variety. All eight of these poems concern Laura, but in quite different ways. Poem 11 (which, by the way, is a *ballata*, a variation on the sonnet form) is addressed directly to her, pointing out that she was kinder and more generous with her presence before the speaker revealed his love for her. Now, he reminds her, she tends to veil herself when he is present, adding to his torment because he can't gaze at her. In Number 12, still addressing her, he speculates on whether her aging may eventually diminish her beauty and thereby lessen his pain. He wonders if such a modification would make him bolder:

> then Love may also grant me timely courage
> to speak at last of my great suffering,
> to tell you of its years, its days, its hours . . .

In a sense, of course, that anticipated moment, "at last," is realized by the present circumstance of the poem, since the lyric itself is speaking about his suffering in the way he hopes he will be able to speak to her, directly and frankly, someday in the distant future. This is a good example of the strategies lyric poems employ to defeat time; two different times cohabit in the poem, anticipating aging, growth, and an improvement in the Laura–Petrarch relationship.

In Number 13 the speaker says that when Laura appears among other women, his desire of her increases by as much as the others fall short of her perfect beauty:

> When now and then among the other ladies,
> Love makes his home within her charming face,
> the ways in which each one can't match her beauty
> renew desire, and my passion thrives.

This time, however, the insight about her superior beauty leads not to the complaint we've come to expect but to celebration:

> I bless the place, the time, I bless the hour
> that raised my eyes so high; and thus I say:
> "Soul, you must give both deep and hearty thanks
> that for that honor you were first picked out."

While poems 11 and 12 were addressed to Laura, 13 is self-divided and turns to self-address ("Soul") as well as to a renewed enthusiasm and energy. But Number 14 recognizes that self-division can be quite painful, and it relapses emotionally, with the speaker now addressing his own eyes. He warns them about the effect of seeing Laura and encourages them to cry and anticipate their eventual "martyrdom."

The next poem, 15, continues the note of despair, using the fact of physical separation from the beloved. Laura is now being directly addressed again. Amor, the love god who figures as an active third party and enemy throughout the sequence, intervenes, reminding the poet of the body-spirit separation all lovers experience. According to Amor, this is a privilege, a rarefaction.

In Number 16 we have an apparent change of scene and subject, as the poet launches into a touching anecdote about an old man setting off on a pilgrimage to see the Veronica relic in Rome. That, of course, turns out to be analogous to the speaker's search for Laura's face, echoing the situation described in poem 11. What has seemed like a shift of attention is eventually a reiteration of the reigning obsession.

In Number 17, still separated by some distance from the lady, the speaker contemplates the combination of suffering and redemption she seems to inspire in him. His dependence on her creates upheavals in his nature and further spirit-body disruptions. In Number 18, still looking back toward her, he takes stock of the damage his passion is doing him and anticipates his own blindness and death. Again, his speaking of these things involves him in paradox, since his claims that "I go in silence" and "what I really want / is solitude in which to shed my tears" are contradicted by the very fact of the poem itself.

This group of poems, chosen from early in the sequence, helps illustrate the variety of approaches—shifts of address, changes of mood, use of anecdote, exploration of the divided self—that Petrarch employs to keep the sequence moving forward without becoming too repetitive. Some readers will find it repetitive anyway, but they will at least want to acknowledge that each poem takes a new tack, not necessarily predictable from the poem preceding it, and that there are surprising changes of tone and direction within the poems as well. We are in the presence, as I've said, of an aesthetic that delights in extravagance, both of representation and of repetition. It values elaboration, imitation, and variation, unlike our own tendency to prefer economy and originality. We need to let that aesthetic carry us where it will, having faith in Petrarch's own standard of excellence. And for all the variations we will encounter, there is of course one constant: always the subject, implied or explicit, is Laura, and always there is the duality that his hopeless love for her visits upon him: a sense of deprivation and sorrow combined with an exhilaration at his spiritual enhancement and artistic growth.

✛

Let us move deeper into the sequence now and look at a group that runs from 107 to 118. These twelve poems begin and end with time references that are quite explicit: in poem 107 Petrarch says he is in the fifteenth year since he fell in love with Laura; by 118 we hear that he has just completed his "sixteenth year of sighs." Thus, among other things, we're aware of the passing of a year as we move through this segment of the sequence and of how long this frustrating passion has preoccupied the poor poet. Fifteen or sixteen years of unrequited love is a great deal, and Petrarch presumably has our sympathy, as well as a measure of impatience for his persistent self-pity. Meanwhile, his growth in self-awareness and spiritual sophistication is an apparent product of the tension in his life and consciousness between change, over time, and constancy as a form of resistance.

Poem 107 concludes that there is to be no escape from the long "war" of love. Everything reminds the poet of Laura, and it's as if he is lost in a forest of the laurel trees that stand for her. They also stand for his poetry, since he has now written over a hundred poems and crowned himself, in effect, with the classical laurel crown awarded to poets.

If he's addressing himself here, he's also addressing the implicit audience for his poems, which by this point were widely circulated and admired. One member of it is Sennuccio del Bene, a fellow poet who is directly addressed in Numbers 108, 112, and 113. Sennuccio is sympathetic and, as both a fellow poet and a fellow lover, can act as a kind of mirror to Petrarch's concerns. He's asked to spare a tear or sigh for the ground where Laura has walked in 108, and in 112 and 113 he is asked to sympathize, to "see how I am treated here" and to recognize that "I half exist." But Number 113 is rather more positive, since Petrarch is also telling Sennuccio about his refuge from the world. He is writing now about his country home in the Vaucluse region of southern France, a rural retreat where he found solace in nature and solitude but where Nature's beauty reminded him continually of his love. In 114, 116, and 117 he sketches in the landscape around the source of the Sorgue, where he had his little house, suggesting that his love is more bearable there than anywhere else. Talking about his pastoral retreat also allows him to cast indignant glances toward the corrupt and crowded papal court at Avignon, which he characterizes as Babylon in 114 and Babel in 117, getting in some political licks at a situation he found deplorable.

In and around these poems is threaded an anecdote about one of his meetings with Laura. In Number 108 he addresses the ground where she has walked, stopping once to turn and look at him. In 109 he revisits the spot where he saw her and gains great peace of mind:

> The visit calms me down, and now those sparks,
> at nones, at vespers, dawn and angelus,
> can fill my thoughts, which have become so tranquil
> that I am free of cares or painful memories.

In 110 he is suddenly made aware of her presence by seeing and recognizing her shadow. Before he has time to realize it, they are face-to-face, and he is enduring the impact of her amazing eyes:

> the way that thunder comes along with lightning
> that's how those eyes, so brilliant, hit me,
> along with a sweet greeting from her lips.

In 111 this episode is narrated further, letting us know that she approached him "where I sat all alone," that she blushed when their eyes met, then spoke briefly to him and went on. The encounter left him "fulfilled with pleasure" because it was a "kindly greeting" that he got from her for once. By 112 he is complaining, again, to Sennuccio, but rather gently, as also in 113.

In Number 115 Petrarch returns to the meeting once more, this time to mythologize it. The sun and Petrarch are both Laura's admirers in this episode, which recalls the myth of Apollo and Daphne (who turned into a laurel tree to escape Apollo's pursuit of her and thereby gave Petrarch one of his many opportunities for punning incessantly on Laura's name), and the fact that Laura smiles on Petrarch is enough to make the sun cloud over, "much annoyed at being bested." His euphoria about this smile carries on into 116, where, as noted before, he introduces us more fully to his valley, with further elaboration in 117.

In 118 we have a kind of retrospective look at the duration of the unrequited love, and the mixed tone and rueful celebration of this lyric mark the distance we have come in the sequence overall:

> I've now passed through my sixteenth year of sighs
> and somewhere up ahead I'll reach the last one;
> and yet it sometimes seems to me as though
> this suffering began just recently.
>
> The bitter now is sweet, my losses useful,
> living itself's a heavy weight—I pray
> my life outlasts this fortune and I fear
> Death may close those eyes that give me speech.

The time behind and the time ahead are surveyed, along with the worry that Laura might die. The speaker is aware of his contradictions—bitter is sweet, "here" makes him wish for "elsewhere," a long period of suffering seems to have begun "just recently"—but as the poem draws to its close, what emerges most clearly to him is the fact that in a world of change he has become a kind of constant, something he can cautiously affirm and enjoy. He's stuck in his love, absurd and unrewarded, but his sixteen years, in which old desires still produce new tears, are acquiring a kind of value he could not have foreseen or understood. The growth of self-awareness and spiritual sophistication that the sequence affords the poet, as mentioned before, is nicely located here in the dynamic between change and constancy.

The self-criticism, openness about pain and failure, and tribute to the person who can offset the speaker's shortcomings is the same mixture we can find in Shakespeare's sonnet sequence, which helps clarify the way in which it is essentially indebted to Petrarch's example. In both cases we gradually learn to value what one critic has called the striking "contrast (or fusion) between proclamations of emotional and spiritual turmoil or despair and the classic beauty of the writing, which combines clarity, ease, order, grace and musicality in constantly changing yet internally consistent variations."[*]

+

For a final sample of the pace and texture of the sequence, let us glance at a late group, from 313 to 321. These nine poems belong to the time after Laura's early death, when Petrarch is mourning her loss, reconciling himself to his own end, and anticipating a reunion with her in Heaven. The mood of the sequence's late poems is somber and muted, but they achieve, again and again, a powerful eloquence centered on loss, aging, and death, with the poet gaining spiritual understanding as he schools himself for what is to come. In Number 313 we get a taste of how retrospective the poet's vision has become:

> The time is gone, alas, when I could live
> refreshed amid the fire; the one I wept for

---

[*] Hainsworth, 25. He further notes that Petrarch was fond of Horace's metaphor for the poet as a bee who collects pollen from many sorts of flowers. "His own pollen came from all sorts of textual and stylistic bric-a-brac—conceits, conversational phrases, echoes of Latin, Provençal, Dante and other Italians, bits of high rhetoric, conventional images, even clichés. The magic lies in how it comes together and also in its awareness of its own problematic status."

passed away, the one I wrote about,
but left me with my pen and all these tears.

Her face is gone, so sanctified and charming,
and as it went, her eyes speared through my heart,
that heart, once mine, which left to follow her,
as if enveloped in her lovely mantle.

The self-division treated earlier has become even more dramatic be-
cause of the barrier between death and life. His heart, we learn, has gone
with Laura, first into the grave and then on up to Heaven. His longing for
her, and for self-completion, is now necessarily a longing for his own
death. In 314 he addresses his mind, recognizing that it had hints of what
was to come, and his soul, which enjoyed the impact of her eyes, "the way
we burned together in the moment," a memory made poignant by the ir-
revocability of death.

In Number 315 he gives a thoughtful self-analysis. Before Laura died,
he was in fact maturing and changing in a way that would have allowed
them a more fruitful relationship, when

Love could be
good friends with Chastity, and lovers might
sit down together and talk naturally.

That prospect created envy in Death, who is personified as a woman
in Petrarch's world, and she intervened. The next poem continues this
theme, adding the lovely image of the cloud dissolving itself in the wind
and offering some poignant conjectures—"She might have waited . . .
I would have talked to her"—about what their lives might have been like
if they had grown old together. What was anticipated clear back in poem
12 never came to pass.

Poems 317 and 318 revisit this subject, the first through a ship and
harbor conceit, the second through an allegory of Laura's death as a vi-
sion of two trees, one fallen and destroyed, the other transported to
Heaven. Number 319 is a moving lament for the passage of time and the
loss of the beloved,

as I go around with graying hair
all I can think about is what she's like
and what it meant to see her lovely veil.

In 320 he revisits her birthplace and feels her death more keenly in the natural surroundings:

> Oh, transitory hopes, oh, crazy thoughts!
> The grass is grieving and the waters troubled,
> the nest is cold and empty where she lay . . .

In 321 he continues to meditate on Laura's birthplace. Seeing it as a "nest" allows him to think of her as a phoenix, rare and rejuvenated, but that miraculous state only leaves him feeling more bereft and desolate, facing a sunset without her, where her "eyes once used to make it day."

Again and again in this part of the sequence he returns to his memories of her living presence, dwelling often on their final parting and his failure to understand its significance. Then, gradually, he acts more and more on his knowledge of her current status, in Heaven, celebrating that and longing for death so that he can join her.

What was once a turbulent rapids has become a steady, majestic river. There is less range of subject and tone, perhaps, but the poems are deeply persuasive in their humanity and curiously comforting in their growing sense of spiritual insight.

✦

One persistent question, not easily answered, is why Petrarch depicts himself so disadvantageously throughout the sequence. His obsession with Laura demeans him considerably, but on top of that we must deal with a self-portrait that continually stresses weeping, sleeplessness, physical debility, naïveté, confusion, and a wounded, bleeding heart. "Get a grip on yourself," we want to say, "stop indulging in all this self-pity!"

A partial answer lies in the courtly love tradition, where the poets explored a deliberate subversion of male dominance and courage, making the women powerful and even warriorlike for a change, exploring the borders of gender and toppling stereotypes. Chivalry had two sides, a traditionally male and stoic aspect and its opposite, an unexpected tenderness and vulnerability, and it was the richer for such ambivalence. Petrarch is obviously comfortable with these traditions, and he is writing for an audience that enjoys their paradoxes and the implicit comedy they tend to produce.

A second answer about the abject self-representation lies in the example of Augustine's *Confessions*, which Petrarch as a Christian humanist was adapting to a more secular format. The whole point of such an account is the miserable behavior of the sinner and the concomitant joy and strength when his conversion comes. It was, again, a pattern that Petrarch and his audience found both congenial and powerful. Thus, the worse Petrarch looks as an earthly lover, trapped in the erotic obsessions of his physical desire for Laura, the more powerful the lesson when he eventually trains himself to despise the world and focus on his salvation, not to mention his eventual reunion with Laura in a heavenly setting, where their love is both pardonable and harmonious.

This is not to say that Petrarch does not complicate the Augustinian pattern, just as Shakespeare, in turn, would complicate Petrarch's. Sin is more interesting and less clearly evil in Petrarch's world, and its identity is more bound up with the meaning of its apparent opposite, heavenly salvation. Laura's beauty is not just a trap, and her attractiveness in this world, which leads Petrarch to a kind of misguided worship and distraction, turns out to be a prefiguring of her heavenly beauty. Far from being totally wrongheaded, his pursuit of her reveals itself gradually as a less enlightened form of what would eventually be both sanctioned and valuable. Erotic love is a training ground, and the lover, while distracted and silly, is also showing good instincts and potential holiness.

We are dealing, in other words, not with oppositions like good and evil, Hell and Heaven, sin and salvation, but with gradations and phases, with life as a pilgrimage that leads us through error and into well-being. It can be relished as an experience that is both painful and pleasurable, misleading and instructive. So powerful is Petrarch's personal account of this process and pilgrimage that he shaped a paradigm still viable for artistic employment. We still have sonnet cycles, and we still have bodies of poetry—Emily Dickinson's is a powerful example—that record the growth and tribulations of the self through time. We are still deeply in this fourteenth-century writer's debt.

✝

The man who put this sequence together was multifaceted. Greatly respected in his own time as a scholar and classicist, associating with princes of the Church and of the world, often called on to consult in matters of statecraft and policy, Petrarch was worldly as poets go, a powerful presence in the turbulent times that saw Italy fragmented and France made the home of the displaced papacy. Petrarch hoped for, and worked toward, an Italy less at the mercy of rivalries and civil conflicts, and a Holy Roman Empire that would bring greater stability to the civilized world. His efforts were often frustrated, but he never gave up on his political ideals, continuing as a voice of reason and conscience to his generation right to the end of his life.

He was widely acknowledged as the leading writer of his time. He worked at length on a Latin epic, imitating Virgil.* He wrote satirical diatribes and verse epistles. He wrote treatises in praise of solitude, reason, and stoic acceptance of the world's vagaries. He may have been best known for an equivalent of our modern self-help books, the popular *De remediis utriusque fortunae* (translated recently as *Petrarch's Remedies for Fortune Fair and Foul*). His long, thoughtful letters to his friends and associates were prized and copied, so that he set himself to collecting and editing them for public consumption. As wars, crusades, plagues, and invasions swirled around him, he often retreated to his country home in the Vaucluse. There he contemplated a beauty that was compounded of that rural landscape, Laura's attractiveness, the classical texts he admired, and the love of God he learned from masters like Augustine and Ambrose. At such times the personal torments associated with the constant feelings of lust in his makeup and the frustration of Laura's unavailability may have seemed minor in comparison to the larger troubles of the world.† Being both familiar and manageable, as a source of poetic in-

---

* The *Africa* was intended to be his ticket to fame, an epic that would recapture the glory of the past. But while it has some fine passages, it is, by common agreement, mostly frigid and dull, boring in the extreme to modern readers. At some level Petrarch must have sensed this, for he tended to keep it to himself, and his anxiety about its success was evident in many of his actions and statements. If it dawned on him that his lyric poems would turn out to be the real testimony to his poetic genius, the recognition came late.

† In retreating to rural solitude, not like a hermit bent on prayer and self-denial but rather like a man who enjoys communing with himself in the friendly presence of nature, Petrarch picked up a classical tradition and founded what we might call the modern tradition exemplified by figures such as Thoreau. Here is a passage from one of his letters about his Vaucluse retreat: "You will see me content with a small but shady garden and a tiny house. . . . You will see me from morn to eve wandering alone among the meadows, hills, springs, and woods. I flee men's traces, follow the birds,

spiration, they could allow him to indulge his playful genius and let his artistic skill merge with his most private thoughts and feelings—made public, of course, through the writing and circulation of the poems. A paradoxical man, surely, this Francesco Petrarca, taking his emotional pulse and moral temperature so often, laughing a little at himself as he went. In old age he grew vain and touchy, and more than a little pompous, but by then his collection of poems from his youth and middle years was mostly finished, a project of retrospective polishing and rearranging.

✛

And what of Laura? She is so much the subject of the sequence, so powerful a presence, that we naturally inquire about the historical person. Was she really as good and beautiful as Petrarch portrayed her? Is his account of her his own projection, too unrealistic to have much connection with the actual woman? Did he, perhaps, as one of his contemporaries teasingly suggested, make her up? °

Many of our answers to these questions must remain conjectural. She existed, surely, and she came from the Avignon area, most probably from the village of Carpentras, where Petrarch lived in his youth. She had blond hair, striking eyes, and considerable composure. She may well have been the Laura—the birth and death dates fit—who married into

---

love the shadows, enjoy the mossy caves and the greening fields, curse the cares of the Curia, avoid the city's tumult, refuse to cross the thresholds of the mighty, mock the concerns of the mob. I am equidistant from joy and sadness, at peace by day and night. I glory in the Muses' company, in bird-song and the murmur of water-nymphs. My servants are few but my books many." From *Familiar Letters*, 6, 3, as quoted in Bishop, 136.

° The suggestion provoked a pained and vigorous denial: "So what do you say? That I invented the beautiful name of Laura to give myself something to talk about and to engage many to talk about me! And that in fact there is no Laura in my mind except the poetic Laurel for which I evidently have aspired with long-continued unwearying zeal; and that concerning the living Laura, by whose person I seem to be captured, everything is manufactured; that my poems are fictitious, my sighs pretended. Well, on this head I wish it were all a joke, that it were a pretense and not a madness! But believe me, no one can simulate long without great effort; to labor to appear mad, to no purpose, is the height of madness. Add that we can in health imitate the behavior of the sick, but we cannot simulate pallor." From *Epistolae Familiares* 2, 9, as quoted in Thompson.

the de Sade family, a name made infamous much later by the notorious Marquis (a historical irony that would have greatly amused both Petrarch and, one guesses, Laura herself). Her marriage, and her preservation of her honor, seems to have composed the main obstacle to any consummation of their relationship.

Even the extent to which she may have reciprocated Petrarch's feelings of admiration is unclear. Sometimes she is kind to him. More often, she is stern, usually because he speaks to her inappropriately of his love. They see each other only occasionally, and these occasions become extremely precious to him. She greets him politely on the street, in passing, and he is enraptured. He sees her in a pageant. He encounters a group of her friends and asks after her, discovering that her husband has confined her to the house. He watches her meet Charles, the Holy Roman emperor. He sees her without gloves on her hands and wishes to keep a glove. She demands it back, but he cherishes the memory. He walks where she has walked and sits where she has sat, just so he can go on thinking about her beauty and her goodness. From time to time, as we have noted, he commemorates the anniversaries of their first meeting, reflecting with melancholy on how long and how fruitlessly he has loved her.

Then, in 1348, while he is away in Italy, she dies suddenly, probably of the Black Death that was ravaging France. Thereafter, his grief and his gradual reshaping of the relationship through attention to her presence in Heaven (with occasional visits in his sleep to comfort him) become his primary poetic subjects. As the sequence closes, Laura merges with Mary, of whose goodness she now seems to him to have been an earthly manifestation. That recognition prepares him for his own death and for their anticipated reunion in Heaven.

To read the sequence in its entirety is to come to feel one knows Laura well, and to admire her for her character. She did not choose to become the object of a famous poet's rapturous attentions, but having been cast in that role she handled it with grace and thoughtfulness.

✢

The structure I have just described, a two-part sequence with the second half shorter (1–263 and 264–366), follows a familiar medieval pattern, devoted to sin and redemption, as well as the classical plot structure, involving complication and resolution, that Aristotle described. Petrarch kept this basic structure intact even as he wrote and added new poems to it, placing them with more regard to the design of the whole than to actual chronology.° The main event that characterizes the change is Laura's death, but Petrarch was careful to start his "resolution" before the news of her death, keeping it on a spiritual as opposed to a material level. It is as if his "conversion" has already begun when she dies, with the death becoming an event that confirms and reinforces his determination to take a new direction.

It should not surprise us that this two-part asymmetric form is also the basic structure of the sonnet, with its eight-line complication, its shift or *volta*, and its six-line resolution. Thus the shape of a life, the shape of a sequence, and the shape of a form that makes up the predominant means of composing it are all in accord with one another. Petrarch writes in other forms, of course, including the sestina, the canzone, the madrigal, and the ballata. But the sonnet is what sustains him, and he records his feelings and experiences in it faithfully, sometimes in groups, sometimes in individual poems.†

Not every poem in the sequence is about Laura; there are political tirades, tributes to other friends, laments for deaths and other losses, advice to those who may or may not ignore it, tributes to nature, meditations on history and mythology, accounts of dreams, occasional poems written to accompany gifts, invitations, apologies for declining invitations, and many other subjects. Always, though, Laura is at the center, an emotional polestar, a source of both stability and torment, love and anger.

We know that Petrarch led a busy life, with much travel and many relationships (including the fathering of two illegitimate children). In the sequence, however, the central drama to which the poems return again

---

° For example, among the last sonnets he wrote was a pair that he inserted into the first half, 194 and 197. See Wilkins, *Making of the "Canzoniere,"* 367.

† Of the 366 poems in the collection, 317 are sonnets, followed by twenty-nine canzones, nine sestinas (one of which is double), seven ballatas, and four madrigals. The sestinas, with their repeating end words and strict patterning, are especially good at reinforcing the obsessive, time-trapped nature of the speaker's dilemma. Some of the canzones choose especially demanding Provençal forms in complex stanzas that match rhymes and repeat difficult patterns. The sonnets, of course, are of the formal Italian type that uses just two rhymes in the octave and two or three in the sestet. Their two-part structure is thus more emphatic than it is in Shakespearean examples.

and again involves a kind of triangle: there is Petrarch, there is Laura, and there is the love god, Cupid or Eros or just plain Love, who rules Petrarch's heart and enslaves him to his love for Laura. Cupid might be thought of as the personified equivalent of some of our modern ideas about biological imperatives and sex drives. He undermines self-control, and he blinds us to larger realities by dominating our senses. A pagan presence in a Christian poem, he is a powerful contradiction to the way that the Church says the world is supposed to work.

The love god's presence also helps focus the lover's anger. By blaming Love and his abusive tyranny, Petrarch can deflect the anger he feels toward Laura and overcome his temptation to resent the fact of her physical beauty. She is the subject of his obsession, but she is not to blame. Cupid is, and Petrarch in turn, for being defeated by him. It is a curious combination of metamorphosis and steadiness; a changeable reality is what gives Cupid his dominance over fickle human beings. But the dominance, in Petrarch's case at least, leads not to fickleness but to fidelity, an unwavering love for Laura and Laura alone. That is the trick the poet plays on the god of love. Eventually, through death and redefinition, his love and fidelity reward him, training the tormented poet to an understanding of heavenly love and heavenly beauty, values which Laura is able to represent fully only after she has left the earth.

The result echoes St. Augustine, but it also invokes poets such as Ovid and Horace, whom Petrarch admired, and it tells a story that seems at times to outdistance in complexity and peculiarity the theology that quite naturally underpins it. Petrarch faces the modern world, but he also faces the medieval world and, beyond it, the classical world. That comprehensiveness accounts in great part for his mastery. Adolfo Bartoli, writing in 1884, put it very well:

> This descent into his own spirit, with its seizing of its griefs and joys, its making of a fleeting moment an immortal poem; this self-scrutiny, turning every impulse into art; this abandonment of medieval symbolism and transcendental idealism; this seeing of humanity plain, feeling it in all its truth—this is what makes Petrarch the first lyric poet of the new time, the heir of antiquity and the herald of the great art of the modern world.°

° From volume 7 of his *Storia della letteratura italiana,* as quoted in Bishop, 254.

✢

Translating is a most peculiar activity. On the one hand it seems inevitably doomed both to inadequacy and to incompleteness. On the other hand it offers a kind of loaves-and-fishes legerdemain: where one poem existed, two now stand, related but different, alike but occupying different linguistic territories and, in some cases, different ages and eras. Is a translated poem the evil twin of the original, or is it a miraculous clone, a musical transposition whereby one valuable thing is replicated, its value effectively doubled? A lifetime of translating—Rilke, Holub, Tu Fu, Neruda, Yu Xuanji—has never completely resolved this question for me. If one could read fluently, confidently, in every known language, one would have no need of translators or translations; one could read Homer on Mondays, Akhmatova on Tuesdays, Swahili poets on Wednesdays, and so on. Barring that, however, this imperfect art is one we at least need to tolerate, perhaps even welcome. And poets, I would argue, are the best equipped to succeed as translators of poetry. Just as you would turn to a composer to get effective musical transposition, you need a poet to wrestle a poem from one language into another, the latter being the one in which he or she has some skill at making poems.

Personally, I translate poems for the same reason that I seek out and read translations: to develop acquaintance with poets and poetry I might not otherwise be able to know. In the case of Petrarch, I began producing versions of his sonnets to share with my students who were trying to understand the tradition in which Shakespeare worked. I wanted something that would feel contemporary to them, written in a living language they would recognize as poetry, and something that would also retain the flavor and distinctiveness of the past. A difficult prescription, surely, but a worthwhile negotiation involving two languages, two times, two sets of possibilities.

My solution was to retain the part of Petrarch's formality that was manageable—a regularity of meter that would also recall Shakespeare's example—without attempting to replicate the difficult rhyme schemes. Italian rhymes much more readily than English, and searching for ways to make a rhyme scheme function can do serious injury to syntax, imagery, tone, and sense. Rhymes do occur throughout my versions, but they are internal rhymes, incidental rhymes, consonantal rhymes, and so forth, free from the demands of strict pattern but part, nevertheless, of an overall musicality.

Meter, while very demanding in its own right, allows for considerable flexibility of expression. Its challenge would keep me alert, I hoped, sensitive to Petrarch's climate and aesthetic, without cutting off access to my own language and my own world, my sense of how to make literary style into a living presence, a voice on the page, speaking authentically to listeners and readers of the same time and place. (The sestinas are the one exception to my consistent commitment to iambics.)

All in all, I have tried to stay close to Petrarch's diction, syntax, and tone, not wishing to impose my own sensibility or vocabulary on what was so well thought out and so remarkably consistent in the first place. My "liberties," where they occur, come from the constraints of meter and the desire to be clear and straightforward. Perhaps it will be useful to illustrate my method with one of Petrarch's better-known sonnets. Here is the Italian of Number 189:

> Passa la nave mia colma d'oblio
> per aspro mare a mezza notte il verno
> enfra Scilla et Caribdi, et al governo
> siede 'l signore anzi 'l nimico mio;
>
> à ciascun remo un penser pronto et rio
> che la tempesta e 'l fin par ch' abbi a scherno;
> la vela rompe un vento umido eterno
> di sospir, di speranze et di desio;
>
> pioggia di lagrimar, nebbia di sdegni
> bagna et rallenta le già stanche sarte
> che son d'error con ignoranzia attorto.
>
> Celansi i duo mei dolci usati segni,
> morta fra l'onde è la ragion et l'arte
> tal ch' I' 'ncomincio a desperar del porto.

An English prose version of this by Robert Durling reads as follows:

> My ship laden with forgetfulness passes through a harsh sea, at midnight, in winter, between Scylla and Charybdis, and at the tiller sits my lord, rather my enemy;

each oar is manned by a ready, cruel thought that seems to scorn the tempest and the end; a wet, changeless wind of sighs, hopes, and desires breaks the sail;

a rain of weeping, a mist of disdain wet and loosen the already weary ropes, made of error twisted up with ignorance.

My two usual sweet stars are hidden; dead among the waves are reason and skill; so that I begin to despair of the port.   (Durling, 334)

Durling's version reconfigures some of the syntax, changing, for example, what is literally "the sail is burst by a wet, eternal wind of sighs, hopes, and desires" into something that is more comfortable in terms of English word order, but it is otherwise extremely faithful.

As it happens, we have a wonderful translation of this sonnet by the sixteenth-century English poet Sir Thomas Wyatt:

> My galy charged with forgetfulness
> Thorrough sharpe sees in wynter nyghets doeth pas
> Twene Rock and Rock; and eke myn enemy, Alas,
> That is my lord, sterith with cruelness;
>
> And every owre a thought in rediness,
> As tho that deth were light in such a case.
> An endles wiynd doeth tere the sayll a pase
> Of forced sightes and trusty ferefulnes.
>
> A rain of teris, a clowde of derk disdain
> Hath done the wered cordes great hinderaunce,
> Wrethed with errour and eke with ignoraunce.
>
> The starres be hid that led me to this pain,
> Drowned is reason that should me confort,
> And I remain dispering of the port.

Wyatt has to leave a few things out, and his first two rhymes may charge his galley with an excess of sibilance, but his language is pungent and direct, a strong response to Petrarch's Italian. Had he done the whole sequence, instead of just a few of the sonnets, I might not have felt the need to undertake this project!

Next, for comparison, is a rhymed version by Thomas Bergin, done in the twentieth century but not untypical of the nineteenth-century fashion for translating Petrarch:

Charged with oblivion my ship careers
Through stormy combers in the depth of night;
Left lies Charybdis, Scylla to the right;
My master—nay my foe sits aft and steers.

Wild fancies ply the oars, mad mutineers,
Reckless of journey's end or tempest's might;
The canvas splits 'gainst the relentless spite
Of blasts of hopes and sighs and anxious fears.

A rain of tears, a blinding mist of wrath
Drench and undo the cordage, long since worn
And fouled in knots of ignorance and error;

The two sweet lights are lost that showed my path,
Reason and art lie 'neath the waves forlorn:
"What hope of harbor now?" I cry in terror.

(Bergin, 334)

This is quite skillful, though I feel that the attachment to traditional En-
glish poetic diction, including contractions such as *'gainst* and *'neath*, as
well as phrases like "wild fancies" and "waves forlorn," makes Petrarch
sound too much like a perfunctory late Romantic. Key details, such as the
facts of midnight and winter, get blurred when presented merely as "the
depth of night." Preserving the rhyme scheme is an honorable challenge,
but it's worth asking whether the matching of *wrath* and *path*, *worn* and
forlorn, and *error* and *terror* really does that much to enhance the poem.
At the same time, it's impossible not to admire the difficult commitment
to rhyme and meter that Bergin manages to sustain here.

Here is my own version, which has benefited, among other things,
from Wyatt's choice of *galley* for the vessel of the opening line:

My galley, loaded with forgetfulness,
rolls through rough seas, at midnight, during winter,
aiming between Charybdis and sharp Scylla;
my lord, ah no, my foe, sits at the tiller;

each oar is wielded by a quick, mad thought
that seems to scorn the storm and what it means;
an endless wind of moisture, of deep sighs,
of hopes and passions, rips the sail in half;

tears in a steady downpour, mists of hate,
are loosening and soaking all the ropes,
ropes made of ignorance, tangled up with error.

The two sweet stars I steer by are obscured;
reason and skill are dead amid the waves;
and I don't think I'll ever see the port.

My hope is that this captures the drama and energy of the original without either modernizing it excessively or leaving it sounding or feeling too archaic. It is a poet's, rather than a scholar's, version—I have found a nice off rhyme in *Scylla* and *tiller*, and I like the contrasting music of, for example, lines 5 and 6—but I have tried to hew very closely to the exact sense of the Italian text.

Readers will judge my success or failure for themselves, but I wish to acknowledge here the value that other translators have brought to my enterprise. Foremost is the aforementioned Robert K. Durling, whose *Petrarch's Lyric Poems*, with facing-page English prose and Italian originals, was invaluable to me. Again and again I strayed from the sensible diction and shrewd syntax of Durling's versions in search of alternatives, only to return eventually to his model and his vision. I have wanted to have poetry where he was content with prose, but little else separates us. His Petrarch is my Petrarch—the man, the writer, the reader, the technician, the jokester—and I am considerably in his debt. Even my explanatory notes tend to echo his, and they largely adopt his format. Why quarrel with success?

Two other recent scholarly translators have treated Petrarch in much the same way I do, faithful to meter but dispensing with rhyme scheme. I encountered James Wyatt Cook's version early on, and kept it at hand, sometimes to quarrel with its choices, sometimes to admire them. Mark Musa's version came to my notice when I was well along in the project, and thereafter I found it quite useful as well. I was interested in the notes and perspectives of these translators, as well as in their solutions to problems of diction and syntax.

I also found, late in the process, a translator who had tried doing a selection from Petrarch in contemporary free verse, Nicholas Kilmer, and another one who has recently attempted to do the entire sequence using off rhymes, J. G. Nichols. While disagreeing with their solutions, I found their efforts instructive. One other book was at hand as I worked, a limited edition of Petrarch sonnets put together by Thomas G. Bergin; this selection assembles formal versions from several centuries, including the version of Number 189 quoted earlier. These examples helped persuade me of the folly of trying to rhyme; they tend to make Petrarch sound like a second-rate Elizabethan poet crossed with a third-rate Victorian. But some surprisingly graceful efforts turned up as well, particularly those of Morris Bishop, who also wrote a charming biography that I found helpful as background reading.

After some pondering, I decided that this need not be a bilingual edition, a choice that makes for a mercifully smaller book. The decision was based partly on the ready availability of the Durling, Cook, and Musa versions, all with facing-page Italian, and partly on the fact that Petrarch's text is now easily available on the Internet, in Seth Jerchower's "Petrarchan Grotto," which can be found at http://petrarch.freeservers. com. It is essentially the same text as Cook's and also quite close to those of Durling and Musa.

Oberlin College's Petrarch connection is of particular interest to me. The greatest Petrarch scholar of the twentieth century, Ernest Hatch Wilkins, happened also to have been Oberlin's president from 1927 to 1945. As I worked, I liked to imagine that his benign shade was occasionally encouraging my efforts. If so, it may have been joined by that of Andrew Bongiorno, from whom I learned about Dante when I became his much younger colleague at Oberlin, and whose high standards of scholarship were always an inspiration to me. I never knew Wilkins, of course, but hearing Bongiorno talk about him gave me familiarity with his scholarly achievements long before I began to think of translating his favorite poet.

My colleague Martha Collins made a particularly significant contribution to this project. She encouraged my commitment to meter and brought her own accurate ear and eye to the careful critique of my efforts, from an early stage on down to the completion. I owe her a great deal. I am also grateful to other readers who helped me polish and refine my efforts, especially Georgia Newman, my wife, and John Hobbs and David Walker, two other colleagues at Oberlin. Jonathan Galassi contributed many excellent suggestions that helped make the translations more consistently faithful to the Italian. Gaetano Prampolini very kindly read this introduction and pointed out some errors. Two monthlong residencies helped give me the time and concentration to complete this project, one from the Bogliasco Foundation in Liguria in 2001, the other a Witter Bynner Fellowship at the New Mexico Institute for the Arts in 2002. For the help and encouragement I received at both places, my deepest thanks.

A Powers Travel Grant from Oberlin College that enabled me to visit sites where Petrarch lived and worked, particularly the Vaucluse and the Fontagne de Sorgue, as well as Mount Ventoux, during the summer of 2002, was also instrumental to the completion of this project.

Finally, if it does not seem too strange and awkward, let me thank my friend Petrarch. To occupy the world of another poet's work at great length is to develop an intimacy that resembles friendship. There are bound to be quarrels and misunderstandings, but there is something that feels like mutual exchange, trust, and candid appraisal. Petrarch enjoyed his friendships and put a high value on them. So do I. Like others, I have found this man fascinating in his flawed humanity, admirable in the honesty and detail of his self-portraiture. His company has been a privilege. To honor it, I would like to close with the characterization that Wilkins used to preface his 1961 *Life of Petrarch*:

> He was and is remarkable for his awareness of the entire continent on which the drama of European life was being enacted; for his awareness of the reality of times past and times to come; for the breadth and variety of his own interest (he was, among many other things, a gardener, a fisherman, and a lutanist); for the high dedication of his writings; for his persistent belief in Rome as the rightful capital of a unified world, governed politically by an Emperor and religiously by a Pope; for his scholarly precocity and for the valiant industry of his old age; for the honors he received and for the hostilities he incurred; for his faithfulness to the study and writing that constituted his most important occupation; and most of all for the vast range, the deep loyalty, and the unfailing helpfulness of his friendships. (v)

Works Cited

Barolini, Teodolinda. "The Making of a Lyric Sequence: Time and Narrative in Petrarch's *Rerum vulgarium fragmenta*," *MLN*, vol. 104, no. 1, January 1989, 1–38.

Bergin, Thomas G. *The Sonnets of Petrarch*. Heritage Press, 1966.

Bishop, Morris. *Petrarch and His World*. Indiana University Press, 1963.

Cook, James Wyatt. *Petrarch's Songbook*. Pegasus Press, 1995.

Durling, Robert K. *Petrarch's Lyric Poems*. Harvard University Press, 1976.

Hainsworth, Peter. "Laden with Oblivion," *Times Literary Supplement*, May 18, 2001, 25.

Kalstone, David. *Sidney's Poetry: Context and Interpretations*. Harvard University Press, 1965.

Kilmer, Nicholas. *Songs and Sonnets from Laura's Lifetime*. North Point Press, 1981.

Lewis, C. S. *English Literature of the Sixteenth Century*. Oxford University Press, 1954.

Musa, Mark. *Selections from the Canzoniere and Other Works*. Oxford World's Classics, 1985.

―――. *Petrarch: The Canzoniere*. Indiana University Press, 1996.

Nichols, J. G. *Petrarch, Canzoniere*. Carcanet, 2000.

Thompson, David. *Petrarch, a Humanist Among Princes: An Anthology of Petrarch's Letters and of Selections from His Other Works*. Harper & Row, 1971.

Wilkins, Ernest Hatch. *The Making of the "Canzoniere" and Other Petrarchan Studies*. Edizioni di Storia e Litteratura, 1951.

―――. *Life of Petrarch*. University of Chicago Press, 1961.

―――. *Petrarch's Later Years*. Medieval Academy of America, 1959.

The Canzoniere, 1–366

1

All you who hear in scattered rhymes the sound
of heavy sighs with which I fed my heart
during the time of my first youthful straying
when I was not the man I've since become:

for the mixed style in which I speak and weep,
caught between empty hopes and empty sorrow,
from anyone who knows of love firsthand
I hope to find some sympathy—and pardon.

I can see now that I was made the subject
of lots of gossip among lots of people;
inside myself I'm often filled with shame;

shame is the fruit of all my clever ravings;
so are repentance and my knowing clearly
that every worldly pleasure is a dream.

2

To make a graceful one his sweet vendetta,
redress a thousand slights in one quick swoop,
Love stealthily picked up his bow, much as
a man who schemes a time and place to hurt.

My vital power was buttressed in my heart
and well defended, there and in my eyes,
until the harsh stroke landed, where before
all arrows that had come had glanced away:

that sudden onslaught and its fell success
left my poor power bewildered and in pain.
It had no time for weapons; it grew weak,

mountain:
Reason

it couldn't help me climb the weary mountain,
it couldn't whisk me from that scene of slaughter.
It meant to help, would like to now, but can't.

3

It was the day the sun himself grew pale
with grieving for his Maker—I was seized
and made no effort to defend myself;
your lovely eyes had held and bound me, Lady.

It didn't seem a time to be on guard
against Love's blows, so I went confident
and fearless on my way. My troubles started
amid the universal sense of woe.

Love found me wholly undefended, with
the way from eyes to heart completely open,
eyes that are now the conduit for tears.

He got no glory by it; I was helpless.
And he let you escape with no attack
when you were well defended, fully armed.

the day: April 6, 1327,
Church of Santa
Clara, Avignon

4

He who showed endless providence and art,
the master craftsman of this shining world,
who made the hemispheres, this one and that,
and proved a Jove, more mild than a Mars,

who came here to illuminate the leaves
that had concealed the truth for many years,
took John and Peter from their fishing nets
and gave them portions of his Paradise;

He, for his birth, did not bestow himself
on Rome, but chose Judea, since he cared
among all states to elevate the humblest.

And now he's given us a sun from one
small village, so that we thank Nature and
the place that gave the world this fairest lady.

leaves: pages
of Scripture

village: probably
Carpentras, near Avignon

5

LAU-RE-TA: Latin
form of Laurette,
i.e., Laura, with
accompanying
reference to the
myth of Apollo and
Daphne, changed
to a laurel tree

When I breathe out my sighs and call your name,
that name that Love has etched upon my heart,
I start it out with something LAUdatory
to get those first sweet accents into sound;

your REgal state, which I encounter next,
doubles my strength for such high enterprise,
but "TAper off!" the ending roars, "her fame
must rest on shoulders better fit than yours."

Thus LAUd and REverence are quickly taught
whenever someone calls you, you so worthy,
oh so deserving of respect and praise,

unless Apollo feels no morTAl tongue
should ever be presumptuous to speak
of his sweet laurel boughs, forever green.

6

My mad desire has gone so far astray
pursuing her, who turned away to flee,
and, free and clear of all the snares of Love,
runs easily ahead of my slow pace,

that when I try to call desire back
and take him home by some safe path, he balks,
nor can I round him up or shepherd him
since Love has made him riotous by nature;

and when he takes the bit by force from me,
then I submit to him and to his mastery;
he carries me toward death against my will

and brings me sometimes to the laurel tree
whose bitter fruit, once gathered and consumed,
deepens one's woes instead of soothing them.

7

recipient unknown

Gorging and sleep and lounging on pillows
have banished every virtue from this world,
and thus our better natures, habit-hobbled,
have let their functions wither and decay;

all heavenly lights by which we see the way
to shape our human lives have been snuffed out;
whoever wants to bring us streams from Helicon
is pointed out and called a prodigy.

Who cares for laurel now? And who loves myrtle?
"Naked and poor, Philosophy, go beg!"
the mob howls now, absorbed by its own greed.

You will have few companions on your way:
It's therefore all the more important, friend,
you not abandon your great-hearted quest.

8

Below the foothills where she first put on
the lovely garment of her earthly limbs—
that lady who can often rouse from sleep
the tearful man who sends us to you now—

we passed our lives in tranquil peace and freedom,
as every living thing desires to do;
we had no fears as we went on our way
of stepping into snares that caught us up.

But for the woeful state to which we're brought
out of our carefree life and to this death,
we have one solitary consolation:

revenge on him who brought us to this end,
for he remains in someone else's power,
facing his own end, bound with a stronger chain.

This sonnet was written
to accompany a gift
of game; the dead
creatures are posited
as the speakers.

9

This sonnet
was written to
accompany a
gift of truffles.

When sun, the planet marking off the hours,
returns again to live in Taurus' house,
vigor spills forth out of his flaming horns
and tricks the whole world out in fresher colors.

And not just things, spread out before our gaze,
the hills and shores, ablaze with their new flowers,
but underground, where daylight never goes,
he makes the depths of earth grow fertile too,

and they produce these fruits and others like them.
The same way she, who is a sun herself,
turns her sweet eyes upon me and stirs up

the thoughts and words and deeds that deal with love:
but any way she rules or governs them,
spring still can never happen in my heart.

10

This sonnet
was written to
Stefano Colonna
the Elder, from
the estate of
his son near
the Pyrenees.

Glorious Column, raising up our hope,
and carrying great Latium's reputation,
who never turned aside from the true path
despite Jove's anger and wind-driven rain:

we have no palaces, arcades, or theaters;
we have instead a fir, a beech, a pine—
the green grass all around, the neighbor mountain
which we climb up and down, making our poems;

these lift our spirits up from earth to Heaven;
and then the nightingale laments and weeps
from shadows every night so sweetly that

our hearts grow heavy, filled with thoughts of love.
Yet all this good you spoil and make imperfect
because, my lord, you do not come and join us!

11

I've never seen you put aside your veil,
for sun or shadow, Lady,
not since you learned about the great desire
that drives all other feelings from my heart.

When all my loving thoughts were unexpressed
(those thoughts that bring my heart desire for death),
compassion toward me shone upon your face;
but ever since Love made you notice me,
your blond hair has been veiled, your loving gaze
has pulled itself away and turned to others.
    What I desired in you has been taken;
that veil controls me now,
and plots my death in weather warm or icy
because it shades the sweet light of your eyes.

This variation on the sonnet form is called a ballata; note the shorter second and twelfth lines.

12

If my life can withstand this bitter torment,
surviving tribulation long enough
to see your later years, my lady, dimming,
the light extinguished from your lovely eyes,

your head of fine gold hair transformed to silver,
your garlands laid aside with your green dresses,
your face drained very slowly of that color
which makes me hesitate and then lament,

then Love may also grant me timely courage
to speak at last of my great suffering,
to tell you of its years, its days, its hours;

if time should be adverse to my sweet wishes,
at least it won't prevent my pain receiving
some small relief from my belated sighs.

13

When now and then among the other ladies,
Love makes his home within her charming face,
the ways in which each one can't match her beauty
renew desire, and my passion thrives.

I bless the place, the time, I bless the hour
that raised my eyes so high; and thus I say:
"Soul, you must give both deep and hearty thanks
that for that honor you were first picked out.

"The loving thoughts that she aroused in you
can make you climb up toward the highest good,
and teach you to hate things most men desire;

she'll fill your mind with a courageous joy,
and lead you thus toward Heaven, a straight path
along which I am moving, high with hope."

14

This is another
ballata, with
shorter third and
thirteenth lines.

My weary eyes, when I direct you toward
the lovely face of her who's murdered you,
be careful, please, I beg you:
Love will assail you, and that makes me sigh.

Nothing but Death can stop my thoughts from taking
the loving road that leads them forward to
a harbor and sweet haven where they'll heal;
but your light, eyes, can be disrupted, lost
to lesser things, for you are made less perfect,
the power that sustains you is too weak.
So go and cry a little now, I say,
before the hours of tears that lie ahead,
take some brief solace here
before you undergo long martyrdom.

15

At every step I make I turn around
then shove my weary body on ahead,
and take a little comfort from your air
that helps me to plod on, crying "Alas!"

I stop, then, in my tracks, to recollect
the awesome presence that I've left behind,
the road ahead so long, my life so short,
and bow my head and burst out into tears.

While I'm lamenting, every now and then,
a doubt arrives to torment me and haunt me:
how can these limbs survive without their spirit?

Love has an answer, though: "Don't you recall?
This is the privilege reserved for lovers,
released from all their human qualities."

16

White-haired and pale, the old man takes his leave
of this sweet place where he has lived his life;
his little family watches in dismay
as their dear father disappears from sight;

and so he drags his ancient flanks along,
through these last days and hours of his life;
his years a burden, and his travel tiring,
goodwill is what he draws on to survive;

he comes to Rome—he must pursue his fancy,
he wants to gaze upon the face of Him
he hopes he'll see eventually in Heaven.

the face: the Veronica,
said to have retained
Christ's likeness, kept
at St. Peter's and an
object of pilgrimage

In just that way, alas, I go and search
in others, Lady, hoping I might find
somehow, somewhere, your much-desired shape.

17

Bitter tears come raining down my face
accompanied by an anguished wind of sighs,
all times I turn my eyes in your direction
who've made me quite alone, lost to the world.

It's true your smile, mild and full of peace,
retains the power to calm my passion down
and free me from the flames that torture me
while I'm intent and fixed on watching you;

but then my spirits are transformed to ice
because we part and those two fatal stars
direct their movements elsewhere, leaving me.

Unlocked and set at large at last, my soul
pulls up within my heart to try to follow,
and its uprooting brings on wild havoc.

18

When I am turned around to see the place
where shines my lady's face, so full of light,
and in my thoughts the light remains and thrives,
burns down and melts, inside me, bit by bit,

I think my heart is going to crack in half,
and fear that I am going to lose my light,
and feel my way, still groping in the dark,
a blind man with no place to go, yet going.

I run away to dodge the blows of death
but not so fast that passion doesn't come
right at my side, the way it always does;

I go in silence, since my fatal words
would make men weep and what I really want
is solitude in which to shed my tears.

19

Some animals there are with eyes so strong
they have no fear of sunlight; others, though,
because they can't exist in such bright light,
don't venture forth until the dusk arrives;

and others still, imbued with mad desire,
plunge toward the fire to enjoy its gleam,
and come upon a force that burns them up;
alas, it seems that I am of this species.

For I lack strength to gaze straight at the light
this lady radiates, and lack the sense
to shield myself in shadows and late hours;

therefore, despite my weak and tearful eyes,
my destiny leads me to seek and see her,
drawn to the thing that I know will consume me.

20

Sometimes, ashamed that I have not been rhyming
to praise your beauty, oh, my gentle Lady,
I let my mind go back to your first sight;
no other beauty moved me after that,

but it's a weight my arms can't really carry,
roughness my file does not know how to hone;
and when it feels its lack of strength, my wit
freezes in place and will not go on working.

Time and again, right on the verge of speech,
my voice has stayed inside me, holding back:
what sound could ever reach to such a height?

Time and again, when I began to write,
I found my pen and hand and intellect
were all defeated in the first assault.

21

A thousand times, oh, my sweet warrior,
to make a pact of peace with your fair eyes,
I've offered up my heart, but you don't deign
to glance down from your elevated mind;

if any other lady wants my heart
she lives in weak and much-mistaken hopes;
and since I hate whatever you don't care for,
I think he never can be mine again.

Now if I drive him off and you won't take him,
he'll have no help in his unhappy exile;
he cannot live alone, nor be with others,

so probably his course of life will fail,
and that would be a fault in both of us;
you more, I think, since he loves you the most.

22

For any animal who dwells on earth,
(except those few who hate to be in sun),
the time for labor is throughout the day;
but then when Heaven kindles all its stars
some go back home, some nest within the forest
and take their rest at least until the dawn.

And I, when lovely day begins to dawn
and scatters shadows from around the earth,
arousing animals in every forest,
can find no truce from sighing with the sun;
and when I see them lighting up, the stars,
I go around and weep and long for day.

When evening comes and drives away the day,
and darkness here is someone else's dawn,
I gaze in sorrow at the cruel stars

that made my body out of feeling earth,
and curse the day on which I saw the sun
until I seem a man raised in a forest.

There is no more ferocious beast in forest
who wanders there by night or roams by day
than she for whom I weep in shade and sun,
past bedtime, always, staying up till dawn,
for though I'm mortal, something made of earth,
my fixed desire comes down from the stars.

Before I come to join you, you bright stars,
or fall back into Love's dense trackless forest,
and leave my body crumbling back to earth,
you'd think that she might pity me, one day;
one day would balance years, and by the dawn
requite me for the setting of our sun.

Love's dense trackless forest: a reference to Virgil's account of the underworld in *Aeneid* 6

To watch it set along with her, that sun,
no one around to witness us but stars,
and just one night; then let day never dawn,
and let her not become a tree, in forest,
escaping, as she did that fatal day
when Lord Apollo followed her on earth!

I will be under earth first, in dry forest,
and day itself be lit by tiny stars,
before the sun will come to such sweet dawn.

23

In the sweet season of my early youth
of passion born and growing like green grass
that would become in time my source of pain—
since singing helps to make my pains less bitter
I'll sing how then I lived at liberty
while Love was merely scorned in my abode.

And then I'll tell how that offended him
and what ensued that served to make of me
a kind of grim example for the world:
although my harsh undoing
is written elsewhere, by a thousand pens,
and almost every valley has been filled
with echoes of my sighs to prove my pain.
But if my memory doesn't help me here
the way it usually does, perhaps my torments
will help excuse me, plus one single thought
which causes so much anguish by itself
it makes me turn my back, forget myself,
because it holds my very being fast
and leaves the rest of me an empty shell.

I'll say that since the day when Love had tried
his first attack, some years had passed, so that
my youthful countenance was altered some
and round my heart the thoughts were frozen fast
to make a surface hard as any diamond
that my firm manner did not serve to weaken;
    no tear yet wet my breast, nor broke my sleep,
and what was insubstantial in myself
seemed like a miracle, observed in others.
Alas, what am I? What was I?
The evening crowns the day, the death the life;
that cruel mastermind of whom I speak
seeing his arrows launched against me
had not yet managed to pierce through my clothes
made his alliance with a potent Lady
against whom wit, and force, and cries for mercy
have not availed to help me, then or now;
these two transformed me into what I am,
a living man turned into a green laurel
that sheds no leaves throughout the winter season.

What I became, when my awareness grew
of this great change I'd undergone, was this:

I saw my hairs transforming into leaves,
the leaves I'd hoped to wear as my own crown,
and then the feet on which I stood and ran,
according to the dictates of the spirit,
   became two roots beside the churning waters
not of Peneus but a prouder stream,
and my two arms transformed to wooden branches!
It gave me no less fear
that hope, all covered in white feathers then,
lay thunderstruck and dead, beyond recovery,
punished for mounting much too far and high;
I knew not where I could recover him.
And thus it was I went alone, and weeping,
by night and day around the place I lost him,
searching the riverbanks, peering in waters,
and since that time my tongue has sung his loss
when it has had the strength; I sing the song
the swan sings, dying, and I have his color.

   I walked along beloved riverbanks
from that time on, and when I wished to speak
I sang in my new voice, beseeching mercy;
but I could never make my amorous woes
resound in such a way, both soft and sweet,
to humble her ferocious heart toward me.
   What was it like to hear? The memory burns me.
But even more than I've already done
I need to sing that sweet and bitter enemy.
Necessity demands it,
although she's quite beyond the power of words.
She who can steal a soul with one swift glance
opened my chest and took my heart in hand,
saying, "Don't speak of this." I saw her next
in such a different form I didn't know her
(oh human sense!) and blurted out the truth,
all fearful, when she changed back to herself
and turned me, oh alas, into a stone:
a partly living, deeply frightened, stone.

She spoke, with such an angry countenance,
it made me tremble from within the stone:
"I am perhaps not who you think I am!"
And I said to myself, "If she should free me
from being stone, no life will make me sad;
come back, my lord, and make me weep again."
 I don't know how I did it, but I moved
my feet and went away, blaming myself,
suspended between death and life all day.
But since my time grows short
my pen cannot keep up with my intention
and I'll omit much that is in my mind
and speak of just a few more special things
that will be wonders to whoever hears them.
My heart was in the grip of death, nor could
my silence act to free it from her hand
or bring me any other kind of help.
Speaking out loud had been forbidden to me,
so I cried out with paper and with ink,
"I'm not my own. If I die, it's your loss."

 I thought that this might change me, in her eyes,
from one devoid of mercy to deserving,
and that hope made me bold; sometimes, however,
while true humility may quench disdain,
it can inflame it too; I learned that later
while dressed in darkness for a season long;
 for at those prayers my light had been extinguished,
and I, not finding anywhere her shadow
or even any trace of where she'd stepped,
like someone bent on sleep
lay down exhausted on the grass one day.
Complaining of the absence of the light,
I let myself dissolve in angry tears
and let them fall wherever they might land;
no snowbank ever shrank beneath the sun
more quickly than I melted there, becoming
a fountain springing from a beech's foot;

I kept that up a long and tearful time.
Whoever heard of man becoming fountain?
And yet I speak of an undoubted fact.

   The soul's nobility derives from God—
for no one else can be such source of grace—
and keeps her thus in likeness to her maker;
and therefore she does not refuse to pardon
whoever comes with humble face and heart
to ask for mercy after much offending.
   And if she manages, against inclining,
to be importuned long, she mirrors Him—
and does this to make sinning still more feared,
for one is not repenting
if he's already bound for the next sin.
Because my lady, finally moved to pity,
had turned to gaze on me and could well see
how much my punishment had matched my sin,
she kindly let me change to my first state.
But nothing in this world can be relied on;
for when I pled again, my nerves and bones
were changed to hardest flint, and thus I stayed
transfixed, a voice, still burdened as before,
calling on Death and only her by name.

   A wandering doleful spirit, I complained
for many years, in caves both strange and empty,
about my unleashed boldness, I recall,
and came eventually to my release
and got my limbs and human movement back
but maybe just so I'd feel sorrow more.
   I let desire draw me on so far
that one day, while I hunted in the woods,
I saw that lovely, cruel, and wild creature
naked at noon and bathing.
No other sight means anything to me
and I so stood and gazed at her, while she
felt shame, and then, to undertake revenge

and camouflage, employed her hand to splash
some water in my face. At this I changed:
I'll tell the truth, though it may seem a lie;
I felt myself drawn out of my own shape
and I became a stag, alone and wandering
from forest unto forest, with my dogs
pursuing me and baying as I fled.

Oh, song, I never got to be the cloud
of gold that came down in a precious rain
to quench Jove's fire, or at least in part;
but I have certainly become a flame,
and I have been the bird that soars above
to raise and celebrate her with my praise;
and never would I trade for some new shape
that laurel I was first, in whose sweet shade
all other pleasures vanish in my heart.

The metamorphoses
referred to are
Daphne, Cygnus,
Battus, Biblis,
Echo, Actaeon,
Danaë, Semele,
and Ganymede.

This is a reply to a
sonnet from Perugia
inviting Petrarch
to drink at Pallas
Athena's fountain.

24

If that much-honored branch that shelters us
from Heaven's anger when the great Jove thunders
had not refused to grant me that green crown
that decorates the writers who make poems,

I might have liked those goddesses of yours
the current world abandons so unjustly;
but that great slight has driven me away from
the goddess who invented olive trees;

the sands of Ethiopia don't boil
under the fiercest of its noonday suns
more than I do at loss of what I love.

You need to find a fountain that's more tranquil,
for mine's bereft of any other moisture
than I provide it with my falling tears.

25

Love used to cry, and I would cry with him
since I was then so often in his company,
to see your soul by strange and bitter habits
escaping all his knots and cunning snares;

and now your soul has been put right by God
on its true path, and I give heartfelt thanks,
and lift my hands to Heaven, deeply grateful
for mercy that attends to human prayers.

If coming back into the life of love
you've found your path disrupted by deep ditches,
and by steep hills that make the going hard,

it's all to show the hard and thorny path,
the steep and alpine slant of the ascent,
by which you can rise up to worth and goodness.

26

recipient unknown,
perhaps the same as
that of Number 25

No ship that ever landed, weather-racked,
storm-drenched from battling waves, its grateful folk
kneeling on land to offer thanks, faith-hued,
could be more glad than I am at this time;

no one set free from prison, who had felt
the rope around his neck, could be more happy
than I to see that fell sword sheathed which had
made war against my lord for such a spell.

All you who praise Sir Love with rhyme and craft,
come celebrate this one who weaves love poems
but strayed awhile from the path we tread;

you know there's more elation up in Heaven
for rescuing one spirit lost—he's more
than nine and ninety who are perfect still.

27

inheritor:
Philip VI
of France

Charlemagne's inheritor, who wears
his predecessor's crown upon his brow,
has taken arms by now to break the horns
of Babylon, and those who take her name;

Christ's Vicar:
Benedict XII

Christ's Vicar, with his ancient holy burden,
the keys and mantle, looks to his first nest,
and if misfortunes don't come to delay him,
he'll see Bologna soon and then great Rome.

lamb[s] and *wolves:*
rival factions in
Florence or Rome

Your lamb, remaining meek and noble both,
beats back the savage wolves, as it should be
with those who put asunder lawful loves;

console her, therefore, she still waits for you,
as Rome herself does, weeping for her bridegroom;

*buckle on your
sword:* join the
Crusade declared
in 1334

and now for Jesus buckle on your sword.

28

This poem was
probably addressed
to Cardinal Giacomo
Colonna, encouraging
him to lead the
Crusade of 1334.

Oh, blessed and lovely soul, which Heaven waits for,
you who go dressed in our humanity
(though not, like others, too much burdened by it):
so that the road ahead may seem less hard,
that road by which we pass on to His realm,
beloved of God, obedient handmaiden,
    behold just now the comfort for your ship,
already sailing from this bad, blind world
unto a better port,
the comfort of this sweet and western wind.
This wind will lead you, freed from former bonds,
through shadowed valleys where we all bewail
our woes and woes of others, taking you
by best and straightest course
to that true Orient toward which you're bound.

It may be that devout and loving prayers,
along with sacred tears that mortals shed,
have had their hearing with the highest Pity;
or maybe their sheer numbers or their force
were never needed for eternal Justice
to keep its course and never swerve aside.
　　But that good King who governs in his grace
in Heaven turns his eyes now toward the place
where He was crucified;
and in the breast of this new Charles breathes
a vengeful spirit that, too long delayed,
made Europe sigh; and thus He aids his bride,
He whose voice alone
fills Babylon with fear and makes it shake.

　　All those who dwell between Garonne and Alps,
between the Rhône and Rhine and the salt sea,
flock to the banners of high Christian calling;
and all who ever cared for valor's meaning
from Pyrenees on to the far horizon
will empty Spain to follow Aragon;
　　and England, and the islands bathed by ocean
between the Pillars and the starry Bear—
as far as knowledge reaches
of muses and their home on Helicon—
all varied in their languages and dress
and in their arms, all spurred by love
to their high undertaking now. What love,
however worthy or well sanctioned,
of men and women ever
gave rise to such a just and lasting anger?

　　There is a portion of the world that lies
always in ice and under freezing snow,
too distant from the visits of the sun;
there lives a people, under cloudy days,
who seem to be the enemies of peace

and have no sense of fear concerning death.
    If they, now more devout than once they were,
gird on their swords in their Teutonic rage,
you'll see how much
you need to prize Chaldeans, Arabs, Turks,
all those who put their trust in pagan gods
from here on to that sea with bloody waves:
a people cowardly, undressed, and lazy,
who fight by archery
and thereby trust the wind to guide their wars.

    It's time, therefore, that we withdraw our necks
out of the ancient yoke, and rend the veil
that has been wrapped around our eyes;
display your noble genius, which you get
from Lord Apollo, whose immortal grace
informs your eloquence and shows its power
    in both your speech and writing, rightly praised.
If reading of Amphion and great Orpheus
no longer makes you marvel,
you will perhaps be even less impressed
when Italy and all her sons awake
and at the sound of your clear summoning
take up their arms for Jesus; for if she,
this ancient mother Italy, sees true,
no other quarrel of hers
had cause so lovely to compel her service.

    To profit from true treasure you have turned
the ancient pages over, and the modern,
soaring toward Heaven, though in earthly body,
and thus you know how from Mars' own son's reign
on to the time of Emperor Augustus,
whose brow was three times crowned with laurel green,
    Rome gave her blood unstintingly to help
when others had been injured; why not now
be grateful, pious, not

just generous, and set about the task
of righting and avenging cruel wrongs
in company with Mary's glorious son?
How then can any enemy have hope
to stand against us
if we have Christ among our fighting ranks?

Consider Xerxes and his reckless daring
when with peculiar bridges he outraged
the sea itself, to tread upon our shores,
and all the Persian women dressed in black
to mourn their husbands' deaths, the while the sea
at Salamis grew red with blood. That omen,
the miserable ruin of those people,
who came, unhappy, from the East, foretells
victory to you and yours;
and so can Marathon and those hot gates
the Lion and his few men held, and more
of which you've heard and read. Therefore it's fit
that you subject both mind and knee to God,
who has reserved
your years in order that you may do good.

My song, you will see Italy, and see
the honored shore concealed from me not just
by mountain, river, sea
but by great Love, who with his noble light
gives me desire where he most inflames me;
nature, I fear, cannot give way to habit.
Go on then, song, with your companions. Love,
who makes us laugh and weep,
does not dwell just beneath the veils of ladies.

29

This canzone follows
a Provençal form in
which the rhymes and
internal rhymes are the
same in each stanza.

Green garments, blood red, black, or purple,
   you never dressed a lady
who twists her hair up in a golden braid
as beautiful as is this one, who strips
my will from me, and from the path of freedom
leads me astray so far that I can bear
   no lesser yoke of any kind.

And if at times my soul will arm itself
   to remonstrate—it judges poorly
when plunged in doubt from all its lamentations—
she'll call it back and then her very look
will summon it, resistless; from my heart
each frenzy is erased, and each disdain
   grows sweeter at the sight of her.

For everything I've suffered, all for love,
   and will still suffer till she heals
my heart, that one who wounded him, a rebel
to all mercy, who still can make him yearn,
there shall be vengeance; that's if pride and anger
don't act to lock humility from showing
   that lovely way that leads to her.

The hour and the day I gazed upon
   those lights, the lovely black and white
evicted me, and Love took up my place
to form the root of this new painful life,
and she in whom our age admires itself;
to see her without being awed, you'd need
   to be made out of lead or wood.

*the lovely black and
white:* Laura's eyes

No teardrop, then, that might pour from my eyes
   (because those arrows in my side
bathe my poor heart in his first wound's own blood)
no tear, I say, can lessen my desire;
the punishment is just: heart makes soul sigh

and it is simply right and fully just
    that she should help to tend my wounds.

Kind stars that did attend the great event
    when one womb had been singled out
and gave its lovely fruit unto this world!
Celestial is what she is, on earth,
and as the laurel keeps its leaf she keeps
her chastity: no wind or lightning storm
    can seem to break or bend her.

I know full well that praising her in verse
    would test the skill of anyone
who sought, however worthily, to write;
what cell does memory own that truly can
contain the virtue that we see in her,
all beauty in her eyes, sign of her worth,
    the sweet key that unlocks my heart?

While the sun turns, Love has no dearer pledge,
Lady, than thou art.

30

I saw a maiden underneath a laurel,
and white she was, and cold as is the snow
which sunlight hasn't shone upon for years;
and seeing her most lovely face, voice, hair
pleased me so much that she is in my eyes
wherever I may go, on slope or shore.

My thoughts will only then have come ashore
when green leaves are no longer on the laurel,
or when my heart is stilled, dried-up my eyes,
or fire freezes and there's burning snow;
there are not, on my head, sufficient hairs
to number days I'd wait, or even years.

But time has wings and thus they flee, the years,
and soon we come, quite soon, to life's last shore—
we may or we may not have grown white-haired—
and still I'll seek its shadow, that green laurel,
in fiercest sun or in the coldest snow,
until my last day comes and shuts my eyes.

There never have been such exquisite eyes,
no, not in this our time, nor in past years;
they melt me just the way that sun melts snow,
which makes a weeping river by the shore
around the foot of a hard-hearted laurel
with diamond branches and with golden hair.

I fear that I must change my face and hair
before some pity rises in her eyes,
my idol, fashioned from the living laurel;
unless I'm counting wrong it's seven years
since I've gone sighing here from shore to shore
by day and night, in heat and in the snow.

On fire inside, although my outside's snow,
alone with all my thoughts and graying hair,
weeping forever, traversing each shore,
hoping that pity might invade the eyes
of someone who may live a thousand years
if that is the true life span of the laurel.

The missing word
laurel in the coda
is supplied by
L'auro, "gold."

Topaz and gold, in sun, against the snow,
are less than is that hair and those fair eyes,
that lead my years so swiftly to the shore.

27

31

This noble soul that starts to move away,
called to the afterlife before her time,
will dwell, if prized the way she should be prized,
in Heaven's choicest regions, those most blessed;

if she should stay where Venus borders Mars,
the sun itself will surely be bedimmed
since choicest souls will flock to see the sight,
and gather round to gaze on this soul's beauty;

if she is set below the sun's fourth sphere,
she'll steal away the beauty of three planets
as fame and great acclaim accrue to her;

at the fifth circle, she'll not dwell with Mars
but will soar higher, I feel sure, until
she'll outshine Jove and every other star!

32

The closer that I come to the last day
which puts an end to all our human misery,
the more I see that Time runs swift and light,
and that my hopes in him are vain and fatuous.

I tell my thoughts: "Not too much further now
will we go on like this, speaking of love;
the hard and heavy burden that we carry
is melting like fresh snow—and we'll have peace,

"because at last we're going to drop the hope
that's made us rave so long, so angrily,
the laughter and the tears, the fear and sorrow:

"we'll see it clearly then, we'll know how much
people run after things that are unstable,
and how their sighs are always sighed in vain."

33

star of love: Venus
as the morning star

that other one:
the North Star,
associated with Ursa
Major and Ursa
Minor. Callisto and
her son Arcas were
transformed by Juno
into constellations
because of Juno's
jealousy of Jupiter's
love for Callisto.

The star of love was flaming in the East
already, and that other one which makes
Juno forever jealous, in the North,
wheeling its outspread rays, all bright and lovely;

the frail old woman was awake to spin,
half-dressed and barefoot, waking up the coals,
and lovers felt the stinging of that moment
that they are so much given to lamenting;

when, worn down to the very nub, my hope
came to my heart by unaccustomed means
(for sleep had closed my eyes, tears kept them wet)—

and changed she was, so different from before!—
and seemed to say: "Why are you languishing?
You still can see these eyes for some time yet."

34

If fair desire's still alive, Apollo,
that burned within you once by Thessaly's waves,
and if through all the years you still have not
forgot those golden tresses that you loved,

among these frosts, these cruel and bitter times,
that last as long as you conceal your face,
redeem the honor of these sacred leaves
where you were trapped, and then I was trapped too;

and by the power of that amorous hope
that once sustained you in your bitter life,
come clear this atmosphere of mist and vapor;

then both of us can see a marvelous thing—
our lady sitting out here on the grass
her arms raised up to give herself some shade.

35

Alone and pensive, crossing empty fields,
I make my way with slow, reluctant steps,
my eyes alert in case I need to flee
if I see human footprints in the sand.

This is my only way to shield myself,
from people's knowing glances, since they read
my miserable bearing, all joy spent,
and know the fires that must rage within.

So I believe the mountains and the shores,
rivers and forests too, all know by now
the sort of life I lead, concealed from people;

yet there's no path so savage or so wild
that Love won't always come and join me there,
discoursing with me, as I do with him.

36

If I could hope by death to free myself
from love that makes me sad and casts me down,
by now I would have used these hands of mine
to lay these limbs in earth and shed their weight;

but since I fear that death would be a passage
from one war to another, grief to grief,
I'm at the pass and find it closed to me.
I half remain, alas, and half cross over.

It's high time that the heartless cord release
the bowstring and its final, fatal arrow,
already wet and red with others' blood,

and I beg Love for this, and beg that deaf one
who's painted me with all her colors and
does not remember she should call me to her.

37

It is so weak, the thread by which it hangs,
this heavy life of mine;
if someone doesn't aid it,
it will come quickly to its journey's end;
for ever since the cruel departure that
I took from my sweet love,
one hope alone remains
and this in fact has kept me still alive;
    it said: "While you're deprived
of your beloved's sight
maintain yourself, sad soul;
how do you know you won't return again
to better times and days,
or if your solace gone might be regained?"
This hope had me sustained a little while;
it's ebbing now. I've lived in it too long.

    Time runs on by, and hours are so swift
to finish up their journey,
I scarce have time to notice
that I run on toward death; one ray of sun
will just have left the East when you already
see it touch the mountains
of the opposite horizon,
coiling across a huge and mighty distance.
    The lives of men are short,
heavy their bodies, frail
their mortal human flesh,
so when I find myself cut off again
from her fair face,
the wings of my desire paralyzed,
my strength deserts me and I do not know
if I can live much longer in this state.

    Each place I visit makes me sad when I
don't see those lovely eyes,
soft eyes that took away

the keys of all the thoughts God gave me once;
and just so my harsh exile will hurt more
whether I walk, or sleep,
or sit, I call aloud,
and all that I've seen since displeases me.
    How many mountains, waters,
how many seas and rivers
hide me from those two lights
that turned my total darkness to a sky
as clear and bright as noon,
so that recalling them destroys me more;
so that my cruel and deeply burdened life
can teach me how much happier I was then.

    Alas, if speaking of it stokes the fire,
renews the burning passion
that was born that day
I left behind my better part, my self,
and if neglect can help love fade away
who takes me to the bait
that helps my sorrow grow,
and why not turn my silence into stone?
    Certainly glass or crystal
were never more revealing
than is my soul, disconsolate,
displaying through my eyes the savage sweetness
living here in my heart,
my poor eyes always ready with their tears
seeking for her by day and then by night
who is alone the cure of their desire.

    Strange pleasure that in human minds is found:
to love whatever thing
that's new and different and
that will produce the thickest crowd of sighs!
And I am one of those whom weeping pleases;
it seems I strive to make
my eyes produce a family

of tears to match the sorrows in my heart.
    Since speaking of her eyes
calls up the passion in me,
and nothing else I do
affects me quite so deeply, I must visit
often where my sorrow
wells up and overflows its boundaries,
and thus my eyes are punished with my heart
because they led me on the road of love.

    Those golden tresses which should make the sun
go filled with envy, and
that clear gaze, serene,
from which the burning rays of Love shine hot,
so hot they're like to bring untimely death,
and words well chosen, rare,
seldom encountered in this world
that gave themselves to me so courteously,
    are taken from me, lost;
and I forgive more easily
all wrongs against me but
the one that takes the kind angelic greeting
that roused my heart;
and thus I think I'm never going to hear
a sound that will encourage me
except the sound that's made by heaving sighs.

    And just so I can weep with more delight,
her slender hands, so soft,
her gracious arms, so white,
and her sweet gestures, just a little haughty,
her lovable disdain, her humble pride,
her youthful and delicious breast,
a citadel of lofty thoughts,
hid from me now by wild and mountainous regions,
    and I don't know if I can hope
to see her once before I die
because from hour to hour

my expectation rises and then falls;
it's never going to see
she whom high Heaven honors, she, the home
where chastity and every virtue dwell,
the place where I have prayed I might dwell too.

    Song, if in her sweet place you run into
our lady, I believe
that you believe she will
reach out to touch you with her lovely hand,
the hand I am so far from;
don't touch that hand, but at her feet, in reverence,
tell her I'll come as quickly as I can,
either as spirit bodiless, or flesh and blood.

38

This sonnet was written to Orso dell' Anguillara, a friend in Rome.

There never was a lake or river, Orso,
nor sea which all the rivers empty into,
nor shade of wall or hill or leafy branch,
nor cloud that spreads above and then rains down,

nor any object else, that blocks out sight,
nor other hindrance I'd complain about,
except the veil that veils two lovely eyes
and seems to say: "Go suffer now, and weep."

And then that lowered gaze that kills my joys,
whether from pride or from humility,
will be the cause of my untimely death.

And I complain as well of a white hand
that always has been quick to do me harm,
rising against my eyes just like a reef.

recipient unknown,
Avignon area

39

I fear their fierce attack, those lovely eyes
where Love and my own death reside together
and I flee them the way a boy flees whipping;
it's years now since I first leaped up and ran.

There is no place too high, too hard to climb,
to which desire will not take me now,
to shun the one who dissipates my senses
and leaves me, usually, as cold as stone.

Therefore, if I've been slow to visit you,
not to be near the one who makes me suffer,
it's something you can probably forgive.

Indeed, just coming back at all, my friend,
to what I flee, and mastering my fear,
is no small pledge of my fidelity!

This sonnet
was written to a
patron in Rome.

birdlime: sticky
substance used
by hunters to
capture birds

40

If Love and Death don't manage to cut short
the new cloth which I've now begun to weave,
and I can free myself from this birdlime
while I am joining one truth with the other,

perhaps I can make something doubly good
between the modern style and ancient speech,
(I tell you this, of course, with trepidation)
that you will hear it all the way to Rome.

But since I lack, to finish up this project
a number of inestimable threads
that were abundant for my cherished father,

father:
probably Livy

why should you keep your hands closefisted now,
against your custom? Please, open them
and you will be amazed by the results.

41

Apollo loved a tree in human form;
when it departs and leaves its proper place,
old Vulcan sets to work: he sweats and pants,
his forge producing bitter bolts for Jove,

who throws them down; it snows and then it rains,
without respecting Caesar more than Janus;
earth weeps, the sun stays far away
because he sees that his dear friend is elsewhere.

Caesar and *Janus:*
July and January

Now Mars and Saturn, evil stars, grow bolder;
Orion, armed, begins to shatter tackle,
the tillers and the shrouds of seamen break.

Aeolus vents his anger: Neptune, Juno
learn how it hurts us when that lovely face,
the one the angels wish for, isn't here.

Aeolus: god of the
winds; *Neptune*
and *Juno:* the sea
and the air

42

But now that her sweet smile, soft and humble,
no longer hides away its novel beauties,
the ancient blacksmith who's Sicilian
flexes his arms in vain at his old forge;

*blacksmith who's
Sicilian:* Vulcan

for Jove has dropped his weapons from his hands
(tempered in Mongibello though they were);
his sister earth is bit by bit renewing
herself beneath Apollo's friendly gaze.

Mongibello: Mt. Etna
sister earth: Latona,
goddess of earth

And from the shore there comes a western wind
so mariners can sail without precautions, while
it wakes the flowers in the grassy meadows;

the harmful planets flee in all directions
dispersed before that lovely face of hers
on whose account I've shed so many tears.

43

Latona's son:
Apollo

Latona's son had looked nine times already
from his high balcony, in search of her,
who made him sigh in vain in times gone by
and now moves sighs of like kind from another;

he tired of searching when he couldn't find
where she was living, near or far, and seemed
like one gone mad with grief who hunts around
to find a much-loved thing that he has lost.

And thus it was that, staying to himself,
he did not see that face return which I
will praise, if I live, on a thousand pages;

it's true as well, that pity had transformed her:
her brilliant eyes were just then shedding tears—
and thus the air retained its former state.

44

Caesar wept for
Pompey, his
son-in-law; David
wept for Absalom
and Saul, cursing
Mt. Gilboa and
making it sterile.

The man whose hands were ready to turn Thessaly
crimson with civil blood sat down and wept
to mourn his daughter's husband's death; he knew
that severed head by its familiar features;

the shepherd too, who broke Goliath's brow,
wept for the rebel son from his own family,
and losing all control in grief for Saul,
took out his anger on a wild mountain.

But you who never blanch because of pity,
you're well defended from Love's deadly bow,
he draws and shoots his arrows all in vain;

you see me torn to death a thousand times
and no tears issue from your lovely eyes;
instead they flash annoyance and disdain.

45

My enemy, in whom you watch your eyes   *enemy:*
gazing on that which Love and Heaven honor,   *her mirror*
enamors you with beauties not his own
happy and sweet beyond all mortal limits.

By listening to him, Lady, you have run me
out of the place where I desired to be—
miserable exile!—even if I'm not worthy
to occupy the place where you now dwell.

But had I been nailed firmly in its place,
the mirror would not then have so defined you
and made you harsh, pleased with yourself, and cold.

You've heard the tale, remember, of Narcissus?   *Narcissus:*
The vanity you practice has one outcome—   *changed to*
though grass does not deserve a flower so fair.   *a flower*

46

The gold, the pearls, the flowers red and white
that winter should have withered and made languid,
are thorns that prick, both poisonous and sharp,
I feel along my breast and in my sides.

Therefore my tearful days are clearly numbered,
since sorrows of this size do not grow old;
but most I blame those mirrors, murderous—
they've worn you out with gazing at yourself.

My lord they've silenced, he who pled my case;
he gave up and grew still because he saw
that your desires ended in yourself;

those mirrors come from waters deep in Hell,
that tinged them with forgetfulness forever,
and they gave birth to my incipient death.

47

Inside my heart I felt my spirits dying,
those spirits that receive their life from you;
and since all earthly creatures have an instinct
to fight off death whenever it approaches,

I let desire, now reined tight, go loose,
and off it went: the path was all grown over,
the path it wants to travel, night and day,
the one from which I try to pull it back,

and there it brought me, tardy and confused,
into the very sight of your bright eyes,
eyes I avoid in order not to pain them.

I cannot live much longer, since your glance
has much to do with whether I survive;
I'll die, unless I follow my desire.

48

If fire never puts a fire out,
nor river can grow dry receiving rain,
but things increase by contact with their ilk,
and even oppositions spur each other;

then you who rule our thinking, oh, great Love,
you who have made me one soul in two bodies,
why do you come in an outmoded shape
and make desire shrink by its own surplus?

Perhaps the way the Nile, thundering down,
makes deaf all those who live too near its noise,
the way the sun blinds those who stare into it,

the way desire, with no sense of limits,
is lost when its objective's too immense,
flies fast, flies hard, and is by that made slow.

49

Although I've tried to hinder you from lying
and honored your achievement, tongue (you ingrate),
you haven't won me honor back; so far
it's mostly been a share of wrath and shame;

the more I call on you to help me out,
entreating mercy, the colder you become,
and if you speak, the words are jumbled up
like someone who is mumbling in his sleep!

You doleful tears, you stay with me all night,
just when I feel the need to be alone,
and then you flee the presence of my peace.

You sighs, who bring me anguish, you as well,
you limp along, so crippled and so slow!
My eyes alone can speak about my heart.

50

At that time when the sky goes slanting quickly
off to the West, and when our day flies off
to people who are likely waiting for it,
a good old woman maybe finds herself
alone and far from home; she's tired, but
her steps redouble on her pilgrimage;
   and then, although alone
and at her twilight hour,
she may well be consoled
by brief repose and by forgetfulness
of all her labor all along the way.
But I, alas, what pain I have by day
seems to grow greater still
when light eternal takes its leave of us.

   And when the sun rotates his flaming wheels
to make way for the night, and there descend

a host of shadows from the highest mountains,
the tiller of the fields collects his tools,
and with some simple tunes he hums or sings,
alleviates the burdens of his mind;
    and then he sets his table
with poor and simple food
(the acorns people praise
while studiously still avoiding them).
Let those who can, be merry when they like,
but I have never had a restful hour,
much less a happy one,
for all the changing of the skies and planets.

    And when the shepherd sees the gorgeous rays
of that great planet sinking toward its nest
and all the eastern pastures growing dark,
he rises to his feet and leaves the grass
and leaves the springs and beech trees, takes his crook
and gently uses it to move his flock;
    then far from other people
he finds a hut or cave
and strews its floor with greens
and stretches out to sleep without a care.
Oh, cruel Love! It's then you urge me most
to hunt the wild creature who destroys me
her voice, her spoor, her tracks;
but you don't help me catch her as she flees.

    And mariners will shelter in a cove
when sun is gone, they'll stretch their tired limbs
and rest upon hard wood and under canvas.
But I, though sun may go beneath the waves,
and manage to leave Spain behind his back,
Granada and Morocco and the Pillars,
    while men, and women too,
the world and all its creatures,
find rest and calm their ills,
I find I cannot shed my mounting grief:
I mourn because each day extends my losses,

and my desire, nearly ten years old,
just keeps on growing greater,
and I don't see who's going to free me from it.

    And (since it eases me to speak of this)
I see the oxen coming home at evening
unyoked, returning from the fields they plowed.
My sighs—why aren't they ever taken from me,
why am I not unyoked at any time?
Why must my eyes be wet both night and day?
    Oh, miserable me!
What was I doing when
I fixed my eyes at first
upon her lovely face as if to sculpt it
and place it in imagination where
it could not be removed except by Death,
who takes away all things?
I'm not sure I believe that Death can do it.

    Song, if being with me
from morning until evening
has made you of my party,
you won't go round and show yourself too much;
and you'll pay little heed to those who praise you;
consider as you move from hill to hill
how fire burns me down
all from this living stone on which I lean.

51

That light that blinds, even when far away,
had it come any closer to my eyes,
then just the way that Thessaly transformed,
I would have changed my kind and shape completely.

And since I can't take on her form and look
more than I have so far, face marked with care

*Thessaly
transformed:*
Daphne
metamorphosed
to laurel

42

(not that it wins me any grace or mercy),
I'd sooner I became the hardest stone,

diamond, perhaps, or maybe lovely marble,
all white with fear, or maybe jasper crystal,
which would enchant the stupid, greedy rabble;

and then I would be free of this harsh yoke
that makes me envy that old man, so tired,
whose shoulders make a shade for all Morocco.

old man: Atlas,
changed to
a mountain

a madrigal

52

Diana's form did not delight her lover,
when just by chance he got a look at her
bathing all naked in the cooling waters,

more than the cruel mountain shepherdess
delighted me while rinsing out the veil
that keeps her golden curls from the wind;

she made me then, despite the sun's hot rays,
shiver a little with the chill of love.

53

Noble spirit, you who rule those limbs
within which dwell a lord who's wise and brave
and unappeasable and peregrine:
now that you've grasped the honored staff of office
with which you can both chastise Rome and teach
her citizens to seek the one true path,
I speak to you because I don't see else
a ray of virtue in this darkened world,
or anyone ashamed of doing evil.
What Italy expects or yearns for, I

don't know; she doesn't seem to feel her woes;
she's idle, old, and slow;
will no one wake her, will she sleep forever?
I wish that I could grab her by her hair!

I have no hope that from her slothful sleep
she'll raise her head, however much men shout,
she's so oppressed, so sorely burdened now;
but Rome, our chief, perhaps by destiny,
is now entrusted to your arms, and you
can use them to awake her, shake her up.
So thrust your hand into those unkempt locks,
those tangled, ancient tresses, and help raise
this poor and slothful creature from the mud.
I who by day and night bewail her torment
entrust my hopes to you, the greater part,
for if the race of Mars
is ever going to see its ancient worth
it seems to me it'll do it in your era.

Those ancient walls the world still fears and loves
and trembles at when it remembers times
now past and gone, turning to look at them;
the stones that once enclosed remains of men
who will be well remembered in the future
unless the universe itself dissolves,
and everything is swallowed up in ruin,
all hope, through you, to renovate themselves.
Oh, faithful Brutus, oh, great Scipios,
how pleasing to you must be these events,
if news of them has come to you down there,
how suitably your office has been filled!
How glad Fabricius is,
to have some word of it, so that he says:
"My Rome will once again be beautiful!"

If Heaven cares at all for earthly things,
the souls who are the citizens up there
and who have left their bodies on this earth

all beg you to conclude the civil strife
because of which the people are not safe,
and pilgrims cannot visit holy sites,
 sites that were once well tended, but in war
have actually become the dens of thieves,
and only goodness finds the doors barred there
where every sort of evil act is practiced
among the statues and denuded altars
(how sharp the contrast is!),
they even signal their attacks and fights
by using bells hung up to worship God.

 The weeping women, the defenseless crowd
of callow youths and old exhausted men
who hate themselves and their protracted lives,
the friars, robed in black or gray or white,
and all the other legions of the sick
and the unfortunate, who call "God! Help!"
 and all the poor and destitute, exposing
their sores and wounds, by thousands and by thousands,
enough to bring a Hannibal to tears.
If you look closely at the house of God
that's all in flames today and you put out
some of those sparks you see,
you'll pacify those wills that are inflamed
and earn some praises for your works in Heaven.

 The bears, the wolves, the lions, eagles, snakes
give frequent trouble to a marble column
and often to themselves do harm as well;
because of them that noble lady weeps
who's called on you to pull up by the roots
the evil weeds that are not going to flower.
 A thousand years and more have passed since she
was first established in that place by those
souls of nobility who've long since died.
Ah, new inhabitants, all much too proud,
Lacking in reverence to so great a mother!

Espouse her, father her:
all kinds of help is looked for at your hand;
the greater Father's bent on other works.

It rarely happens that injurious Fortune
fails to oppose high deeds and undertakings,
for she agrees unwillingly to glory.
Now smoothing out the way for you to come
she makes me overlook her past offenses
because for once she's acting in support;
    because, within the memory of the world,
no mortal man has ever had a path
as clear and open as this is to you
to make yourself the benefit of fame;
for you can raise her up, if I'm correct,
restore this noble monarchy at last.
Such glory for you when
they say: "Some helped her in her youth and strength:
He rescued her from death in her old age."

Above the rock Tarpeian, Song, you'll see
a mounted knight whom all Italia honors,
who cares for others more than for himself.
Tell him: "One who has yet to see you close,
who loves you from a distance, through your fame,
says Rome forever will
with eyes of sorrow, brimming with her tears,
beg you for help from all her seven hills."

In May 1347 the tribune Cola di Rienzo tried to restore the Roman republic and temporarily gained control of the government; Petrarch was enthusiastic about the attempt, but Cola's oppressive government turned supporters against him and he was gone within a year. Chronologically, then, this poem belongs much further on in the sequence, being ten years later than, for example, Number 50. The animals in the sixth stanza represent various Roman families; the column stands for the Colonna family.

54

Because she bore Love's ensign in her face
a foreign beauty moved my foolish heart
and made all others seem to me less worthy;

but as I followed her across green grass
I heard a voice say loudly, from far off:
"How many steps you're wasting in that wood!"

I stood then in the shadow of a beech,
all pensive, and began to gaze around me,
and realized that this path was full of peril;
and just as it struck noon I came back home.

55

That fire which I thought had spent itself
—the season cold, my age no longer fresh—
now flares back up, with anguish to my soul.

They had not been extinguished, I see now,
those embers: they were simply covered over;
I fear my second error may be worse!
The tears I shed, by thousands and more thousands
run from my eyes, their source within my heart,
and that's where all the sparks and tinder are:
not just the former fire, something fiercer!

Shouldn't a fire reasonably be quenched
by all the water that my eyes pour forth?
Love—and I clearly should have sensed this sooner—
wants me distempered by a paradox,
and uses snares of such variety
that when I most believe my heart is free
he most entraps it with that lovely face.

56

If I do not deceive myself too much,
counting the hours with my blind desire
that still torments my heart, now is the time
mercy and I were promised—and it's passing.

What shadow is so cruel it withers seed
just when the longed-for fruit is right at hand?
What beast is loose, and roaring in my sheepfold?
What wall is raised between the hand and harvest?

Alas, I do not know. But I do know
that Love has led me into joyous hope
so he could make my life more sorrowful;

and now I recollect what I have read:
no one deserves to be considered happy
until his day of final parting comes.

57

My good luck is both late and very sluggish;
my hope's uncertain, passion swells and rises,
so leaving's painful, waiting's painful too;
and then they vanish, swift as running tigers.

The snow, oh misery, will be black and warm,
the sea without its waves, Alps full of fish,
the sun will go away and lie down there
where Tigris and Euphrates share a source,

before I find my peace or truce in this,
or Love and Lady change their well-known ways,
who plot, conspire, and are cruel to me;

and if I chance to come to any sweetness,
my taste will not enjoy it, trained to bitter;
that's how their favors promise to reward me.

58

gift: pillow, book, cup, and poem ("me")

Use one of these to rest your cheek, my lord,
made weary by your weeping, it's my gift;
take care in time to come, protect yourself:
that god you follow leaves you pale and wan;

the second helps to block that left-hand road
where Love's own couriers ply their cunning trade;
be your same self, August and January,
since time for that long path is running short;

the third will help you mix a drink of herbs
to purge your heart of all its sore afflictions;
the taste is sweet, though sour at the first.

And put me there where pleasures are stored up,
that I need not fear Styx's ferryman—
if that is not a hope that's too immodest.

not fear Styx's ferryman: the poem hopes for immortality. Its recipient was probably Agapito Colonna, disappointed in love.

59

another ballata

Although another's fault removes from me
what drew me first to love,
it doesn't take away my firm desire.

Among the golden tresses hid the noose
by which Love caught and bound me,
and from those lovely eyes came freezing ice
that passed into my heart,
    and with the power of such sudden splendor
that just the memory of it
empties my heart of all but that desire.

The lovely sight of that blond hair is gone,
alas, quite taken from me,
the gaze of those two chaste and lovely lights
has fled and left me saddened,
    but since by dying well I gain some honor,
neither my suffering nor my death
can make me wish that I were free again.

60

The noble tree I've loved so many years
(times when its lovely branches gave me shelter)
helped my weak wit to flower in its shade
and added that way to my store of troubles.

For when I'd come to feel a total trust,
it turned its very wood from sweet to bitter;
my thoughts began to gather round one subject
and now can only prate of their misfortunes.

What might some lover say, who'd gotten hope
from reading youthful rhymes of mine and then
lost everything he had because of her?

"Then let no poet gather from it, nor
Jove give it favor! Let the sun's anger
beat down and shrivel all of its green leaves!"

61

The day, the month, the year, oh, bless them all,
the season and the time, the hour and moment,
the gorgeous countryside, the very spot
where two eyes struck me first and bound me fast;

and bless the first sweet palpitation that
swept over me as I grew one with Love,
and bless the bow that shot, arrows that pierced,
and wounds so deep they went down to my heart.

And bless the flock of words I've scattered round
as I pronounced my lady's name again,
the sighs and all the tears and the desire;

and bless the pages, too, pages where I
have gained some fame for her, with all my thoughts
which are of her alone, excluding others.

62

Father of Heaven, after days now lost,
after the nights spent raving with desire
that burned incessantly within my heart
when I saw graceful gestures that destroyed me,

be pleased that finally, by your great light,
I may embrace a different way of life,

adversary: Satan

my bitter adversary now disarmed,
his nets at last all spread for me in vain.

eleven years:
i.e., Good
Friday, 1338

It's now eleven years, my gracious Lord,
that I've been subject to this ruthless yoke
that is most fierce, always, to the submissive:

on my unworthy misery, please have mercy,
and lead my thoughts back to a better place,
remind them: this day you were on the cross.

a ballata

63

Casting your eyes upon my strange new pallor
which makes most people cognizant of death,
you felt a twinge of pity, and from that,
spoke to me kindly, keeping me alive.

The fragile life that dwells inside of me
was freely given, gift of your bright eyes
and your soft voice, the accents of an angel;
I recognize my being stems from them,
for they woke up my soul, the selfsame way
you rouse a lazy creature with a stick.
      You hold the keys, dear lady, of my heart
there in your hand, a fact that makes me happy,
prepared to launch my boat in any wind,
because what comes from you is my sweet honor.

64

If you got free by any strange behavior—
your eyes downcast, a bending of your head,
or flight more swift than anybody else's,
frowning the while at my honest prayers—

if by that means, or any other way,
you could escape and get out of my breast,
where Love goes right on grafting laurel branches,
I'd say disdain on your part would be just;

because no noble plant should have to grow
in arid soil like mine; it's natural
that you'd desire to live somewhere else:

but since it's fate and since it seems you can't
be somewhere else, have care, my dear,
not to despise your present habitation.

65

Alas, I was not careful at the first,
the day Love came to wound me, he who has
controlled my life and step by step climbed up
to seat himself upon its very summit.

I didn't understand his file's power
would work to take away the strength and firmness
that I'd built up in my well-hardened heart,
but that's just what my excess pride has brought me.

Defense of any kind is too late now,
except to measure how much or how little
Love pays attention to our mortal prayers:

and I don't pray, since it's impossible,
that my poor heart might burn less furiously;
I simply pray that she should share the fire!

66

The burdened air and unrelenting cloud
compressed from without by the rabid winds
must soon transform themselves into a rain;
following that we'll have crystalline rivers
and instead of lush grass in the valleys
there'll be nothing to see but frost and ice.

valleys: especially
the Vaucluse, to
which Petrarch
moved in 1340

Down in my heart, which is colder than ice,
lie heavy thoughts, the looming kind of cloud
that rises sometimes from these hollow valleys,
closed off all around from the loving winds,
surrounded at times by stagnating rivers,
while there falls from the sky the gentlest rain.

It passes in almost no time, hard rain;
and warmth takes care of the snow and the ice,
which gives a proud appearance to the rivers;
and no sky ever had so thick a cloud
that when it encountered the fury of winds
it didn't flee from the hills and valleys.

But I am not helped by the flowering valleys;
I weep when it's clear, I weep in the rain,
and in freezing winds and in warming winds;
on the day that my lady melts her ice
and comes out of her veil, that usual cloud,
the sea will be dry, and the lakes and rivers.

As long as the sea receives the rivers
and beasts still favor the shady valleys,
she'll have before her lovely eyes a cloud
that makes my eyes give birth to constant rain,
and her breast will be full of that hard ice
that genders in mine such sorrowful winds.

Well may I pardon each one of those winds
for the love of one between two rivers,

*between two
rivers:* the Sorgue
and the Durance

who shut me in green, and in the sweet ice,
so that I've drawn, in a thousand valleys,
the shade where I've been; neither heat nor rain
can alarm me, nor sound of shattered cloud.

But cloud never fled from the driving winds
as on that day, or rivers from the rain,
or ice when the sun opens the valleys.

67

By the Tyrrhenian Sea, on its left bank,
where waves are shattered, crying in the wind,
I suddenly caught sight of that high branch
of which I have to write on many pages.

Tyrrhenian Sea: the
northwest coast of Italy

high branch: laurel

And Love, that boiled within my breast just from
the memory of her hair, was urging me
ahead when suddenly I tumbled into
a stream concealed by grass, like some dead body.

Alone between the forest and the hills,
I winced with shame; it doesn't take much, really,
to act upon a tender heart like mine.

At least I've switched from wet eyes to wet feet:
a change of style might prove to be useful
if I can go dry-eyed through gracious April.

This sonnet was
written on a
visit to Rome,
probably in 1341.

68

The sacred prospect of your city makes
my evil past a matter for complaint,
exclaiming: "Get up, wretch, what's going on?"
and shows the way that I could mount to Heaven.

Another thought, however, jousts with this one,
and says to me, "Why are you fleeing?
Don't you recall that this is near the time
we should return and gaze upon our lady?"

I hear his reasoning and turn to ice
like one who suddenly has heard bad news
and felt the shock run down and wring his heart.

The first thought comes again, the second flees.
I don't know which will win, but I do know
that's how they fight, and not just this one time.

69

I know quite well that natural advice
has never been much good against you, Love,
so many little traps and phony promises,
so often the fierce nip of your sharp claw.

But lately, and I marvel at this fact
(I speak of it as one who was involved,
it happened to me on the salty seas
between the rugged Tuscan coast and Elba),

I got free of your hands and took a journey,
a stranger and a pilgrim, incognito,
whirled round by winds, among the waves and skies,

when suddenly your ministers appeared
as if to show me I can't fight my fate
and it's no good to hide or run away.

70

Alas, I don't know where to put the hope
that now has been betrayed so many times!
For if there are no listeners with pity,
why crowd the heavens with such frequent prayers?
But if it happens I don't lose the chance
to finish up these songs
before my death comes round,
may it not make my lord displeased to hear
me say one day, among the grass and flowers:
"It's just and right that I rejoice and sing."

It stands to reason I should sing sometimes
since I have sighed so often and so long,
and it would take forever to make up
smiles equivalent to all my sorrows.
But if some verse of mine could give delight
to those amazing eyes,
some sweet thing I composed,
oh, then I'd be above all other lovers!
And further blessed when I might say sincerely:
"A lady bids me, so I wish to speak."

My yearning thoughts, you've led me, step by step,
to muse in such an elevated fashion:
but look, my lady has a heart of stone
so hard that I can never penetrate it.
She doesn't even deign to glance so low
as to take note or heed
our words; Heaven's opposed,
and I am worn out from opposing it,
so hard and bitter I am well prepared to say:
"I'm ready to be harsh now in my speech."

What am I saying? And where am I now?
And who deceives me but myself and my
inordinate desire? Scan the skies
from sphere to sphere: no planet makes me weep.

Each stanza
concludes with
a line from
another poem:
one thought to
be by Arnaut
Daniel; one
by Cavalcanti
("Donna me
prego"); one
by Dante; one by
Cino da Pistoia;
and the last from
Petrarch's own
poem Number 23.

And if a mortal veil obscures my sight
why blame that on the stars
or any lovely thing?
There's one who lives in me both night and day
and pains me, having weighed me down with pleasure:
"Her presence sweet, her soft and lovely gaze."

All lovely things that help adorn our world
came forth in goodness from the Maker's hand:
but I, who cannot see beyond the surface,
am dazzled by the beauty right at hand,
and if I ever manage to return
to the true, first splendor
I cannot keep it fixed
because my eye is weakened by my guilt,
not by the day it saw angelic beauty:
"In the sweet season of my early youth."

71

 Because our life is brief
and my wit quails at this high enterprise,
I do not have much confidence in either;
but my pain will be known, I hope,
there where I wish it understood, and where
it must be heard, a pain cried out in silence.
 Amazing eyes, where Love has made his nest,
I turn to you again: my feeble style,
sluggish in itself, is driven by great joy;
for anyone who speaks of you
acquires noble habits from his subject,
and lifts on wings of love,
leaving ill thoughts behind him as he goes.
Raised by such wings, I've come to you to say
things I have carried hidden in my heart.

Not that I do not see
how much my praise does injury to you;
but I cannot resist the great desire
I've carried in me since
I saw you first, saw what no thought can match,
let alone speech, my speech or any other's.
    First cause of my sweet bitter state,
I know you are the one who understands me.
When in your burning rays I melt like snow,
your noble scorn, perhaps,
finds my unworthiness to be offensive.
Oh, if my prudent fear did not
temper the burning fire that consumes me
how much I'd welcome death! Under those rays,
I'd rather die than have to live without them.

    That I am not undone,
so frail an object in a fire so mighty,
is not perhaps from any worth of mine;
but just a little fear I have
which chills the hot blood raging in my veins
strengthens my heart that it may flame on longer.
    Oh hills, oh valleys, rivers, forests, fields,
oh, you who've witnessed my unhappy life,
how many times you've heard me call for death!
Ah, destiny of sorrow,
staying destroys me, fleeing does not help!
But if a greater fear
did not constrain, some short and speedy means
would find a way to end this bitter anguish,
the fault of someone totally indifferent.

    Sorrow, why do you lead me
off of my path, to say what I don't wish to?
Please let me go where pleasure wants to take me.
Oh, eyes serene beyond
the mortal race, I don't complain of you,
nor yet of him whose knots have bound me fast.

You can see clearly all the different colors
that Love paints in my face from time to time
and you can guess how he treats me, within,
where day and night he stands
with all the power he's amassed from you,
you lights both blessed and joyous
except that you can never see yourselves,
though when you turn my way you get some sense
of what you are from seeing my response.

If you could know as we
who gaze at it, the beauty that I speak of,
so goddesslike, incredible, divine,
your measurement of joy
would vanish from your heart; therefore, perhaps
your vigor is protected from your beauty.
Happy the soul who sighs for you, however,
you heavenly lights to which I owe my life
since nothing else affords me earthly joy.
Alas, why am I seldom
rewarded with what never satisfies me?
Why not more often notice
how Love of you is tearing me to pieces,
and why remove so suddenly the good
that helps my soul survive its awful times?

I say that now and then,
thanks to your aid I feel within my soul
a strange new sweetness, unaccustomed,
and one that takes away
all other burdens of depressing thoughts,
trading a thousand thoughts for one alone.
This little bit of life restores my joy,
it's all I need, and if I could sustain it,
there'd be no state on earth to equal mine.
But such an honor might
make others envious, swell me up with pride;
therefore, alas, it's needful

to limit laughter with a bout of weeping
and interrupt those flaming thoughts to bring
me to my senses, back to myself again.

    The amorous disposition
that dwells within you shows itself to me
and draws all other joys out of my heart;
and that's when words and deeds
come forth from me and help inspire hope
that, though flesh die, I may become immortal.
    When you appear, my grief and anguish flee,
and when you leave, they come right back again;
my memory, however, still infused
with love, can bar the door,
and they can't penetrate beyond my skin.
Thus if I bear good fruit
of any kind, the seed comes first from you;
I am dry land that you can till and cultivate,
and if some good results, the praise is yours.

    Song, you don't calm me down, but rather
you kindle me to say what steals my self:
be sure then that you'll not exist alone.

72

    Gentle my lady, I can see
a sweet light in the movement of your eyes
that points the way by which I might reach Heaven;
and, as it always does,
within, where I sit down alone with Love,
your heart is shining almost visibly.
    This is the sight that moves me to do good
and guides me forward toward a glorious goal;
this separates me from the vulgar crowd.
No human tongue could hope

to indicate what those two holy lights
can make me feel,
both when the winter scatters frost around
and later, when the year grows young again,
as in the time when I first learned desire.

    I think: "If up above,
where the eternal mover of the stars
shows forth his handiwork to us on earth,
there's something else this fair,
unlock the doors of this my prison here
which bars me from the path to such a life!"
    Then I revert to my recurrent war,
with thanks to Nature and my day of birth
which destined me for so much precious good,
and she who raised my heart
by filling it with hope (for up to then
I was a burden to myself,
but since, I have been pleasing even me),
filling my heart with thought so high and gracious,
the heart whose key those lovely eyes possess.

    A state so joyous, neither
Love nor turning Fortune ever gave
to gratify their friends in this wide world;
I would not trade them for
one glance from eyes that nourish my repose
the way a tree grows upward from its roots.
    Lovely angelic sparks that bless my life,
that kindle and ignite the bliss which burns,
sweetly consuming me: while other lights
will fade and then go out,
yours grows more bright and clear with time; it shines
and then, down in my heart,
such sweetness rains that every other thing
and every other thought is left behind,
and nothing's there except yourself and Love.

No matter how much sweetness
existed in the hearts of lucky lovers
and managed to be stored up in one place,
it simply won't compare
to what I feel at those rare times when you
direct toward me the black and white of Love;

    and I believe that from my infancy,
my swaddling clothes and crib, this remedy
was sent by Heaven to redress my faults and ills.
Your veil, then, does me wrong,
so does your hand, when either comes between
your eyes and my delight,
and thus by day and night, to ease my breast,
my giant passion spills itself around,
taking its cue from your retiring face.

    Because, distressed, I see,
that Nature's gifts to me aren't worth a thing,
don't make me worthy of so dear a glance,
I force myself to be
someone who may be worthy of high hope
and of the noble fire in which I burn.
    Then if through toil I can make myself
quick to do good and slow to do the opposite,
disliking all the things the world desires,
perhaps the reputation
could help me to a kind and lenient judgment;
the end of all my weeping,
my sad heart knows, will come from nowhere else,
will come from lovely eyes, trembling at last,
the final goal of every courteous lover.

    Song, your sister has gone on ahead;
I feel another coming from your home,
and to that end I'm going to rule more paper.

*black and white
of Love:* Laura's
eyes, the subject
of Numbers 71,
72, and 73, known
as "the canzoni
of the eyes"

your home:
his inspiration
or his head

73

    Since it's my destiny
that burning passion forces me to speak
just as it always forces me to sigh,
Love, you who rouse me to it,
please be my guide and help me find the path
and harmonize my rhymes with my desire;
    but not so much as to untune my heart
with too much sweetness, as I fear it might be
from what I feel where others' eyes can't reach;
speech kindles me and spurs me,
nor do I find, as used to be the case,
my wit will quench the fire
that rages in my mind (for which I fear
and tremble); I melt to hear the sound
of my own words, a man of ice in sun.

    At first I thought I'd find
through speech some respite for my hot
desire, some truce or armistice;
this hope emboldened me
to discourse of my feelings; now, however,
it leaves me, in my need, and quite dissolves.
    But I must still pursue my undertaking,
continuing to sound my notes of love,
so potent is the will that drives me forward;
reason is dead and gone,
who used to hold the reins but couldn't manage.
Let Love at least instruct me
what I should say, how I might sing so that
if it should strike the ear of my sweet foe,
she might befriend, not me perhaps, but pity.

    I say: "While in those days
when men went out pursuing greater honor
their industry betook them many places,
to far-off lands, across

the hills and seas, seeking for honored things,
hoping to pluck the rarest flowers of virtue,
    I find that Nature, God, and Fortune
have worked to put all virtues in one place,
those holy lights that give my life its meaning,
which means I need not travel,
passing across this country or that shore,
because I come back always
to lights that are the fountain of my life,
and if I start to gravitate toward death,
it is their sight that brings me back to health."

    As in the tearing winds
the weary helmsman lifts his head at night
to those two lights that always mark the pole;
so in this tempest I endure,
this storm of love, that pair of shining eyes
become my constellation and my comfort.
    Alas, but most of what I get I steal
now here, now there, as Love incites me to,
rather than any sort of gracious gift;
the little worth I have
I take from them as my perpetual norm;
since first I saw them I've
not gone one step toward good without their help;
I've made them stand upon my very summit,
for on my own I have no sense of worth.

    I never could imagine,
much less elucidate, the full effects
those soft eyes have upon this heart of mine;
all other life-delights
pale in comparison for me, I know,
and every other beauty comes behind.
    A tranquil peace, one free from any pain,
like that which is in Heaven, for eternity,
comes forth from them and from their lovely smile;

if I could see, see steadily,
how Love so sweetly manages their life,
for just one day, up close,
with not one turn of a supernal sphere,
nor be distracted by myself or others,
or even by the blinking of my eyes!

*supernal sphere . . .
blinking:* Petrarch
imagines time
stopping while
he gazes at Laura.

    Alas, I go on wanting
that which can't be, by any means or way,
and I live on desire, well past hope.
If that one knot could be
untied, the one that Love has bound my tongue with
when too much light has overcome my sight,
    if it were loosened, I'd be bold to speak
words that might have such a strong effect
that everyone who listened to them wept.
But my deep wounds, by their
intensity, distract my injured heart
and I grow pale and wan,
and my blood hides away, I know not where,
and I am not myself; it seems to me
this is the blow that Love has killed me with.

    Song, my pen has surely gotten weary
from all this sweet conversing with you here,
although my thoughts continue talking to me.

74

I'm weary now of thinking how my thoughts
of you are always weariless, and how
I have not yet abandoned life to flee
from this great burden of depressing sighs;

and how I'm always going on about
your face, your hair, your penetrating eyes,
and how my tongue and voice are never tired
of sounding out your name by night and day;

and how it is my feet are not worn out,
from following your footsteps everywhere,
a waste of time and energy for sure;

and asking where the ink comes from, the pages
I fill with words of you (if I offend,
the blame is Love's, not a defect of art).

75

Those lovely eyes that hurt me are the only
things that could heal the wound they've made; but not
the power of herbs, nor any magic art,
nor healing stone from far beyond our sea;

they've cut me off from any other love
and only one sweet thought can soothe my soul,
and if that's all my tongue can talk about,
then mock the escort, do not blame the tongue.

These are those lovely eyes that made my lord's
exploits victorious on every side,
and most especially upon my flank;

these are the lovely eyes whose burning sparks
shine always in my heart, which helps explain
why I do not grow tired praising them.

76

Love took me in with all his promises,
coaxing me back into my former prison,
then handed all the keys to her, my enemy,
who always keeps me banished from myself.

I wasn't quite aware of what was happening
till I was in their power; now, distressed
(who will believe this even if I swear it?),
I have regained my liberty, though sighing;

and like true prisoners, who go on suffering,
I wear my chains, or most of them; my heart
is plainly written in my eyes and forehead.

You'll say, as soon as you perceive my color,
"If I have any judgment in these matters
this man was just a little way from death."

77

Polyclitus:
Greek sculptor

A thousand years could Polyclitus study,
along with others famous in his art,
and never glimpse a fraction of the beauty
that has made such a conquest of my heart.

Simon: Simone
Martini, who
apparently sketched
Laura's portrait

But certainly my Simon was in Heaven,
the place from which this noble lady comes;
he saw her there, he captured her on paper,
to show her lovely face down here on earth.

This work could only be imagined there
in such a place as Heaven, not with us,
here where the body always veils the soul;

a noble act, and he could not have done it
after he got back here, to heat and cold,
and saw the world once more with mortal eyes.

78

When Simon came upon that high conceit
and took his pencil up on my behalf,
had he been able to grant voice and mind
as well as form to that amazing image,

he might have saved my breast from many sighs
that make what others love feel base to me.
For in her picture here she looks quite modest
and her expression seems to promise peace;

when I address her, then, to make my case,
she seems to listen with a willing air,
if only she could answer to my words!

Pygmalion, you should celebrate your statue,
since you received, maybe a thousand times,
what I desire to have just even once!

79

My fourteenth year of sighs: if its beginning   *fourteenth*
is any forecast of its end and middle,   *year:* 1341
no breeze or cooler spell can rescue me,
as my desire seems to burn and grow.

Love, who is never absent from my thoughts,
under whose yoke I never can breathe easy,
renders me less than half of what I should be,
turning my eyes once more toward what destroys them.

And thus I go on day by day; I weaken,
and no one knows about it except me
and she whose simplest glance can melt my heart;

I've coaxed my soul to come along this far,
and it can't go much further on, I think,
since death's approaching and life runs away.

80

He who decides to entrust his life
to treacherous waves and close to the rocks,
preserved from death just by a little boat,
cannot be very far from his own end;
he ought then to turn back to find the port
now while the tiller still governs the sail.

The gentle breeze to which I trusted sail
and tiller, embarked on an amorous life
and hoping to come to a better port,
has steered me up against a thousand rocks,
and I carried the cause of my woeful end
not just around me but right in the boat.

Closed in for a long spell in this blind boat,
I drifted on and did not watch the sail
that carried me off to a premature end,
but it pleased Him then, who had given me life,
to summon me back, away from the rocks,
and let me glimpse it far away: the port.

As in the night a light in some far port
is seen way out at sea by ship or boat
unless it is obscured by storm or rocks,
so I could glimpse, beyond the swollen sail,
ensigns and banners of some other life
that made me sigh, desiring my own end.

It's not that I am certain of that end,
for while I'd like, come dawn, to reach that port
the journey's long within so short a life;
and I'm afraid, when viewing this frail boat,
and see that it's too full of wind, my sail,
a wind that's driving me on toward the rocks.

May I escape alive from doubtful rocks
and may my exile come to a good end;

how happy I'd be then to furl the sail
and cast my anchor in a friendly port!
But I am burning in a blazing boat,
finding it hard to leave my former life.

Lord of my end, Lord of my very life,
before I split my boat upon the rocks
guide safely to the port my tattered sail.

81

I am so weary from my ancient bundle,
the sins I lug, and all my evil habits,
I fear I'll lose my way and fall at last
into my mortal foe's most potent grasp.   *foe:* Satan

It's true, a great friend came to free me once;   *friend:* Christ
His was the highest and most gracious courtesy;
and then He flew away, out of my sight,
and I have tried in vain to find and see Him.

But His voice echoes still, down in this world:
"Oh, you who labor, here's the way for you;
come to me now unless the pass is blocked."

What grace, what love, oh, what high destiny,
will give me wings and make me like a dove,
so I can rest and rise up from the earth?

82

I do not tire, Lady, of my love,
nor will I ever, long as I shall live;
but my self-hatred now has reached its limit
and I am sick of all the tears I shed;

I'd rather that my tombstone was left blank
than that your name be carved on marble as
the source of loss, at that time when my spirit
is parted from the flesh it lives with now.

If one heart full of faithful love, therefore,
can please you without tempting you to torture,
then let it please you to have mercy on it;

if your disdain should seek to glut itself
some other way, it's wrong and it will fail;
for that I'm thankful to myself and Love.

83

As long as my two temples are not white
(though time is learning how to grizzle them),
I will not feel secure to risk myself
where Love employs his arrows and his bow.

Not that I really fear he'll hurt me more,
maim me or kill me while I am still snared,
or split my heart, since he's already pierced it,
and filled it with his cruel poisoned darts.

Tears do not run down from my eyes these days,
but they do know the way there, notwithstanding,
and nothing acts to block their path just yet;

the fiery ray can surely make me hot,
but it can't burn me now; the cruel image
bothers my sleep but cannot break it off.

84

"Go on and weep, my eyes: accompany
the heart whose death you've helped to bring about."—
"Yes, that's exactly what we do, but we
have to lament another's error more."

"It was through you that Love first made his entry,
and still he comes, as if it were his home."—
"We opened up to him because of hope
that stirred within the man who's dying now."

"Oh, you can claim these faults were just the same,
but you went first and you were very greedy
for that first sight that brought us both to ruin."

"What makes us sad beyond these other things
is just how rare true justice is these days,
when some must take the blame for others' faults."

85

I've always loved, I go on loving still,
and I'll love even more, day after day,
that sweet place I return to, full of tears
at times when Love comes over me with sadness;

and I am fixed to love the time, the hour,
that took away my base and mundane cares,
most of all she whose lovely face makes me
in love with goodness by her great example.

But who'd have thought these things would so converge,
knocking my heart this way and that, here, there,
all these sweet enemies I love so much?

What force you conquer me today with, Love!
And had not hope grown greater with desire,
I would fall dead where I most want to live.

86

I'll always hate the window from which Love
has shot a thousand arrows at me now,
because they haven't killed me, none of them,
and yet it's good to die when life has peaked;

but staying longer in my earthly prison
has brought me countless evils, sad to say;
I'm pained the more because they'll stay with me:
the soul can't be untangled from the heart.

Oh, miserable soul, you should have known
by now, through long experience, that none
can turn Time back, and none can rein it in!

I've warned you many times with words like these:
"Begone, sad soul; for he who is well past
his happiest days is not departing early."

87

As soon as bowstring's loosed and arrow flies,
an expert marksman knows at some great distance
which shot is wasted, which shot has a chance
to find the target he intends to strike;

the same way, Lady, as you felt the shot
pass from your eyes straight to my inner parts
you knew you'd hit the heart and that it would
weep from its wound, tears everlastingly;

and I am sure, observing this, you said:
"Unhappy lover, where's his passion headed?
Here is the arrow Love will kill him with."

Now, though, because they see how pain can rule me,
what my two enemies will do is not
design my death, just elevate my torment.

88

Since what I hope for is so long in coming
and what remains of life is much too brief,
I wish I'd had the sense to turn back sooner
and faster than a gallop, made retreat;

I do flee now, of course, but weak and lame
where passion has deformed me on one side,
escaped to safety, bearing on my face
the scars I got in Love's unlovely wars.

And thus I counsel: "You who go that way,
turn back your steps, and you whom Love inflames,
do not go on in those ferocious fires,

for even though I live, I am but one
of thousands. None escaped. The enemy
was strong, though wounded in her heart."

89

I fled the prison in which Love had held me
for all those many years, slave to his will;
it would take long to tell you all, my ladies,
how much I found my liberty unwelcome.

My heart was telling me that he could live no more
out on his own, and then along the way
I saw the traitor Love so well disguised
he could have fooled a wiser man than I.

This led to many sighs and to my saying:
"Ah me, the yoke and all the chains and shackles
were sweeter far to me than going free!"

Oh, miserable me, I saw too late,
and now I struggle to escape the error
in which I wrapped myself so willingly!

90

Her golden hair was loosened to the breeze
that twined it in a thousand lovely knots;
a bright light burned unmeasured in her eyes
that are so sparse and grudging of it now;

it seemed to me (I'm not sure if she meant it)
her faced showed pity, coloring a bit;
and I, who had love's tinder in my breast,
is it surprising I went up in flames?

Her walk was not a mortal being's walk,
it had an angel's form, and her words too
were different from a merely human voice:

a spirit all celestial, a living sun
was what I saw; and if she's not so now,
a wound's not healed because a bowstring's loosened.

91

This sonnet was
probably written to
Petrarch's brother
Gherardo on the
death of his wife.

The gracious lady whom you loved so much
has suddenly departed from our midst,
and, as I dare to hope, risen to Heaven,
since all her actions were so sweet and gentle.

It's time to find the two keys of your heart,
which she possessed in life, recover them,
then follow her, a straight and open road:
no further earthly weights need hold you down.

Since you're disburdened of your greatest care,
you won't have trouble setting down the rest,
and rising like a pilgrim, unencumbered;

now you can see how all created things
run toward their deaths, and how carefree the soul
needs to become to make the dangerous crossing.

92

Weep, ladies, weep, and let Love weep as you do;
weep, lovers all now, all across the land,
since he is dead, who meant to do you honor
within this world, as long as he was living.

And as for me, I hope my biting sorrow
will not be such that it obstructs my tears,
that it will have the courtesy to let me
sigh all the sighs that will unpack my heart.

Weep, rhymes, as well, let all the verses weep,
because our loving master, master Cino,
has now departed newly from our midst.

Weep too, Pistoia, and your perverse people;
you've lost a neighbor who was kind and gentle;
and Heaven rejoice, where he has now arrived.

This sonnet was
written on the death
of the poet Cino da
Pistoia, 1270–1336.

93

How many times Love has instructed me:
"Write what you've seen, write it in golden letters,
how I can make my followers change color
and in one moment leave them dead or living.

"There was a time you felt it in yourself,
a loud exemplar in the lovers' chorus;
and then a project freed you from my grasp,
and then I overtook you as you fled,

"and if those lovely eyes wherein I showed you
my very self, sweet fortress where I lingered
when I broke up the hardness of your heart,

"if they restore my bow, that shatters all,
perhaps your face will not remain so dry,
for I am fed by tears, as you well know."

94

When through my eyes, down to my deepest heart,
the image of my lady overmasters me,
all else departs, which leaves the stricken soul
unable to empower lifeless limbs;

and from that miracle a second comes:
sometimes the power that is driven out,
fleeing itself, comes to a separate place
that takes revenge and makes the exile sweet;

two faces, then, take on the same dead color,
because the vigor that gave life to them
resides no longer where it used to be.

I recollected this the other day
seeing a pair of lovers so transformed
their faces looked the way mine usually does.

95

If I could get my thoughts down in these verses
the way I have them captured in my heart,
there's no soul living that could be so cruel
as to lack pity nor dissolve in grief.

But you, blessed eyes, from whom I took that blow
against which there's no armor, shield, or helmet,
you see me wholly, outside and within,
even when no laments express my sorrow.

Because your vision lights me up inside
as sunlight does through glass, let that suffice
to show my love without my even speaking.

Mary and Peter were not harmed by faith;
alas, it's just my own that is so hurtful.
I know you understand this, no one else.

96

I'm so defeated by this endless wait
and by the drawn-out war of my own sighs,
that I have learned to hate what I desired
and all the snares that bound my willing heart.

That lovely smiling face of hers, however,
I carry as a picture in my heart
and everywhere I look it's what I see,
which drives me back into my first tormentings.

I went awry when first my former road
was blocked to me, my road of freedom;
it makes no sense to chase what takes the eyes;

my soul ran free before, and much at risk,
where she now goes around at someone's bidding,
despite the fact that she's sinned only once.

97

Ah, liberty, sweet freedom, how you've shown,
by leaving me, my former situation
when that fell arrow made the first great wound
from which I cannot ever hope to heal!

My eyes grew so enamored of their woe
that reason's curbs and reins are no avail
for they dislike all other mortal works
because I trained them to from the beginning!

I cannot seem to listen but to those
who speak about my death; her name alone
is what I fill the air with, its sweet sound;

Love doesn't send me elsewhere, and my feet
do not know any other road; my hands
can use a paper only for her praise.

98

This sonnet was
written to Orso
dell' Anguillara,
who was apparently
unable to attend
a tournament
because of illness.

Your charger, Orso, can be given reins
that will control his course, but who can curb
your heart till he cannot get loose again
if he desires honor, hates the opposite?

Don't sigh; he cannot lose his fame and worth
even if you're prevented from attending,
because his glory argues his inclusion
and says that no one else precedes him there.

May it suffice that he'll be in the field
on the elected day, bearing the arms
he rightly owns by time, love, strength, and birth.

And he'll cry out: "My lord and I both burn
with noble aspiration, though his absence
means he can't follow me, which makes him sick."

99

recipients unknown

Since you and I have proved so frequently
how false our hopes have been, lift up your hearts
and help them find a state where they are happy
because they seek the highest good of all.

This mortal life is really like a meadow
whose grass and flowers also hide a serpent,
and anything that entertains our eyes
is there to snare our minds and souls the more.

You therefore, if you ever hope to have
a peaceful mind before your final day,
must emulate the few and not the mob.

Someone could well accuse me: "Brother, you
keep pointing out the way, astray yourself,
and maybe even now more lost than ever."

100

That window where one sun is visible
when it shall please her, and the other one
that's visible at noon, and then the window
that cold air rattles when the north wind blows,

also the stone where, when the days are long,
my lady sits conversing with herself,
and all the places where her lovely body
has cast its shadow or set down its foot,

and that cruel pass where Love took me in ambush,
and this fresh season that, year in, year out,
passes the anniversary of my wounding,

that face of hers as well, and all those words
that are fixed deep within my heart—these things
have made my eyes too apt to weep these tears.

This sonnet describes north and south windows at Laura's house, part of a list of things associated with her.

101

Alas, I know that she who pardons no man
makes all of us her melancholy prey
and that the world quite rapidly forgets us
and only briefly keeps its faith with us;

there isn't much reward for so much yearning
and now the last day thunders in my heart.
But Love still doesn't want to set me free
and still exacts his tribute from my eyes.

I know our days, our minutes, and our hours
pack off our years, and I am not deceived
but subject to a power more than magic's.

My passion and my reason have been fighting
seven plus seven years; reason will win
if souls down here can understand what's best.

she: Death

102

When the Egyptian traitor handed him
the honored head of Pompey, Caesar wept,
or so we're told; he hid his boundless joy
behind external tears, concealing it;

and Hannibal, when he could see that Fortune
had turned so cruel to his afflicted empire,
laughed in the midst of his lamenting people,
to vent his bitterness another way;

and thus it happens—every soul may cloak
the passion of the moment with its opposite,
a face that's clear or else a face that's dark.

Thus if at any time I laugh or sing
you may be sure I do it as a way
to cover up my weeping from the world.

103

In May 1333, Stefano
Colonna defended
himself against two
members of the Orsini
family by killing them.

Hannibal won but later did not know
how to make proper use of his good victory;
be careful then, my lord, that you yourself
do not experience something of that sort.

mother bear:
the Orsini clan

The mother bear is raging for her cubs
who found a bitter harvest this past May;
her teeth and claws grow harder, and within
she fuels her rage and plots revenge on us.

So therefore, while her recent sorrow burns,
do not put up your honorable sword;
but let it take you where your fortune beckons:

along the straight and narrow road where you
can earn a fame and honor that will last
beyond your life a thousand thousand years.

104

The longed-for virtue that was flowering in you
when Love began to battle with you, now
produces fruit that's worthy of the flower
and makes my hope begin to be fulfilled.

My heart then prompts me to put pen to paper
and write a verse to amplify your fame,
for even sculpture may not last enough
to give a person life through solid marble.

Do you believe that Caesar or Marcellus,
Paulus or Africanus, grew so famous
because of any hammer's work, or anvil's?

No, my Pandolfo, such stuff's far too frail
to last for long, whereas our kind of study
makes men immortal and brings lasting fame.

This sonnet
was written to
Pandolfo Malatesta,
ruler of Rimini.

Marcellus et al.:
Roman generals

our kind of study:
poetry and literature

105

    I never wish to sing   the way I used to
I wasn't understood   somebody scorned me,
one can be heartbroken   in a pleasant place.
    Sighing all the while   does no good.
It's snowing in the mountains   everywhere;
and dawn is quite close by   so I'm awake.
    A sweet and honest act   is something noble;
a lady who is lovely   pleases me
if in her face she shows   a haughty disregard
unless she's proud and stubborn.
Love needs no sword to govern his domain.
Whoever's lost his way   let him turn back;
and he who has no house can sleep on grass;
who has no gold, or loses it,
can quench his thirst by drinking from a glass.

    My trust was in St. Peter   but no more,
figure me out if you can   I understand.

canzone frotolla:
a poem of intentional
obscurities, maxims
and proverbs, and
constantly shifting
subject matter

A rotten tribute is   a heavy load to bear.
    As fully as I can   I free myself.
I hear Apollo's son   fell in the Po, died,
and that the blackbird has   now crossed the stream.
    Hey, come and take a look   (I'd rather not, myself),
it's not a joke, a rock   among the waves
or else, in branches, birdlime!   And I'm hurt
when overbearing pride can hide
a wealth of virtues in a lovely lady.
Some people come   when no one's called to them;
others you beg for disappear and flee;
and some melt from the ice
and others long for death, both night and day.

    Proverb: "Love who loves you"   ancient fact;
I know exactly what I say   I'll drop it,
people need to learn some things   at their expense.
    A humble lady makes   her sweet friend grieve.
Assessing figs is difficult;   it's prudent
to undertake no task   too hard to do,
    and pleasant homes exist   in every country.
Hope, when it is infinite,   usually kills,
and there were times when I   would dance that dance.
What little bit is left of me
ought to please someone if I give it to him.
I put my faith in Him   who rules the world
and shelters His disciples in the woods
to lead me with His flocks,
wielding His shepherd's crook of mercy.

    Not everyone who reads   can understand,
and he who sets up nets   may well catch nothing;
who tries to be too subtle   breaks his neck.
    Don't let the law be lame   when folks are waiting.
To have good health you might   go many miles.
Some things seem marvelous   and then we hate them;
    a cloistered beauty is   the sweetest, softest.
Blessed be the key that slipped   into my heart
and turned the lock and gave   my soul its freedom
from very heavy chains

releasing from my breast unnumbered sighs.
There where I grieved the most   another suffers,
and makes my sorrow sweet by having shared it;
and so I offer thanks to Love,
because I feel it not and yet it's there.

    And in the silence, words   wise and proficient
become the sound that takes   all other care
the darkened prison where   there shines a light;
    nocturnal violets growing   on the bank,
and wild beasts at large   within the walls,
and fear, sweet fear,   and lovely customs,
    and from two fountains grows   a peaceful river
flowing where I want it   gathering there;
Love and Jealousy walked off   taking my heart,
the stars of that fair face
that lead me forward on a level path
along toward my own hope   my pain concluded.
Oh, hidden sweetness and your close companions—
now peace, now war, now truce,
do not desert me in this earthly garb.

    For all my injuries past   I weep and laugh
because I set such store   in what I hear;
I like the present some   and look for better,
    and I go counting years   silent and crying.
And I construct my nest   on a fair branch
in such a fashion thanking   the grand refusal
    that finally overcame   the hardened feelings
and in my soul engraved: "I would be heard of
and pointed at for that,"   and she's erased
(I'm driven to extremes
that I am going to say it): "You were not bold enough!"
She pierced my side and then   she healed it too,
I write more in my heart than on this paper,
she makes me die and live;
she makes me freeze and then she makes me burn.

106

A little angel, new, on nimble wings,
came down from Heaven to the springtime shore
where Fortune had me walking, all alone.

Because she saw I had no company or guide
she spread a lasso she was making out of silk
out on the grass with which the way was green.

She caught me then; I wasn't sorry later
because so sweet a light was in her eyes.

107

I don't see anymore how to escape;
her eyes have been at war with me so long
that I'm afraid, alas, the ongoing torment
will kill my heart, which never knows a truce.

I'd like to flee, but those inspiring rays
shine in my mind by night and then by day,
so bright that in this fifteenth year they dazzle
more than they did even on that first day;

and their resemblances are scattered round
so that I cannot turn without a glimpse of light,
that light or else a like one, lit from it.

From just one laurel tree a forest grows
so green my enemy, with magic arts,
leads me at will, astray among the branches.

108

More fortunate than any other earth,
you ground, where Love once made her pause her foot
and turn those holy lights in my direction
that make the air around her all serene:

a solid diamond statue would wear out
before I could forget her deed, so sweet
that it has filled my mind till now
and never will desert my memory;

however many times I see you yet
I'll still bend over you to trace her foot
recalling where it made its gracious turn.

But since Love doesn't rest in worthy hearts,
ask my Sennuccio, when you see him next,
for just a little tear, or for a sigh.

This sonnet is
addressed to
the soil where
Laura walked.

109

When Love, alas, decides to reassault me
(a thousand times, it seems, by night and day)
I come again to where I saw those sparks
that make the fire in my heart immortal.

The visit calms me down, and now those sparks,
at nones, at vespers, dawn and angelus,
can fill my thoughts, which have become so tranquil
that I am free of cares or painful memories.

The gentle breeze that from her shining face
moves when she speaks her words, so clear and wise,
creates fair weather when she breathes it forth,

and is so much a thought of Paradise
that its pure air can always bring me comfort
and my hurt heart breathes easy nowhere else.

Sennuccio:
Sennuccio
del Bene,
Florentine poet
and Petrarch's
good friend

110

my accustomed place: presumably the Vaucluse

Pursued by Love to my accustomed place
I was like one who is prepared for war,
who fortifies the entrances and passes,
and thus I stood, armed with my ancient thoughts.

I turned and saw a shadow on the ground
off to the side, created by the sun,
and recognized it: hers, who as I judge,
is worthy to be thought of as immortal.

I said to my own heart, "Why do you quail?"
and yet before that thought was fully shaped
the rays that melt me were unleashed in full;

the way that thunder comes along with lightning
that's how those eyes, so brilliant, hit me,
along with a sweet greeting from her lips.

111

The lady whom my heart is always watching
appeared to me where I sat all alone
with lovely thoughts of love, and I, in homage,
moved toward her with a pale and reverent brow.

As soon as she was conscious of my state
she turned to me and with her color changed
in such a way as would have disarmed Jove
in greatest fury, killing his dread wrath.

I trembled as, conversing, she passed by
because I couldn't bear to hear her speech
or look directly at her brilliant eyes.

And now I find myself fulfilled with pleasure
as I look back upon that kindly greeting
and feel no pain, nor am I like to soon.

112

Sennuccio, just see how I am treated here
and what my life is like: I live in flames
and burn and suffer just the way I used to,
because the slightest breeze can spin me round.

I saw her humble, then I saw her haughty,
now harsh, now gentle, cruel, then full of mercy,
now clothed in virtue, now decked out in mirth,
one minute tame, the next a wild thing.

Here she sang sweetly, here she was seated,
here she turned back and here she paused her step,
here with her lovely eyes she pierced my heart;

she said a word here, smiled here, I think,
and here she frowned. Wrapped in these thoughts, alas,
is how our lord Love keeps me, night and day.

Sennuccio: see
Number 108

breeze: l'aura,
pun on Laura

113

Here where I half exist, my dear Sennuccio
(would I were here completely, and you happy),
I came to flee the storm and mighty wind
that suddenly have made the season harsh.

Here I am safe, and wish to tell you why
I do not fear the lightning as I did,
and why my passion hasn't lessened any
but looks as though it never will be quenched.

No sooner had I come into Love's region
and saw the birthplace of the sweet, pure breeze
that calms the air and sends away the thunder,

than Love, who rules my soul, relit the fire
and drove away my fear. What might I do
if then I got to look into her eyes?

*storm and mighty
wind:* probably
the corrupt papal
court at Avignon;
see the next poem

breeze: Laura

114

Babylon: Avignon

From wicked Babylon, that's lost all shame,
from which all good has long since fled away,
now sorrow's dwelling, mother of all errors,
I've run away, to rescue my own life.

here: Vaucluse;
see Numbers
116 and 117

I'm here alone, and as Love leads me on,
I gather rhymes and verses, herbs and flowers,
conversing and recalling better times,
the only thing that can sustain me now.

I do not care about the mob, or Fortune,
nor very much about myself, nor do
I feel much heat, inside myself or out;

I ask for just two people in my life:

her: Laura

him: probably
Cardinal Giovanni
Colonna, whose
foot was gouty

I'd have her heart be pacified and kind
and him I'd want with his foot whole again.

115

Between two lovers once I saw a lady
all virtuous and proud; she had with her
that lord who rules among both men and gods;
the sun was on one side, I on the other.

When she could see that she had been left out
from the bright sphere of her more handsome friend,
she turned her eyes to me, quite happily,
and I could wish she'd always be no fiercer.

The jealousy that on first sight was born
to see a rival of such height and power
transformed itself to joy within my heart;

his face, meantime, so tearful and so sad,
was covered over by a little cloud,
and he was much annoyed at being bested.

116

Full of that sweet, ineffable delight
that came to my eyes from her lovely face
on that day when I'd willingly have closed them,
never to gaze again at lesser beauties,

I went away from what I yearn for most;
I've trained my mind to contemplate her only
and it sees nothing else; what isn't she
it hates and scorns from long-established habit.

Into a valley closed off on all sides
that cools my weary sighs, I came alone
except for Love, all full of care and late;

valley: Vaucluse,
to which Petrarch
moved in 1337

I find no ladies here, just rocks and fountains
and then the very likeness of that day
that shapes my thoughts, wherever I may look.

117

If the rock that mainly shuts this valley
(from which it seems to take its very name)
responded with its scornful nature, turning
its back to Babel and its face toward Rome,

this valley: Vaucluse

Babel: the Papacy
at Avignon

my sighs would have a better path to travel
toward where their source of hope is living now;
right now they travel scattered, yet arrive
where I have sent them, not one fails to get there;

and over there they have so sweet a welcome
not one of them, I note, ever returns,
they have such rich enjoyment where they stay.

My eyes sustain the pain, for when dawn comes
their passion for the lovely places lost
brings tears to me and labor to my feet.

118

I've now passed through my sixteenth year of sighs
and somewhere up ahead I'll reach the last one;
and yet it sometimes seems to me as though
this suffering began just recently.

The bitter now is sweet, my losses useful,
living itself's a heavy weight—I pray
my life outlasts this fortune and I fear
Death may close those eyes that give me speech.

I'm here, alas, and wishing I were elsewhere,
and wish I wished for more, yet cannot wish,
and since I can't do more, do what I can;

and these new tears, shed for these old desires,
prove that I'm still the thing I used to be,
a thousand things have changed, but I have not.

119

A lady much more splendid than the sun—
more blazing and quite comparable in age—
using her famous beauty
attracted me while young into her ranks.
This one is in my thoughts, my works, my words,
for she's among the great world's rarest things;
along a thousand roads
she's always gone before me, proud and gay.
For her alone I turned from what I was,
endured her gaze up close, and afterward,
in honor of her love,
set myself difficult tasks and undertakings
so that, if I achieve the longed-for harbor,
I hope through her to live,
long after people take me to be dead.

This lady led me on for many years
full of a youthful burning longing,
and, as I understand,
only to ask me for more certain proof—
    she'd let me glimpse her shadow, veil, or robes,
sometimes herself, but with her face concealed;
and I, alas, believing
I saw a lot, passed through my younger years
    contentedly—the memory makes me happy,
especially now that I can see her better.
A short time past, I'm saying,
she showed herself more fully than before,
showed much to me, and turned my heart to ice,
and that is still the case,
and will be always, till I'm in her arms.

    But neither fear nor cold could hinder me
from giving so much daring to my heart
that I fell at her feet
to draw a greater sweetness from her eyes;
    and she, who had removed the veil from mine
addressed me, saying: "Now, friend, you can see
how beautiful I am,
and ask me for whatever fits your years."
    "Madonna," said I, "for a long time now
I've set my love on you; it so inflames me
that while I'm in this state,
I cannot wish that anything be altered."
And then, with voice of such a wondrous temper,
she answered, with a look
that left me always between fear and hope:

    "Few are there in this world, among the crowd,
who hearing the discussion of my worth
have not felt in their hearts,
at least a short time, something of a spark;
    "but my opponent, who hates all that's good,
douses those sparks, whereby all virtue dies;

another lord takes over
who promises a life more easygoing.
      "Love, who unsealed your mind at first,
tells me the truth about you, and I see
your great desire makes you
worthy of some most honorable end;
and as we are already special friends,
as sign, you'll see a lady
who'll make your eyes more fortunate and happy."

      I tried to say "That is impossible,"
when she said: "Look up now (lifting your eyes
to a more secret place)
upon a lady who has shown herself to few."
      Quite suddenly ashamed, I bowed my head,
feeling within a new and greater fire,
and she was much amused,
saying to me: "I see now where you stand;
      "just as the sun, with its more powerful rays,
makes every other star retire and vanish,
likewise the sight of me
is much diminished by this greater light.
But I don't fault you or dismiss you for it,
for she and I (she first),
were born together from a single seed."

      That helped to break the knot of shame
that had been tight around my tongue when I
first felt abashed
because I knew that she had noticed it,
      and I began: "If what I hear is true,
blessed be the father and blessèd be the day
that have adorned the world with you,
and all the times when I have run to see you!
      "And if I ever strayed from the true path
it pains me more than I can ever show;
but if you think me worthy
to hear more of your nature, why, I burn to!"

She watched me pensively and answered,
her sweet regard so steady
that face and words both sped straight to my heart.

    "Because it pleased our everlasting father
to have it so, we each were born immortal.
Poor things, what good is that
to you? Better for you if we did not exist.
    "Beloved, lovely, young and full of charm:
that's what we were at first; we've come to this:
that this one beats her wings
and wants to fly to her old hiding place;
    "but on my own I'm just a shade. And now
I've told you everything that you can grasp."
She moved away then, saying,
"Don't worry; I'm not leaving you just yet,"
and gathered up a garland of green laurel
and with her own hands made
a wreath of leaves and put it round my temples.

    Song, to whoever calls your speech obscure,
answer: "I do not care, because I hope
another messenger
will soon announce the truth in clearer voice;
I came ahead to wake men up, if he
who sent me on this errand
did not mislead me when he launched me forth."

the first lady:
Glory; the second
lady: Virtue;
Petrarch was
crowned Poet
Laureate in
Rome on Easter
Sunday, 1341.

120

Antonio de Ferrara,
hearing a rumor of
Petrarch's death, had
written a canzone
mourning him.

Those verses full of pity where I saw
your ingenuity and deep affection
displayed such strength that I was quickly moved
to take my pen and make a swift response,

her final bite:
Death's

assuring you that I'm among the living,
have not yet felt her final bite whom I
and all the world await, though there's no doubt
that I was at her threshold, without fear;

then I returned—I'd seen, written above it,
the information that my term of life
(although I couldn't read the day or hour)

had not yet finished its determined course.
I want you thus to calm your troubled heart
and seek some other man more worth this honor.

a madrigal

121

Now look at this, Love: how a youthful woman
scorns your supremacy, cares naught for my illness,
and feels secure between two enemies.

You are in armor, she has just a gown,
loose-haired and barefoot in the grass and flowers,
ruthless toward me, and arrogant toward you.

I am a prisoner, but if pity has preserved
your bow for you, and one or two sharp arrows,
for both yourself and me, my lord, revenge!

122

For seventeen long years the heavens have rolled
since I at first caught fire, still not quenched;
but when I start to contemplate my plight
I feel a chill within these flames of mine.

The proverb's true: your hair is going to change
before you'll change your habits; senses wane,
but human passions keep their strength and force:
the bitter shadow of the heavy veil.

heavy veil:
the human body

Oh me! Alas! And when will that day come
when I can gaze back at my misspent years
and step out of the fire, the long sorrow?

Or will I ever even see the day
when that sweet face's air, those eyes,
will please me much, but only as they ought to?

123

Her lovely paleness made a cloud of love
that covered her sweet smile—so majestic
it stirred my heart and brought him out to meet it
right in the middle of my rapturous face.

I learned then how they apprehend in Paradise,
as mercy showed quite clearly in her thought
while I alone was able to perceive it
because I gaze at nothing else on earth.

Each look angelic, every humble gesture
that ever came forth from a loving lady
would seem like scorn compared to what I speak of.

Her lovely gaze was fixed upon the earth,
and as her silence spoke it seemed to say:
"Who separates me from my faithful friend?"

124

Love, Fortune, and my mind—which now avoids
all that it sees and turns back to the past—
afflict me so that sometimes I must feel
envy for those who've reached the other shore.

Sir Love torments my heart, and Fortune
takes from it all its comforts, while my mind
weeps foolishly and pines; as a result,
I live at war, contending with my sorrow.

I do not hope that sweet days will return;
instead I think they'll go from bad to worse,
the midpoint of my course is now well past.

I see all hope, alas, crash through my hands;
it isn't made of diamond, merely glass,
and all my thoughts, I see, must break in two.

125

 If the thoughts that hurt me,
since they're so sharp and pungent,
could dress themselves for once in their true colors,
 the one who burns me up
and flees might share the pain,
and wake Love up from where he's sleeping now;
 my weary footsteps wouldn't
be so lonely then,
across the hills and fields;
my eyes would be less wet
if she burned too, who stands there now like ice
and leaves me not a jot
that isn't flame or fire.

 Because Love fights and bests me
and strips away my skill,
I speak in acrid rhymes that lack all sweetness;

but branches do not always
reveal in leaf or flower,
or in rough bark, their native strength and vigor.
    Let Love, who sits in shade,
and let her eyes as well,
see what my heart conceals;
if sorrow overflows
and happens to bring tears and lamentations,
that must pain me, and others,
because I can't be smooth.

    Sweet and delightful rhymes
that I resorted to
upon Love's first assault, I with no weapons:
    will no one come to shatter
the stone around my heart
so I can pour my feelings forth again?
    Because it seems to me
there's someone in my heart
who always wants to paint
and speak about my lady;
I can't describe her by myself; I come
undone, I fall apart,
my comfort runs away.

    Like a child held down,
and with his tongue tied up,
who cannot speak and yet feels he must talk,
    desire drives me on
and I must speak, in hope
my enemy will hear before I die.
    If she gets all her pleasure
from her own face alone
and shuts all others out,
then maybe you, green shore,
will listen to my sighs and send them on
so it will be recalled
that you were good to me.

You know quite well no foot
has ever touched the earth
that matches hers in beauty when she trod you;
    therefore my tired heart
and my tormented body
return to share their cares with you again.
    I wish you had concealed
some lovely footprints still
among the flowers and grass,
so that my bitter life
might come in tears and find a place to rest!
My doubtful wayward soul
finds comfort as it can.

    Each place I chance to look
I find a sweet repose
and think: "Her eyes' bright light shone on this spot."
    Each grass or flower I pick
persuades me it was rooted
in earth on which she took her usual walk
    along the river meadows,
fresh, flowering, and green,
and sometimes stopped to rest.
So nothing's really lost,
and knowing more would likely spoil things.
Oh, blessèd spirit, what
can you pass on to me?

    Poor little song, you turned out pretty rough!
I think you sense your worth:
stay right here in these woods.

126

    Clear waters, fresh and sweet,
where she who is my lady,
my only one, would rest her lovely body;
    gentle branch that pleased her
(with sighing, I remember)
to make a column she could lean against;
    grass and flowers which her gown,
graceful and rich, concealed,
and her angelic breast,
sacred, brilliant air
where Love had those fair eyes unlock my heart:
listen all together
to these my mournful words and dying speech.

    If it's my destiny
and Heaven deems it so
that Love will shut these weeping eyes of mine,
    let kindness act to see
my body buried here
and let my soul go naked to its home;
    my death will be less harsh
if I can keep my hope
until that fearful pass,
because my weary spirit
could never sail to a more restful port,
or in more tranquil grave
flee from my poor, exhausted flesh and bones.

    The time will come, perhaps,
when she'll come back again
to her old haunts, that wild gentle thing,
    and she will seek me out
as on that blessèd day
and turn her loving and expectant gaze
    to search me out—oh, pity!—
and see that I am dust
among the stones. Then Love

will make her sigh so sweetly
that she will win me grace at last in Heaven
and force my fate to change,
wiping her eyes upon her lovely veil.

From lovely branches fell
(how sweet to recollect this)
a rain of flowers on her precious bosom,
    and she sat humbly there
in such a cloud of glory,
a loving nimbus that surrounded her;
    some flowers on her skirt
and some in her blond hair—
like pearls set on gold
they seemed to me that day;
while one was landing gently on the earth,
another twirled around,
as if to say, "Now here is where Love reigns."

How often I would murmur
at that time, full of awe:
"This person clearly had her birth in Paradise!"
    Her bearing, clearly godlike,
her face and words and smile,
so filled me with forgetfulness,
    and so divided me
from images of truth,
that I would utter, sighing,
"How did I get here? When?"
believing that I must have gone to Heaven.
That's why this grass delights me;
there is no other place where I find peace.

If you had beauties equal to desires,
you could go boldly
out of this wood and move among mankind.

127

In that direction where I'm spurred by Love,
I must conduct these aching, painful rhymes,
which take their cue from my afflicted mind.
Which one goes first and which shall be the last?
He who converses with me on my woes
leaves me uncertain by confused dictation.
    I find my painful story is inscribed
down in my heart, written in his own hand,
and I go back to read it there; however,
I'll speak it out as well,
because my sighing brings relief, and talking helps.
I say: Although I look
at many different things, gazing intently,
I only see one lady, her fair face.

    Because my cruel misfortune banished me
far from my greatest good, to show me
how proud, disturbing, and implacable it is,
memory's all that Love will let me live on:
thus when I see a world of youthful aspect,
starting again to clothe itself in green,
    to that same season I can call a girl
whose beauty's now transformed her to a lady;
when once the sun has mounted to its zenith,
it warms the world below,
it's like the flame of love deep in the heart;
but while the shorter day
laments the sun's retreat, a stepping backward,
I see her coming to her perfect days.

    When I see leaves upon a branch, or gaze
at violets, growing on the earth in spring,
when cold grows less and better stars grow potent,
I still see green and violet in my eyes,
the colors Love was armed with when he came
to start the war he still pursues today,

and that sweet tender bark that covered then
those youthful limbs and now, today, encloses
the noble soul who dwells there and whose beauty
makes other pleasures seem
just vile: I recollect so strongly
her humble bearing then
which had begun to flower, sooner than her years,
and still remains the source and balm of woe.

Sometimes I look at freshly fallen snow
on distant hills, all brilliant in the sunlight,
and think of how Love's sun can melt my snow,
considering that face that's more than human,
which has the power to wet my eyes far off
and up close dazzles them and kills my heart;
between that white and gold are colors that
come always, yet I think no mortal eye
but mine has glimpsed or understood their hue;
as for the hot desire
that flames within me when she sighs or smiles,
everything disappears
and my forgetfulness becomes eternal:
summer can't change it, winter keeps it here.

And after rain at night I never see
the wheeling stars pass through the clearing air,
showing their lights between the dew and frost,
without considering her lovely eyes,
the one support on which my wan life leans,
the way I saw them once behind a veil;
and as the sky displayed their beauty then
I see them still, they glitter with her tears
and that same brilliance makes me burn forever.
Chancing to see the dawn,
I sense the advent of the light that holds me;
watching the evening sunset,
I seem to watch her as she takes her leave
and plunges all the world in utter darkness.

If ever I saw white and crimson roses
gathered by virgin hands and then arranged
fresh in a golden vase, I thought at once
that I was looking at the face of her
who easily excels all other wonders
by virtue of three excellences gathered:
        blond tresses loose about her neck and throat
where any milk will suffer by comparison,
and then her cheeks, which glow with a sweet fire.
And if I see the wind
stirring the white and yellow meadow flowers
I think about the place
where that first day I saw that golden hair
disheveled in the wind as I caught fire.

        Maybe I thought that I could count the stars
and catch the ocean in a little glass
when I conceived this most peculiar notion
of saying in a page or two how many
places this woman, flower of all beauty,
has shed her dazzling light upon the world,
        because I never want to part from her;
nor shall I leave her—if I tried to flee
she'd block my way to Heaven or on earth;
she's always present to
my weary eyes, her image quite consumes me,
and thus she stays with me,
I'll never see another, nor desire to,
nor could my sighs form any other's name.

        Song, you know very well that what I say
is nothing when compared to all the thoughts
I have to carry with me night and day;
and yet the love I bear
has helped me to survive this endless war;
I'd have been dead by now
bewailing all the sorrows of my heart,
except that thoughts of her have kept me living.

128

This is Petrarch's
most important
political poem,
addressed to the
warring factions of
Italy. It was probably
written during the
siege of Parma,
1344, composed at
Selvapiana, on the Po.
German mercenaries
were being widely
employed by the
warring city-states,
and they were
notorious for
surrendering too
readily ("Bavarian
deceit / that throws
its hands aloft").

Italy, my Italy, though speech cannot
cure all the mortal wounds
that seem to me to fill your lovely body,
maybe my sighs at least can hope to aid
the Tiber and the Arno,
the Po as well, where I sit grieving now.
    Ruler of Heaven, I pray
the mercy that first brought You here to earth
may turn now to Your loved and sacred country.
You see, my noble Lord,
what petty causes can bring savage wars;
these hearts that fierce, proud Mars
makes closed and hardened now,
open them, Father, soften and free them;
and let Your truth be heard
through me, although my tongue is hardly worthy.

    All you whose hands, by Fortune's means, now hold
the reins of power for
these lovely regions, for which no pity moves you,
what are these foreign swords doing among us?
And why should our green plains
be colored red by this barbaric blood?
    A foolish error blinds you:
you see so little, thinking you see much,
looking for love and trust in venal hearts;
who has the most retainers
is most surrounded by his enemies!
Oh, deluge gathered up
in what strange wilderness
to come and flood our sweet and verdant fields!
And if by our own hands
we bring this on, who do we think will save us?

    Nature provided well for our protection
when she put up the shield
of Alps between us and the raging Germans;

but blind desire, set against itself,
has found a clever way
to make this healthy body sick again.
    Now inside the same cage,
the savage beasts are mingled with the flocks
which means the gentler, better ones will groan;
and all this comes about
from the descendants (sharpening our grief)
of those same uncouth people
whom Marius split open,
so much that memory still recalls his deed
when, thirsty and worn out,
he drank from streams that were half blood, half water.

Marius: a Roman consul, the victor in a battle with the Teutonic tribes in 102 B.C.

    I will not speak of Caesar, who once turned
the green fields red with blood
that poured from veins he'd opened with our steel.
It seems (who knows by what malignant stars)
the heavens hate us now,
and thanks to you, to whom so much was trusted.
    Your warring wills lay waste
the fairest regions that the world can find.
What fault, what judgment, or what destiny
makes you attack your neighbors
and persecute the poor and the afflicted,
seeking in foreign parts
to hire mercenaries
who want to sell their souls and shed some blood?
I'm trying to speak the truth,
not out of hate for others or contempt.

    And can't you see, after so many proofs,
Bavarian deceit
that throws its hands aloft and jokes with Death?
The mockery outweighs the shame of loss.
But your own blood is shed
more freely, since these quarrels are your own.
    From dawn to nine o'clock
please think about yourselves and you will see

that anyone who holds himself so cheap
can't be expected to hold others dear.
Oh, noble Latin blood,
throw off these harmful burdens, do not make
an idol from a name
that's empty and all vain;
and if that savage people from the north
look smarter than we are,
that shows our sin, it doesn't stem from nature.

"Is this ground not the ground that I touched first?
And isn't this my nest
in which I found myself so sweetly nursed?
Is not this my own country, which I trust,
a kind of mother to me,
the place where both my parents have been buried?"
By God, let this sometimes
fill up your mind and let you look with pity
upon the tears of all the sorry people
who put their hope in God
and next in you. If you would demonstrate
some signs of piety,
men would arise again
and take up arms; the battle would be short,
since ancient valor still
exists, not dead yet in Italian hearts.

My lords: consider how time flies with us
and how our lives, so brief,
are running past, while Death is at our backs.
You're present now, but think of your departure,
when naked and alone at last,
your souls must venture on that dangerous path.
As you pass through this valley,
suppose you overcome your hate and anger,
those winds that blow against a peaceful life;
and take that time you spend
in giving pain to others and convert it
to some good action of

the hand or of the mind,
some worthy praise, some well-rewarding study:
down here one can rejoice
and find the road to Heaven free and open.

My song, I ask that you
speak out your message diplomatically,
because you go among a haughty people
whose wills are full, I fear,
of ancient and uncivilizing customs,
always the enemies of truth.
But you must try your luck
among the few who cherish magnanimity;
say to them: "Who'll protect me?
I wander, crying out: Oh, peace, peace, peace!"

129

From thought to thought, from peak to mountain peak,
Love moves me forward, while each beaten path
I find contrary to a tranquil life.
If on some solitary slope I find
a spring or river, or a shady valley
between two hills, my soul seeks refuge there;
as Love dictates, it laughs
or weeps, now fearful, now assured, and then
my face, which follows as the soul leads on,
is cloudy and then clear,
but stays the same for just the briefest moment.
So anyone who knows of life would say:
"This man is burning and his state's erratic."

Among high mountains and in tangled woods
I find some rest; populous places, though,
are deadly enemies, they hurt my eyes.
And every step I take gives birth to new
thoughts of my lady, which can change to pleasures

the torments that I bear because of her;
    and then I wouldn't trade
the bitter sweetness of this life of mine,
because I say: "It seems that Love preserves you
against a better time;
though worthless to yourself, perhaps you're dear
to someone else." I take this thought and sigh:
"Could that perhaps be true? But how? Or when?"

    Where some tall pine or hillside makes for shade
I often stop, and staring at a stone
I try to call her lovely face to mind.
    Then coming to my senses once again
I find my breast awash with pity, saying:
"Alas, how came you here? How far she is!"
    But while I can stay fixed,
my yearning mind on that first thought, and gaze
at her, and let myself forget myself,
I feel Love close at hand
and do not mind the error of my soul;
she's all around me, she's in everything,
and all I ask is that illusion last.

    I've seen her many times (who will believe me?)
in clearest water, and on greenest grass,
and in the trunks of birches, seen her living,
    and in a cloud, so white and lovely that
Leda would say her daughter's beauty fades
the way a star does when the sun comes up.
    And when I find myself
in wilderness or on deserted beaches,
the thoughts of her are even more amazing.
But when the truth dispels
that sweet deception, in that very place
I sink down cold, dead stone upon live rock,
a statue which can weep and think and write.

    Up where the shadow of no mountain reaches,
upon the highest and most open peak
is where my strong desire seems to draw me.

*Leda would say her
daughter's beauty
fades:* her daughter
was Helen of Troy.

There I can use my eyes, surveying all,
to take the measure of my losses, then
weep to release my gathered clouds of sorrow,
 because I gaze and think
of how much air is standing there between us:
her lovely face, so near and yet so distant.
I softly tell myself:
"What do you know, you fool? Perhaps out there
someone is sighing at your distant absence."
And in this thought my soul begins to breathe.

 Oh, song, beyond the Alps,
where skies are both more happy and serene,
you'll see me by a running stream once more,
where you can sense the breeze
distilling from a fresh and fragrant laurel;
that's where my heart is, with the one who stole it:
what's left of me is just a kind of ghost.

130

Since Mercy's road is closed to me, I've come
along a desperate way, far from those eyes
in which were stored (I know not by what fate)
the rich reward of all my faithfulness.

I feed my heart with sighs, that's all it asks,
I live on tears, I think I'm born to weep;
I don't complain of that, since in my state
weeping is sweeter than you might believe.

One image has me rapt, and one not made
by Zeuxis or Praxiteles or Phidias,
but by a better craftsman, higher mind.

Zeuxis et al.: classical
Greek painters
and sculptors

What Scythia or what Numidia
can keep me safe, if Envy, still not sated
by my rough exile, finds me out in hiding?

Scythia and
Numidia: traditionally
remote regions

131

I'd sing of Love in such a novel fashion
that from her cruel side I would draw by force
a thousand sighs a day, kindling again
in her cold mind a thousand high desires;

I'd see her lovely face transform quite often
her eyes grow wet and more compassionate,
like one who feels regret, when it's too late,
for causing someone's suffering by mistake;

and I'd see scarlet roses in the snows,
tossed by the breeze, discover ivory
that turns to marble those who see it near them;

all this I'd do because I do not mind
my discontentment in this one short life,
but glory rather in my later fame.

132

If it's not love, what is it then I feel?
But if it's love, by God, what sort of love?
If good, why kill me with its bitterness?
If bad, why is each torment then so sweet?

If I burn willingly, why weep and howl?
And if against my will, what good's lament?
Oh living death, oh you delightful pain,
how can you rule me if I don't consent?

And if I do consent, why then I'm wrong
thus to complain. Amid contending winds
I am at sea, and my frail boat is rudderless,

empty of wisdom, and so prone to error
that I myself do not know what I want,
burning in winter, shivering in summer.

133

Love sets me up, a target for his arrows,
like snow in sun, like wax in fire, like clouds
before the wind; and I'm already hoarse
begging for mercy, Lady. You don't care.

The deadly shot came at me from your eyes,
nor time nor place protect me from its blow;
from you alone come forth (you take it lightly!)
the sun and fire and wind that make me thus.

Thoughts are the arrows, and your face, the sun;
passion's the fire; armed with those weapons
Love spears me, dazzles me, and melts me down;

and your angelic song, your very words,
your own sweet breath (I can't defend myself),
these make the breeze that drives my life to flight.

the breeze: l'aura,
one of the puns
on Laura's name

134

I find no peace, and yet I am not warlike;
I fear and hope, I burn and turn to ice;
I fly beyond the sky, stretch out on earth;
my hands are empty, yet I hold the world.

One holds me prisoner, not locked up, not free;
won't keep me for her own but won't release me;
Love does not kill me, does not loose my chains,
he'd like me dead, he'd like me still ensnared.

I see without my eyes, cry with no tongue,
I want to die and yet I call for help,
hating myself but loving someone else.

I feed on pain, I laugh while shedding tears,
both death and life displease me equally;
and this state, Lady, is because of you.

135

Whatever's strange and rare,
existing in whatever wondrous region,
if truly understood will prove
to most resemble me: your doing, Love.
There where the day comes forth
there flies a bird that all alone, no mate,
dies willingly and then
renews itself and comes to life again.
        Thus my desire acts,
turns to the sun and reaching then the summit
of its high thoughts, burns itself up again
and is consumed by fire
and so reverts to its original;
it burns and dies and incarnates itself
and lives again   competing with the phoenix.

There is a stone out there,
somewhere in the Indian Ocean, that's
so bold that it draws iron
and pulls it out of wood, and ships go down.
That's me, among the waves
of weeping, where that lovely rock
has pulled me to its hardness
and brought my life to shipwreck once again.
        Thus a stone has robbed
my soul (stealing my heart—hard once, it held
me up, where I now break and scatter),
a stone more greedy for
my flesh than iron. Oh, ignoble luck,
that in my flesh I'm hurried toward the shore
by that live   lodestone of sweet calamity.

Out in the farthest west
there is a wild creature who's more gentle
and quiet than the rest,
but sorrow, pain, and death live in her eyes;
the sight must be most wary

that turns in her direction; it can see
the rest of her quite safely
if it is careful not to meet her eyes.
    But I'm disastrous, heedless,
I always seem to run straight toward my pain
and know how much I've suffered and will suffer;
but my desire, greedy thing,
both blind and deaf, transports me so that her
charming eyes and holy face will kill me
this wild beast   angelic in her innocence.

    Somewhere in the south
a fountain gushes (for the sun it's named),
a fountain that by nature
boils at night and is ice-cold by day;
and it grows colder as
the sun mounts up and as the light grows stronger.
That is what happens to me,
for I'm a fountain occupied by tears:
    I lose that lovely light
that is my sun, it leaves, I'm sad, alone,
my eyes are desolate and dark night comes,
that's when I burn; but if
the gold and living radiance of that sun
appears to me, I change, inside and out,
and turn to ice   so frozen I become!

    Epirus has a spring,
whereof it's written that, despite its cold,
spent torches can
rekindle there, and flaming ones go out.
My soul, which had not yet
been damaged by the flames of love, approached
to just a little distance
from the cold one for whom I ever sigh,
    and then burst into flames;
such pain the stars and sun have never seen,
it would have moved a marble heart to pity;

and having caused the blaze,
then frozen lovely virtue put it out.
How often she has lit and quenched my heart
I know, who felt it   and it makes me angry.

Far out beyond our shores
two springs are in the Fortunate Isles,
twin fountains; he who drinks
from one dies laughing, while the other rescues.
That kind of fortune marks
my life, because I could die laughing from
the pleasure that I take
if cries of sorrow didn't temper it.
Love, you who guide me
even to shades of fame, hidden and dark,
let us not speak about this spring; it brims
but has its greatest flow
when Taurus joins together with the sun:
my eyes weep always, but they weep the most
in that same season   when I saw my lady.

If anyone asks, dear Song,
what I am up to, say: "Next to a huge stone
in a closed valley where the Sorgue comes forth,
he sits; there's no one there to see him,
except for Love, who never goes away, and
the image of a person who destroys him;
he, for his part   flees all other company."

The natural wonders are drawn from Pliny: the phoenix in Arabia; the magnet in the Indian Ocean; the catablepa, a creature whose glance could kill; the fountain in Africa said to be hot by night and cold by day; the fountain at the shrine of Zeus in Dordona that could ignite and quench torches; and the pair of fountains in the Canary Islands. The final fountain, *"this spring,"* is the Vaucluse, where Petrarch lived. The sun is in Taurus around mid-April.

136

May fire from Heaven rain down on your tresses,
oh, wicked one, since evil gives you pleasure;
once you ate acorns, drank from streams, who now
grow rich and great from others' poverty,

you nest of treason, hatching from yourself
most of the ills that now afflict the world,
you slave of wine, of soft beds and of feasting,
in whom intemperance finds its highest power!

Young girls and old men chase around your chambers,
the while Beelzebub, living in their midst,
brings bellows, fires, and mirrors to their revels.

You were raised not on pillows, under shade,
but naked to the winds, barefoot in thorns;
may your life's stench rise up until God smells it!

wicked one:
whore of
Babylon, here
personifying the
papal court at
Avignon; *ate
acorns,* etc.:
refers to the
poverty of the
early Christian
Church

137

Rapacious Babylon has stuffed her sack
with God's great anger and with wicked vices
until it's fit to burst; she's made her gods
Venus and Bacchus, not Jupiter or Pallas.

I wait for justice, struggling, growing weary;
yet I foresee a sultan who will rule her
and take his court (not soon enough for me)
where it belongs, way over there in Baghdad.

Her idols shall be scattered on the earth,
her lofty towers, enemies of Heaven,
burned with their keepers, both outside and in.

Then lovely souls and virtue's intimates
will rule the world; we'll see a golden age
and the return of ancient worthiness.

Babylon: the
papal court
at Avignon

sultan: the
pagan nature
of the court will
become clear
and remove
to the world
of idolatry
associated
with Muslims.

138

This sonnet is addressed to the papal court at Avignon; Constantine was thought to have first given sovereignty to the Popes. He is in Hell, where Petrarch assigns them, too.

Fountain of sorrow, dwelling place of anger,
school of all errors and heresy's temple,
once Rome, now false and wicked Babylon,
on whose account there are such tears and sighs:

confusion's forge and foundry, cruel prison
where good expires, infamy is nourished,
hell for the living: it's a great miracle
that Christ has not shown anger at you yet.

Begun in chaste and humble poverty,
you lift your horns against your founders now,
you shameless whore! Where do you place your hopes?

In your adulterers, in evil spawned
from ill-got gains? Constantine won't return.
Let the sad realm that holds him take you too!

139

This sonnet is addressed to friends left behind in Italy.

The more I spread my wings, filled with desire
to join you, flock of friends, the more my fortune
entangles me with birdlime, checks my flight,
and holds me back or makes me go astray.

My heart, whom I send out against his will,
is always with you in that open valley
where land and sea embrace: possibly Venice
where land and sea embrace so tenderly;
I left him weeping there the other day.

to the left: west, toward Provence
I went off to the left while he went straight;
force carried me, while he was led by Love;
Jerusalem: the Promised Land; *Egypt:* slavery
he toward Jerusalem and I toward Egypt.

But patience is a comfort in our sorrow;
for by long habit, now routine between us,
we never are together very long.

140

Love that lives and reigns in all my thoughts
and makes his seat of power in my heart,
sometimes appears in armor on my brow
and camps there, setting up his banner.

Then she who teaches us both love and patience
and wants my great desire, kindled hope,
to be reined in by reason, shame, and reverence,
grows angry at our boldness, hot within.

Which makes Love flee in terror to my heart;
abandoning all enterprise, he weeps
and shakes; hides there, and will come forth no more.

What can I do, when my lord is afraid,
except stay with him till the final hour?
For he dies well who dies while loving deeply.

141

The way a simple butterfly, in summer,
will sometimes fly, while looking for the light,
right into someone's eyes, in its desire,
whereby it kills itself and causes pain:

so I run always toward my fated sun,
her eyes, from which such sweetness comes to me,
since Love cares nothing for the curb of reason
and judgment is quite vanquished by desire.

And I can see quite well how they avoid me,
and I well know that I will die from this,
because my strength cannot withstand the pain;

but oh, how sweetly Love does dazzle me
so that I wail some other's pain, not mine,
and my blind soul consents to her own death.

142

Toward the sweet shadow of those lovely leaves
I ran, in flight from a relentless light
that burned me, even here, from the third Heaven;
snow was already fading from the hills
thanks to the loving breeze which starts the season,
and in the meadows grew green grass and branches.

The world had never seen such graceful branches
nor had the wind blown through such tender leaves
as showed themselves to me in that first season;
and thus it was, in fear of that hot light,
I chose for safety not the shade of hills
but of that tree most favored by high Heaven.

A laurel, then, protected me from Heaven,
and thus quite often, longing for its branches,
I've strayed through woods and wandered over hills;
but never since have I found trunk or leaves
so honored by the bright supernal light
that they did not change color with the season.

Therefore, more firmly, season after season,
in answer to a call I heard from Heaven
and guided by a clear and mild light,
I came back always, pledged to those same branches,
both when the earth is scattered with their leaves
and when the sun is greening all the hills.

Woods, rivers, rocks, and fields and trees and hills,
all the creation, must give way to seasons,
vanquished by time, and thus from these green leaves
I ask forgiveness that, beneath the heavens,
ever-changing, I sought to fly those branches
and their birdlime, soon as I saw the light.

It was so pleasing to me first, that light,
that full of joy I traveled across hills
in order to approach those lovely branches.

Now life grows short; now place and season
direct me to another path to Heaven
and show me fruit as well as flowers and leaves.

Some other love, new leaves, another light,
another climb toward Heaven, other hills
I seek (the season's right), and other branches.

143

Now when I listen to you speak, so sweetly,
like Love himself, inspiring his disciples,
my passion, kindled, showers out such sparks
that they might even set the dead on fire;

that's when my lovely lady comes to mind
and those few times when she was kind to me
before I woke again, not to the sound of bells
but to the noise of sighs, my own, of course.

I see her turn, her hair stirred by the wind,
and it's as if she walks into my heart,
so beautiful, the one who keeps its key.

But my profound delight, which ties my tongue,
has not the means or strength to publish her
and show what she is like, enthroned within.

listen to you: another
love poet, unidentified,
possibly Sennuccio del
Bene, to whom the next
poem is addressed

144

I never saw the sun come up so fair
when all the sky is free of mist and clouds,
nor after rain the great celestial arc
spread itself out through air with many colors,

as on that day when I took on my burden
and saw her lovely face transform itself
blazing before me (and my words here fail me)
as something that no mortal life could match.

I witnessed Love, moving her lovely eyes
so gently then that every other sight
has ever since seemed dark to me in contrast,

Sennuccio; I saw Love, saw the bow
he drew—my life was safe no more, and yet
it seems to long to look on him again.

145

Oh, put me where the sun kills flowers and grass
or where the ice and snow can overcome him;
or put me where his chariot's mild and light,
where he's restored or where he's kept from us;

give me bad fortune or a run of luck,
put me in clear, sweet air, or dark and heavy;
set me in night, in daytime long or short,
in ripe maturity or early youth;

put me in Heaven, earth, or the abyss,
or mountain peaks or in low, swampy valleys;
make me move freely or transfix my limbs;

give me obscurity or lasting fame:
I'll still be what I've been, live as I've lived,
trilustral: fifteen   I'll still continue my trilustral sighing.
years; one lustrum
is five years.

146

Oh, noble spirit warm with burning virtue
for whom I fill so many pages still,
oh, sole unblemished home of chastity,
strong tower built on your deep worth's foundation,

oh, flame, oh, roses spread on a sweet drift
of living snow, whose mirror makes me better,
whose pleasure makes me raise my wings to fly
up to that lovely face, brighter than sunlight:

with your name, if my rhymes could reach so far
and still make sense, I would fill Thule and Bactria,
the Nile and the Don, Atlas, Olympus, Calpe.

Thule: farthest north; *Bactria:* east of Persia; *Calpe:* Gibraltar

Since I can't take it to the world's four corners,
I'll say it to the lovely country which
the Apennines divide, the sea and Alps surround.

the lovely country: Italy

147

When my desire, which rides me hard and rules me
with two hot spurs as well as a hard bit,
runs wild from time to time, outside the law,
as if to give my spirits what they want,

he finds a person who can read my brow
and see the fear and boldness of my heart;
and he sees Love, who comes to chasten him,
by flashing lightning from her angry eyes.

At that, like someone dodging thunderbolts
from angry Jove, he hastens to retreat,
showing how fear can quickly curb desire;

but cooling fires and shivering bouts of hope
that happen in my soul, so glass-transparent,
can sometimes brighten her sweet face again.

148

Not Tesin, Po, Varo, Arno, Adige, Tiber,
Tigris, Euphrates, Nile, Ganges, Indus, Hermus,
Danube, Don, Alpheus, Garonne that breaks the seas,
Timavus, Rhône, Rhine, Seine, Elbe, Loire, or Hebrus—

nor ivy, fir, pine, beech, or juniper—
could ease the fire that wearies my sad heart

like the fair stream that sometimes weeps with me
and the slim tree my verses celebrate.

I find this helps me during Love's assaults,
which make me spend my time all dressed in armor
while life goes past me, taking giant leaps.

Then let this laurel grow on this fresh bank,
and may the man who planted it enjoy
sweet shade, soft waters, writing happy thoughts.

149

From time to time it seems her form and smile,
sweet and angelic, grow less harsh toward me,
the air of her fine face
clears like the sky, her happy eyes grow brighter.

These sighs, what are they doing with me now,
that used to come from sorrow
and once made very clear
the desperate, anguished nature of my life?
Happens I turn my face in her direction
to try to ease my heart,
it seems that Love is there
lending his aid and taking up my cause.

Yet I don't think this war is going to end
or any tranquil peace come soothe my heart:
my passion burns the more
the more I'm tempted by my hopefulness.

150

"What are you doing, soul? What do you think?
Will we have peace? A truce? Or always war?"—
"I do not know our future, but I see
our torment doesn't please her lovely eyes."—

"What does that help, if with those eyes in summer
she turns us into ice, to fire in winter?"—
"Not she, but he who has control of them."—
"What's that to us, if she sees and is silent?"—

has control:
the love god

"Sometimes her tongue is silent while her heart
cries out, and though her face is dry and gay
she's weeping where your gazing cannot reach."—

"My mind is still not satisfied, and sorrow,
which gathers there, and stagnates, must burst out;
it's hard for one who's wretched to have hopes."

151

No tired helmsman ever fled to port,
escaping angry waves and looming storm,
so readily as I flee my dark thoughts
to where my passion spurs me and inclines me;

no holy light has conquered mortal sight
more fully than has hers my own dim eyes
with rays sweet, fair, soft, black, and white, and mild
from where Love gilds and sharpens his fell arrows.

He isn't blind; I see him, with his quiver,
naked except for where he's veiled by shame;
a boy with wings, not painted but alive.

And he shows me what he conceals from many;
for bit by bit, within her lovely eyes,
I read the things I say or write of Love.

152

This humble wild thing, with tiger's heart, or bear's,
who comes in human form or angel's shape,
spins me around too much, in tears and laughter,
in fear and hope, and makes my state uncertain.

If soon she doesn't take me or release me,
but keeps me still reined in, between the two,
by that sweet poison running through my heart
and all my veins, Sir Love, my life is over.

My frail and weary strength cannot survive
among so many changes; all at once
it burns, it freezes, blushes and turns pale.

It hopes to flee, and thereby end its suffering,
like one who's failing hour to hour; for he
is powerless who cannot even die.

153

Go forth, hot sighs, and reach to her cold heart,
break up the ice that fights against her pity;
if mortal prayers are listened to in Heaven,
let me have death or mercy for my torment.

Go forth, sweet thoughts, and speak of what exists
there where her lovely gaze cannot extend;
if still her cruelty offends, or my ill star,
why then, we'll know we're past all hope and error.

You both can say, although perhaps not fully,
that our condition is as dark and troubled
as hers is now quite peaceful and serene.

Be confident, and go, for Love comes with you;
my cruel fortune may yet terminate
if I can read good weather in my sun.

154

The stars, the heavens, and the elements
contested, using all their arts and care,
to make that living light where Nature and
the sun are mirrored; nothing matches it.

The work's so high, so lovely and so new,
that mortal gaze cannot stay fixed on it
because her eyes, beyond all measure, can
rain down Love's sweetness and his endless grace.

The air affected by their rays burns clear
with chastity, transfigured so completely
it's quite beyond our reach of thought or word;

a place where base desires don't exist,
just love of honor, virtue. When else, ever,
was low desire thus destroyed by beauty?

155

Caesar and Jove were never so much moved
(the one to wound, the other one to thunder)
that pity would not help put out their anger
and make them lay their usual weapons down:

my lady wept, and my lord wished me there
to see her and to hear her lamentations,
to fill me up with sorrow and desire,
to probe my very marrow and my bones.

That weeping Love depicted—no, he sculpted
so I could see it, and those words he wrote
upon a diamond set within my heart,

wherewith he comes back, often, with his keys,
strong and ingenious, and draws forth from it
the precious tears, the long and heavy sighs.

156

I saw on earth angelic attributes
and heavenly beauties unmatched in this world,
the memory both pleases me and pains me:
all else I see seems shadows, dreams, or smoke.

And I saw weeping those two lovely lights
that have a thousand times provoked the sun
to envy; and heard words mixed up with sighs
that would make mountains move and rivers stop.

Love, wisdom, valor, piety, and sorrow—
these made a sweeter music when she wept
than any to be heard throughout the world;

the heavens were so taken with the sound
that no leaf stirred upon a single branch
so great a sweetness filled the air and wind.

157

That always cruel and yet honored day
engraved its living image on my heart
in such a way no wit or skill can tell;
but I revisit it in memory.

Her gestures, marked with gracious pity, and
her bittersweet lamenting, which I heard,
made me unsure: a mortal or a goddess?
She made the sky grow clear and bright all round.

Her head was finest gold, her face warm snow,
her eyebrows ebony, her eyes two stars
where Love has never bent his bow in vain;

pearls and crimson roses formed the words
that gathered her exquisite sorrow up,
her sighs were flames, her tears were precious crystal.

158

No matter where I turn my weary eyes
as if to rest them from their endless longing,
I find that someone paints a lady's portrait
as if to keep my passions fresh and green.

someone paints:
the imagination

With graceful sorrow she breathes forth, it seems,
a deep compassion, wringing noble hearts,
and in my ears, beyond the sense of sight,
I seem to hear her speech and holy sighs.

Love and the truth were with me when I spoke
of beauties that were matchless in this world
and never yet encountered under stars;

nor had such sweet, devoted words been heard,
nor had the sun seen tears so beautiful
issuing forth from such attractive eyes.

159

What part of Heaven was it, what Idea,
where Nature found the pattern of that face,
that lovely visage that she brought down here
to show the capabilities up there?

What nymph beside a spring, what goddess in
what woods, has ever loosed such golden hair?
What heart has ever housed so many virtues
(although their sum is guilty of my death)?

They search in vain, who never saw her eyes,
if beautiful divinity's their goal,
especially if they never saw them moving;

nor can they know how Love both kills and heals
if they have never listened to her sigh
or hearkened to the sound of her sweet laughter.

160

Both Love and I are full of sheer amazement,
like someone who has seen something fantastic,
watching her speak or laugh, gazing on her
who's like herself but not like any other.

Out of the clear serene, her tranquil brow,
shine the two stars that guide me with their light
so much so that there is no other source
that might inflame someone to noble love.

It's such a miracle when on the grass
she blossoms like a flower, or when she
presses her bosom to a green tree's branch!

What sweetness in the spring to see her walking
alone and pensive, picking buds and weaving
a garland for her shining golden curls!

161

Oh, scattered steps, oh, ardent, craving thoughts,
oh, stubborn memory, wild eagerness,
oh, powerful desire, feeble heart,
and oh, my eyes, not eyes but running fountains—

leaves: laurel   oh, leaves that honor brows of fame and glory,
single symbol: oh, single symbol of twofold importance;
perhaps of   oh, life of laboring, oh, sweet mistaking
Heaven   that sends me questing, over shores and mountains;
and earth

oh, lovely face, where Love has placed his spurs
and reins as well, so he can prod and guide me
just as he pleases while I can't unseat him;

oh, noble, loving souls, if you exist,
anywhere in the world, you shades and dust,
ah, stay so you can witness all my suffering!

162

Lucky, happy flowers, and well-born grass
whereon my lady's apt to walk in thought,
and shore, that listens to her sweet words spoken
and keeps some imprint of her lovely foot,

and slender trees, green leaves on unripe branches,
delicate violets, pale in forest light,
the shady woods where sunlight filters through
and helps the saplings grow into tall trees,

oh, gentle countryside, and river pure,
bathing her lovely face and brilliant eyes,
taking your worth from their illumination;

how much I envy you your dear, chaste contact!
By now there's probably no stone among you
that hasn't learned to burn with my same passion.

163

Love, you who can see clearly all my thoughts
and those harsh steps where you alone can guide me,
look searchingly into my heart's recesses,
open to you, though they are hid from others.

You know what I have suffered in your service
and still, day after day, you climb these mountains
with no attention to my great fatigue
or to the awful steepness of the trail.

I do see in the distance that sweet light
you drag me toward, while goading me so harshly,
but I lack wings like yours with which to fly.

And yet you satisfy my wild passions
by giving me a great love to consume me,
and I don't think she minds my sighs at all.

164

Now that the heavens, earth, and winds are silent,
and sleep restrains the birds and wild beasts,
night drives her starry chariot overhead,
and in its heavy bed the sea lies waveless.

I am awake; I burn, think, weep; and she,
sweet pain who ruins me, is always there
before my eyes; I am at war, I'm wounded;
thinking of her is all the help I get.

Thus, from one clear and living fountain
come both the sweet and bitter in my life;
one single hand can pierce me and then heal me,

and since my suffering has no end in sight,
I die a thousand times a day and then
I am reborn, still distant from true health.

165

As her white foot moves forward through cool grass,
her sweet and quiet walking starts to spread
a power, emanating from her soles,
that acts to open and renew the flowers.

Love only bothers trapping noble hearts
and doesn't try to wield his power elsewhere;
he makes such warmth rain down from her sweet eyes
that I forget about all other bait.

Her words are matched exactly with her gait
and with her gentle glance at things around,
and with her measured, modest, mild gestures.

From four such sparks, though not from them alone,
comes this great fire in which I live and burn,
for I've become a night bird in the sunlight.

166

If I'd remained within that selfsame cave
in which Apollo turned into a prophet,
Florence might have a poet of her own,
not just Verona, Mantua, Arunca.

But since my land no longer grows good reeds
from water of that rock, another planet
must be my guide as I reap thorns and thistles
from this bare field of mine with my hooked sickle.

Dry olive tree, the waters trickle elsewhere
that flowed down from Parnassus and helped make
it flower, flourishing in other times.

Bad fortune or my own mistakes deprive me
of all good fruit, if great eternal Jove
will not let grace from Heaven rain on me.

*Florence might have
a poet:* presumably
Dante does not qualify
because he wrote in
the vernacular;
Verona: Catullus;
Mantua: Virgil;
Arunca: Juvenal

olive tree: sacred
to Athena/Minerva;
Parnassus: sacred
to Apollo, source of
poetic and prophetic
inspiration, i.e.,
"that selfsame cave"

167

Maybe Love makes her drop her lovely eyes
toward earth, and uses his own hands to shape
her vagrant breath into a sigh, releasing it
in a clear, soft, divine, angelic voice;

sweetly my heart is being stolen from me,
my thoughts and wishes altering, within;
I say: "They're going to finish plundering:
Heaven's designed this martyr's death for me."

The sound, though, ties my senses up with sweetness
and keeps my soul, though eager to depart,
rapt in the act of listening, feeling blessed;

so I live on, and thus she winds the spool
of my appointed life, and then unwinds it,
this heavenly siren, peerless in our midst.

siren: myth of Er, who
governs a heavenly
sphere and whose
music constitutes its
harmony; she and the
three Fates rule the
spindle of necessity,
to which the heavenly
spheres are attached.

168

Love sends me that sweet thought, the one which is
a confidant of old between us two,
and comforts me, says I was never closer
to having what I yearn for than right now.

His words, I've found, are sometimes true and then
are sometimes false; I don't know what to think,
and so I live somewhere between the two:
no yes or no rings honest to my heart.

Meantime the days go by, and in my mirror
I watch myself approximate that season
that contradicts his promise and my hope.

Well, let it come. I'm not the only one
who's aging. My desire doesn't age,
but how much time, I wonder, have I left?

169

Full of one longing thought that sends me far
from others, lone wayfarer in the world,
from time to time I even hide from me,
still seeking only she whom I should shun;

then she walks by, so cruel and so sweet
that my soul flutters, trying to take flight;
she leads a mob of armored sighs around,
this lovely enemy of Love and me.

If I'm not wrong, I can make out a gleam
of pity on her proud and cloudy brow,
which partly clears the sorrow in my heart:

I gather up my soul at that, and when
I feel I'm ready to explain my sorrow,
I have so much to say I can't begin!

170

How many times, using my faithful guides,
have I learned courage from her kind expression,
to meet my enemy with skillful words
and take advantage of her humble bearing.

my faithful guides:
i.e., his eyes

But then her eyes expose that thought as useless,
since all my fortune, all my destiny,
my good, my ill, my life, my death, are placed
by Love, who has that power, in her hands.

Result: I've never managed to bring forth
a word that anyone but I could fathom,
because Love's made me quivering and weak.

And I see well how burning love can tie
one's tongue up, steal away one's breath: he who
can say he's burning isn't much on fire.

171

Love's put me in the grasp of fair, cruel arms
that kill unjustly, and if I protest,
my suffering is doubled; better, then,
to die in loving silence, as I'm used to;

for she could burn the Rhine up with her eyes
and break his icy ridges when he's frozen;
her pride is so connected to her beauty
that it displeases her to know she's pleasing.

My own wit won't reduce or wear away
the lovely diamond that makes up her heart;
the rest of her is moving, breathing marble;

but she can never, by contempt or by
the darkened looks she gives me, take away
the hopes I harbor or the sighs I sigh.

172

Oh, Envy, you old enemy of virtue,
so eagerly opposed to good beginnings,
along what path did you so silently
enter that lovely breast, with what art change it?

You pulled up my salvation by the roots:
you made her think I was a lucky lover,
she who had heard my chaste and humble prayers,
and now appears to hate them and reject them.

But even if, with cruel and bitter gestures,
she weeps about my luck, laughs at my weeping,
she cannot alter any thought of mine;

a thousand times a day she may destroy me,
and I'll still love her and have hopes of her;
when she affrights me, Love will give me courage.

173

Admiring the clear sun of her great eyes,
where there is one who makes mine wet and bloodshot,
my weary soul takes leave of my poor heart
and sets out for its earthly paradise;

one who makes
mine wet:
the love god

then finding that it's full of sweet and bitter,
it sees the world is made of spiderwebs,
and it complains to Love accordingly,
about his searing spurs and his hard bit.

Between these opposite and mixed extremes,
with frozen passion, then with kindled longing,
it stays part happy and part miserable;

its happy thoughts are few, its sad ones many,
and mostly it repents its bold endeavors;
such is the fruit that springs from such a root.

174

Cruel star (if heavens have indeed the power
they're thought to have), beneath which I was bred,
cruel cradle where I lay, newborn, and cruel
earth on which I later set my feet,

and cruel lady, she who used her eyes
(the bow that loved to have me as a target)
to make the wound I've mentioned to you, Love,
since with those very weapons you could heal it.

But you enjoy my pain, it pleases you;
that's not her case, I think, she's not that harsh;
the blow is from an arrow, not a spear.

And that consoles me: better pine for her
than be with someone else. By your gold arrow
you swear that that is true, and I believe you.

175

When I recall the time and place where I
first lost myself, and think of that dear knot
Love tied me up with, using his own hands
(making the bitter sweet, weeping a pleasure),

I'm tinder, sulfur, and my heart's a fire
lit by those gentle words I always hear,
such flames that I enjoy the conflagration,
and live on it and care for little else.

The sun that seems to shine for my eyes only
still warms me with her beams when evening comes
just as she did quite early in the day;

and from afar she so ignites and kindles
that memory survives, still fresh and whole,
to make me see the time, the place, the knot.

176

woods: the
Ardennes,
probably
c. 1333

Right through the midst of savage, hostile woods,
where even men at arms travel at risk,
I walk secure, and nothing can alarm me,
except the sun, whose rays are living Love.

And I go singing (oh, my foolish thoughts!)
of her, whom Heaven cannot keep me from;
she stays before my eyes, accompanied
by maids and ladies who are firs and beeches.

I seem to hear her when I hear the branches,
the breeze, the leaves, the birds' complaints, the waters
that run with murmurs soft among green grass.

Seldom has silence or the lonely horror
of shady forests thrilled my heart so much,
except this fear that I may lose my sun.

177

In just a single day I have been shown
a thousand slopes and then a thousand rivers
by Love, who gives his followers winged feet

third sphere:
the planet
Venus

and wingèd hearts, to fly to the third sphere.

Sweet to be in this famous Ardennes forest,
alone, unarmed where Mars can lie in ambush;
a ship adrift, dismasted, rudderless,
filled with a host of grave and secret thoughts.

But now, at this dark day's approaching close,
recalling where I came from, on what wings,
I start to falter at my own great daring;

the lovely country, the delightful river,
welcome me back and reassure my heart,
already turning to the source of light.

178

Love spurs me on and reins me in at once,
comforts and terrifies, burns and freezes me,
is kind, then scorns me, summons and dismisses,
thrills me with hope, then fills me up with sorrow,

now high, now low, he leads my weary heart;
until my wandering desire's lost
and starts to hate its only source of pleasure,
and most peculiar notions fill my mind.

A kind thought shows my mind the river crossing
(not through the water pouring from the eyes)
where it might get to where it feels contentment;

river crossing:
perhaps to the
realm of virtue

but then, as if a great force turned it back,
it has to go along another path,
agreeing to slow death, against its will.

179

*This sonnet is a
reply to one by
Geri Gianfigliazzi,
a Florentine poet,
using the same
rhyme words.*

Geri, when my sweet enemy gets angry
the way she sometimes does, in her great pride,
I have one comfort keeping me alive,
and by its strength my soul can go on breathing:

whichever way she turns her eyes in anger,
as if she thought to take my life and light,
I gaze right back with such humility
that she relents and throws away her scorn.

Were that not so, I'd no more go to see her
than I'd seek out Medusa's face, the one
that turned so many victims into marble.

You try this too; all other aids are useless,
as far as I can see, and flight won't help
because our lord has speedy wings to chase us.

180

This sonnet was
written while
Petrarch was sailing
east on the Po.

Po, you can bear my outer shell along
upon your rapid current's forceful waves,
but the spirit housed within the shell is not
subject to your force, or to anyone's;

he moves straight on ahead, he does not tack
to port or starboard, straight into the wind,
golden foliage: toward golden foliage, beating his strong wings
Laura's hair against the wind and water, sail and oars.

Monarch among the rivers, proud god, you
who greet the sun when it is bringing day
a fairer light: Laura and leave behind a fairer light, to westward:

horn: a traditional you carry on your horn my mortal part;
feature of river gods the spirit part, befeathered by his love,
is flying back to where he started from.

181

Love spread out in the grass a graceful net
gold and pearls: Laura's of gold and pearls, underneath a branch
hair, braided with pearls; of that same evergreen I love so well,
evergreen: the laurel tree despite the ways its shadows make me sad.

The bait was seed he scatters and then reaps,
bitter and sweet, my fear and my desire;
such gentle, quiet notes had not been heard
since that first day when Adam came awake;

bright light was growing all around and making
the sun itself grow dim; she held the rope
in hands that rival ivory and snow.

And so I fell, into the net, and I've
been trapped by her sweet bearing, and her words,
and by desire, pleasure, and my hope.

182

Love fires up my heart with ardent zeal,
then makes it shrink again with icy fear;
he makes my mind uncertain which is greater,
the hope or fear, the mighty flame or frost.

I shiver when it's hot, I burn in cold,
I'm filled with fear and also with desire,
as if a lady seemed to have concealed
a full-grown man beneath her dress and veil.

My own especial pain's the first of these:
I burn by day and night, an illness sweet
beyond all comprehension, verse, or rhyme;

the other pains are less; the flame itself
sees everyone alike; who thinks to fly
up toward her light would spread his wings in vain.

183

If that sweet glance of hers can murder me,
and little words, so soft and sweet and gentle,
and if Love gives her total mastery
when she just speaks or simply when she smiles,

then what, alas, will happen to me if
through some mistake of mine or some bad luck
she who protects me now should take away
the pity from her eyes and thus dispatch me?

That's why I tremble, feel my heart freeze up,
if her expression changes in the least,
a fear that's born of long experience:

All women are by nature changeable;
I know quite well that any state of love
may not persist for long within their hearts.

184

Nature, and Love, and that sweet, humble soul
where all high virtues congregate and rule,
contrive to thwart me: Love intends to kill me,
promptly, ingeniously, as is his style;

Nature sustains that soul by just a thread,
so delicate that it can bear no strain;
she's shy and shows no tendency to dwell
in this fatiguing life, so low and vile.

And thus the spirit's failing, hour by hour,
within that graceful body that has been
the mirror and the mood of loveliness;

unless, alas, Pity can rein in Death,
I see how vain the state of hope has grown
on which I have been trying to survive.

185

golden feathers:
Laura's hair

The golden feathers that surround her white
and noble throat array this artless phoenix
with such a precious necklace that each heart
is sweetened by it, though my own's consumed;

they make a kind of natural diadem
that lights the air all round; Love's soundless flint
draws out of it a subtle, liquid fire
that burns me even in the coldest frost.

A scarlet dress, hemmed with cerulean
and scattered roses, veils her lovely shoulders:
new garment for a beauty without equal!

Fame says the phoenix lives in distant mountains
among the spicy reaches of Arabia,
but this one's cruising proudly through our skies.

186

If Homer and then Virgil had but seen
that sun my eyes are able to enjoy,
they would have bent their skill to make her famous,
mingling their separate styles into one:

that would enrage Aeneas; and Achilles,
Ulysses, all the demigods make sad;
and he who ruled the world so well for six
and fifty years, and whom Aegisthus killed.

he who ruled: Augustus

whom Aegisthus killed:
Agamemnon

That ancient flower of virtue and of arms,
how similar his star was to this new one
that now embodies chastity and beauty!

ancient flower:
Scipio Africanus,
Roman conqueror
of Carthage, whom
Ennius celebrated
in a long poem

Ennius praised him with a clumsy song,
and I praise her; oh, may I not displease,
and may she not despise my celebration!

187

When Alexander saw the famous tomb
of fierce Achilles, we are told he sighed:
"Oh, lucky man, who found so clear a trumpet
to write so splendidly of your great deeds!"

trumpet: Homer

But this dove, pure and white, whose living equal
has not existed ever in this world,
is barely echoed in my feeble style.
That's how our destinies are various;

for she deserves an Orpheus or Homer
or homage from the shepherd Mantua loves,
she's worth their singing, always, just of her;

*shepherd Mantua
loves:* Virgil

a crooked star, determining her fate,
made her unlucky: to have one adore her
who sings her praise, but mars it by his crudeness.

188

Life-giving sun, you loved that branch at first
which I love now: it's she who thrives alone
in her sweet place, who has no equal since
Adam first saw his lovely curse, and ours.

Let's stay and gaze at her, I beg of you,
oh, sun, for you still run away and darken
the hillsides all around, take out the day,
and take from me what I desire most.

The shadow growing from that sloping hill
there where my gentle fire glows and sparks,
where this great laurel was a little sapling,

grows longer as I speak, steals from my eyes
the happy sight of that most blessed place
there where my heart is dwelling with his lady.

189

My galley, loaded with forgetfulness,
rolls through rough seas, at midnight, during winter,
aiming between Charybdis and sharp Scylla;
my lord, ah no, my foe, sits at the tiller;

each oar is wielded by a quick, mad thought
that seems to scorn the storm and what it means;
an endless wind of moisture, of deep sighs,
of hopes and passions, rips the sail in half;

tears in a steady downpour, mists of hate,
are loosening and soaking all the ropes,
ropes made of ignorance, tangled up with error.

The two sweet stars I steer by are obscured;
reason and skill are dead amid the waves;
and I don't think I'll ever see the port.

190

A white doe on green grass appeared to me;
she had gold horns and stood between two rivers,
beneath a laurel, in a place I knew,
at dawn and in a season still unripe.

gold horns: Laura's braids; *rivers:* the Sorgue and the Durance

Her look was sweet and proud, so that I left
all other tasks to follow her, just like
a miser seeking out a treasure, who
sweetens the pain of labor with delight.

Around her lovely neck: "Let no one touch me,"
the words spelled out in diamonds and topaz.
"It pleased my Caesar to create me free."

diamonds and topaz: loyalty and chastity

Caesar: God? or Laura's husband?

Already it was noon. My eyes were weary
but hadn't gazed their fill when suddenly
I fell into the water and she vanished.

191

Just as eternal life means seeing God
and wanting nothing else (nor could one want to),
so, Lady, seeing you can make me happy
in this my very brief and fragile life.

Nor have I ever seen you lovelier
than you are at this hour, if my eye
tells my heart truly, hour of blessed thoughts,
surpassing every hope and all desire!

If this would last I wouldn't ask for more,
for if some beings live on odors, as
they tell and it's believed, and some on fire,

and some on water, with their touch and taste
thriving somehow on things that lack all sweetness,
why shouldn't I be nourished seeing you?

192

Love, let us pause to contemplate our glory
and see things high and strange, past Nature.
See sweetness that rains down upon her here,
see light that shows us Heaven come to earth;

see how much skill has gilded and made pearly
and ruddy-hued that body, surely matchless,
which moves sweet feet and lively eyes throughout
the shady cloister of these lovely hills!

Green grass and flowers of a thousand colors
scattered beneath that black and ancient oak
entreat her lovely foot to step on them;

the sky's aswarm with sparks, with shining fire,
and seems to be rejoicing everywhere
at being made so clear by eyes so fair.

193

I feed my mind upon a food so noble
I don't need Jove's ambrosia or nectar;
for simply gazing makes oblivion rain
into my soul; all other sweetness: Lethe.

I hear words spoken, write them in my heart
so I can look them up again and sigh,
transported by Love's hand I know not where,
tasting a double sweetness in one face;

for that voice, pleasing even Heaven, utters
words so exquisite, words so enchanting,
who hasn't heard it never could conceive it.

Together then, in one hand, is collected
all that our Art, our Wit, Nature, and Heaven
could hope to find accomplished in this life.

194

This noble breeze that clears the hills again,
arousing flowers in the shady woods:
I recognize from its soft breath the one
on whose account I labor and grow famous.

To find someplace my weary heart can rest
I flee my sweet and native Tuscan air;
to bring some light to dark and torpid thoughts
I seek and hope to see today my sun,

in whom I find so many sweetnesses
that Love leads me by force to her again,
then dazzles me and makes it hard to flee.

To get away I would need wings, not armor;
but Heaven decrees that this light shall destroy me,
torment me at a distance, burn close up.

breeze: L'aura, the pun on her name; the same pun opens Numbers 196, 197, and 198.

195

My face and hair are changing, day by day,
but that can't make me shun the baited hook
or keep me from the green and birdlimed branches
of that same tree that knows not sun or frost.

tree: the laurel

The sea will lose all water, sky all stars,
before I lose my fear and my desire
for her good shade, lose both the love and hate
for this love-wound that I conceal so badly.

I do not hope to put away my labors
till I'm deboned, demuscled, and defleshed,
or else my enemy takes pity on me.

All other things impossible could happen
before another she, or Death, might heal
the wound her eyes first made upon my heart.

196

The tranquil breeze that passes, murmuring,
through verdant foliage, blows across my brow
and calls me to remember that first time
when Love gave me the deep, sweet wounds I bear

and makes me see the lovely face she hides,
and still withholds from jealousy or anger;
her golden hair, braided with gems and pearls,
or loosened, and more blond than burnished gold,

which she shook free so sweetly and then gathered
with such a charming gesture that my mind
still trembles when I think of it again.

Time braided up that hair in tighter knots
and bound my heart as well, so strong a cord
that death alone can manage to untie it.

197

The heavenly breeze that sighs in that green laurel
where Love once struck Apollo in his side,
has placed about my neck a yoke so sweet
that I regain my liberty too late,

controlling me the way Medusa ruled
that Moorish giant whom she turned to flint;
I can't shake loose that lovely knot that rivals
the sun itself, as well as gold and amber:

I mean that hair of hers, the curled blond snare
that softly ties my soul and binds it tight,
leaving it no armor but humility.

Her very shadow turns my heart to ice,
blanching my face with fear, but it's her eyes
that have the power to harden both to marble.

that Moorish giant: Atlas, whom Perseus turned into a mountain by holding up the severed head of Medusa

198

The soft breeze spreads and vibrates in the sunlight
the gold that Love is spinning here by hand;
using her lovely eyes and gorgeous hair
he binds my weary heart, sifts my light spirits.

I have no marrow in my bones, or blood
within my veins, that does not tremble if
I come into her presence, she who weighs
my life and death upon a fragile scale;

I see those two lights burning that engulf me,
I see those knots that bind me with their shine
now on the right-hand shoulder, now the left.

I can't explain what I don't understand,
my intellect is snuffed by two such lights,
oppressed and wearied by such steady sweetness.

*the gold: l'auro,
so that the first
two lines of the
poem pun twice
on her name,
l'aura and l'auro*

*knots:
Laura's braids*

199

Oh, lovely hand that grasps my heart, enclosing
my life entire in a little space,
oh, hand where Heaven and Nature have put all
their art and labor, to enhance their glory,

soft fingers like five Oriental pearls,
bitter and harmful only to my wound,
quite gentle otherwise and just now naked,
which Love allows as if to make me rich.

White, delicate, and precious little glove,
that covered flawless ivory and fresh roses,
who in the world's seen spoils sweet as these?

I wish I had a part of that fine veil!
Oh, fickleness of human life and fate,
that would be theft; she'll come and take it back.

200

Not just that single naked hand
that now reclothes itself, to my deep sorrow,
the other too, and those two arms, are quick
to squeeze and wring my timid, humble heart.

Love sets a thousand snares, and none in vain,
among these beautiful new virtuous forms
that so adorn her vesture, high and heavenly,
that human wit or style can add nothing:

her tranquil eyes, her starry brows, her fine
angelic mouth, a mouth that's full of pearls
as well as blooming roses and sweet words

that make one shake with wonder, marveling,
and then her forehead and exquisite hair,
at noon in summer vanquishing the sun.

201

embroidery: the
glove mentioned
in Number 199,
which Petrarch
apparently wanted
as a keepsake and
Laura insisted on
taking back

My luck, along with Love, had blessed me so
with an embroidery of gold and silk,
I'd almost reached the limits of my joy
by saying to myself, "Just think who wore this!"

And now I cannot bring that day to mind
when I grew rich and poor all in one moment,
without becoming filled with rage and sorrow,
divided evenly by scorn and shame

that I did not secure my noble spoils
when that was needful, or was not more steady
against the force of just one little angel,

or that I didn't flee, wings on my feet,
and take my vengeance on at least that hand
that has provoked so many tears from me.

202

From ice that's clear, alive, and smooth and shining
the flame appears that kindles me and melts me,
and it so dries and drains my heart and veins
that I decline, invisibly, and perish.

Death has already raised his arm to strike
and he pursues my life, which flees from him,
as angry heavens thunder, lions roar,
and I am trembling, silent, filled with fear.

Pity, allied with Love, could still arrive
to save me; they could make a double column
between my weary soul and Death's fell blow;

but I don't think it will, nor do I see it
there on her face, my enemy and mistress;
I don't blame her, I blame my heavy fortune.

203

Alas, I burn, and no one will believe me;
or everyone believes me except her,
the one, of all, whom I would have believe
and who does not, although she watches it.

Infinite beauty with so little faith,
do you not see my heart's truth in my eyes?
My star is ranged against me or I'd surely
find mercy at the fountainhead of pity.

This ardor, which you care so little for,
and all your praises in my well-known verses,
might start a blaze within a thousand hearts;

for in my thoughts I see, oh, my sweet fire,
a tongue grown cold in death, two eyes shut down,
and embers burning on, long after us.

204

You, Soul, who see so many different things
and hear and read and speak and write and think,
and you, my roving eyes, and other senses,
who bring her holy words into my heart:

how strongly do you wish that you had come
later or sooner to this road we travel
if it would mean you'd miss those lovely lights
or trace the footprints of those well-loved feet?

Now, since we have clear light and such good signs
we must not lose our way in that brief journey
which may allow us an eternal dwelling:

push on toward Heaven, then, oh, tired heart,
pass through the clouds and mist of her disdain,
and trace her chaste steps toward a light divine.

205

Sweet angers, sweet disdains, sweet peace accords,
sweet ill, sweet suffering, sweet weight of pain,
sweet speech, conversing, sweetly understood,
and now a soothing breeze and now sweet fire!

Soul, don't complain of this, be still and patient,
and temper the sweet bitterness that's harmed us
with all the honor, sweet, in loving her,
to whom I said: "It's you alone who please me."

Perhaps someday some person will remark,
sighing, and colored with sweet jealousy:
"This man endured much pain for noble love."

Another adds: "Oh, Fortune, foe of eyes!
Why did I never get a chance to see her?
Why couldn't she live later or I sooner?"

206

If I said that, then may the one whose love
I live by and would die without despise me;
if I said that, my days be sad and numbered,
my soul the servant of some vile power;
if I said that, may stars be armed against me,
and my companions be
Terror and Jealousy,
and let my enemy
be crueler still and yet more beautiful!

If I said that, then let Love use up all
his golden arrows on me, lead on her;
if I said that, let earth, sky, men, and gods
reproach me while she grows more pitiless;
if I said that, let her use her dark torch
to lead me straight to death,
stay just that way she is,
and never may she show
some kindness to me in her words or deeds!

If I said that, let me go down a road
that's short and rough and full of things I hate;
if I said that, let flames of passion grow
in me to match the growing ice in her;
if I said that, may my eyes never see
the clear sun, or his sister,
no lady, or a maiden,
but just the kind of storm
the Pharaoh saw when he pursued the Hebrews!

If I said that, let pity for me die
and courtesy, with all the sighs I've breathed;
if I said that, may she speak just as harshly
as she was tender on the day she won me;
if I said that, let me disgust her, her
whom I would love, alone,
though locked in some dark cell

This poem is based
on a Provençal form
that uses rhyming
stanzas and a riddling
manner; what he was
presumably reported
to have *said* was that
he loved someone
other than Laura and
was using his love
for her as a pretext.

golden arrows . . .
lead: Cupid's way
of creating love
and hate

from day of weaning till
my day of death—which I might engineer!

But if I didn't say it, may she soften,
the one who opened up my youthful heart
to sweetness, and still steer my weary ship
using the tiller of her natural mercy;
don't let her change, but still be as she was
when I could do no more
(for I had lost myself
and have no more to lose):
it does great harm to overlook such loyalty.

I didn't say it, and indeed I could not
for gold or cities or for castles, no;
let truth prevail, still seated in its saddle,
let falsehood fall, all beaten, to the earth!
You know, Sir Love, what's in me; if she asks
tell what you should of me;
I'd say myself that he
who has to suffer is
more blessed, three-, four-, sixfold, if he dies first.

for Rachel, not for Leah: Jacob served seven years to marry Rachel and then another seven years when the girls' father, Laban, tried to substitute Leah; Elijah's fiery chariot carried him off to Heaven.

I've served for Rachel, not for Leah, could
not live with any other;
I would be ready, sure,
if Heaven called us both,
to go with her upon Elijah's chariot.

207

I thought by now perhaps that I could live
as I have lived these past few years, without
new studies and without new stratagems;
but now that I don't have the help I'm used to,
my lady's aid, perhaps you'll understand
where you have led me, Love, teaching such art.
    I don't know if I should

be angry that you'd make me, at my age,
go steal her lovely light,
without which I would live in dreadful pain.
I wish I'd learned in youth
the style I must try to take on now,
because there is less shame in youthful failings.

Her gentle eyes, which nurtured me with life,
were so forthcoming to me at the first
with their divinity and lofty beauty,
that I was like a man of little wealth
who's greatly helped by secret patronage;
I did no harm to them, and none to others.
    Now, to my own distress,
I have become importunate and nasty;
a beggar who is starving
is capable of actions that he'd hate
in anybody else.
If Envy's made a fist of Pity's hand
my weakness and love's hunger should be blamed.

For I have tried a thousand ways to find
if any mortal thing could help me live
a single day without them. But my soul,
because it can find respite nowhere else,
still hurries after those angelic sparks,
and I am made of wax and seek the fire;
    I try to reckon where
what I desire most is least well guarded,
and like a bird that is
most quickly caught where he is least afraid,
so at her lovely face
I steal a glance, and then another glance,
and by them I am nourished but inflamed.

I feed on my own death, and live in flames:
strange feast, and most amazing salamander!
But it's no miracle, just someone's will.
I bleated with his flock a little while,
a happy lamb, but at the end, it seems,

salamander: thought
to be able to survive
and thrive in fire

154

both Love and Fortune treat me like the rest:
    violets and roses in spring,
and in the winter lots of ice and snow.
Thus if I try to snatch
some food with which to nourish my short life,
she should not call it theft,
so rich a lady surely should not mind
if someone lives on what is hers, unmissed.

    Who does not know what I live on, and have
since that first day I saw those lovely eyes
that made me change my life and change my ways?
Who understands the ways and means of men
from searching earth and sea and every shore?
Along a river one man lives on scent
    as I by fire and light
nourish and soothe my weak and starving spirits.
Love (I have to tell you),
it doesn't suit a lord to be so stingy.
You've arrows and a bow,
so kill me by your hand and not by yearning:
a decent death can crown a life with honor.

    A covered flame is hottest; as it grows
it can't be hidden long and it will out.
I know this, Love, I feel it at your hands;
you saw it well when I blazed silently;
my own cries pain me now, and I go round
annoying others near and far away.
    Oh, world, oh, senseless thoughts,
oh, my strong fate, where do you carry me?
oh, such a lovely light,
that made a steady hope live in my heart
and bind it and oppress it,
and give her strength to lead me to my death!
The fault is yours, while mine's the loss and pain.

    For loving well my gift has been this torment,
I'm asking pardon for another's crime;
for mine, I guess, because I should have turned

one man lives on scent: a race near the Ganges, as reported by Pliny

my eyes from too much light and stopped my ears
against the sirens; and I can't repent
because my heart is brimming with sweet poison.
    I wait for him to shoot
the final shot, who hit me with the first one:
and if I understand,
he can show pity if he kills me quickly,
since he's not going to treat me
in any way that's different from now;
escape from sorrow makes a good death welcome.

    My song, I will stand firm
upon this field, since fleeing is dishonor;
and I reproach myself
for my complaints because my fate is sweet,
my sighs and tears and death.
Love's servant, you who read these lines, know this:
this world contains no good to match my ill.

208

Swift river, coming from your Alpine source,
gnawing your way (from which you get your name),
by night and day, descending in your passion
to where I'm led by Love, you just by Nature:

go on your way; no sleep or weariness
can check your course; before you meet the sea
and pay him homage, gaze around you where
the grass is greener and the air more clear.

There is that sweet and living sun of ours
adorning and beflowering your left bank;
my being tardy bothers her (I hope!).

Then kiss her foot, her white and lovely hand;
tell her (as if your kiss could turn to speech):
"The spirit's willing, but the flesh is weak."

gnawing: pun
on Rodano, the
Italian name for
the Rhône, and
rodendo, gnawing

left bank:
i.e., Avignon

"The spirit's willing":
Matthew 26:41

209

sweet hill country:
Vaucluse

The sweet hill country where I left myself
when I departed what I can't depart from,
is all around, before me as I go; behind
is that sweet burden Love's assigned to me.

Inside myself, I marvel at myself,
the way I move and yet can't move away from
the sweet yoke I have tried to shake in vain;
the more I distance it, the more it's with me.

The way a deer can have a poisoned arrow
fast in its side: it feels its pain still more
as it runs faster, trying to escape:

so I, that arrow in my left-hand side
that somehow pains me and delights me too,
am hurt by sorrow, worn out by this fleeing.

210

Ebro: the Hebrus;
see Number 148

Not from the Spanish river Ebro to
the Hydaspes in India, each slope,
each shore, Red Sea and Caspian, Heaven
and earth, is there but one—a single phoenix.

Crow . . . raven: omens

Parcae: the Three Fates,
who measure, wind, and
cut the thread of life

deaf as asps: asps
were thought to cover
one ear with their tail
and put the other ear
to the ground to
avoid hearing spells
against them.

Crow on my right, raven on my left, who
sings my fate? Which of the Parcae spools it?
For I alone find pity deaf as asps,
a man of misery wishing to be happy.

I do not want to speak of her; who sees
her feels his heart fill up with love and sweetness,
she has so much, bestowing it on others,

and then, to make my sweetness turn to bitter,
pretends she doesn't care, and doesn't notice
my temples blooming white before their time.

211

Desire spurs me on, Love guides and escorts,
Pleasure cajoles me, Habit is my transport;
Hope flatters me and flirts and reaches out
with her right hand to help my weary heart;

the poor fool grasps it and will not be shown
how blind and treacherous is this guide of ours;
the senses are in charge, and reason's dead;
each hot desire's going to breed another.

Virtue and honor, beauty, noble bearing,
and words too sweet have brought me to these branches,
and gently caught my heart upon this birdlime.

In 1327, at precisely
the day's first hour, April 6, I entered
this labyrinth, and I've found no escape.

212

Blessed in sleep and languishing, contented,
embracing shadows, chasing summer breeze,   *breeze: l'aura,*
I swim a sea that has no shore or bottom,   a pun on Laura
plow water, build on sand, write on the wind;

and I gaze yearning at the sun that has
destroyed my sight already with his brightness,
and thus pursue a wandering, fleeing doe,
hunt with an ox that's lame and sick and slow.

Blind and worn out to everything except
my harm, which I seek trembling day and night,
I cry to Love, my lady, and to Death;

thus twenty years of hard and heavy labor,
have gained me only tears and sighs and sorrow:
under this star I took the bait and hook!

213

Graces that bounteous Heaven grants to few,
virtues too rare among the human race,
under blond hair a mind of wise old age,
a godlike beauty in a humble lady,

a charm both singular and most uncommon,
and singing that you feel caress your soul,
celestial walk, a lovely, ardent spirit
that breaks up hardness and makes pride bow down,

and those great eyes that can turn hearts to stone
and light up the abyss, turn night to day,
move souls from bodies, passing them to others,

and conversation full of sweet, high insights
and sighs that sweetly interrupt themselves:
by these magicians I have been transformed.

214

days: seven-year
stages of life

A soul had been created in a place
three days before, to find what's high and new
and learn to scorn the things that many prize;
this soul, uncertain of her fated course,
alone and thoughtful, young and very free,
came in the springtime to a lovely wood.

A tender flower was born within that wood
the day before, and rooted in a place
that could not be approached by souls still free;
for there were snares there of a form so new
and so much pleasure hastening one's course
that losing freedom there seemed like a prize.

Dear, sweet, and high, and most fatiguing prize,
that took me quickly into that green wood,

used to diverting travelers from their course!
I've searched the world since then from place to place
to see if verses, gems, or herbs of new
concoction mixed could make my mind feel free.

But now, alas, I see my flesh will free
itself from that one knot for which it's prized
before the medicines, old ones or new,
can heal the wounds I took on in that wood
so thick with thorns; because of them my place
is hobbling lame, when once it was swift course!

that one knot:
joining soul
and body

All filled with thorns and brambles is the course
I must complete, just when a light and free
foot is what's needed, sound in every place.
But you, dear Lord, who can be said to prize
pity, extend your right hand in this wood:
may your sun conquer this strange shadow new.

Protect my life from these distractions new
that have dislodged my life from its true course
and left me dwelling in a shadowed wood:
release me, if you can, and make her free,
my wandering consort; yours be the prize
if I find both of you in better places.

Behold in place my conflict rare and new:
Am I worth prizing? Have I run my course?
Is my soul free, or captive in the wood?

215

In noble blood a quiet, humble life,
a lofty intellect and a pure heart,
the fruit of age within the flower of youth,
a happy soul within a thoughtful face—

all gathered in this lady by her planet,
or by the King of stars—and the true honor,
well-deserved praises, merit, and great worth
such as would tire any godlike poet.

For Love has joined with chastity in her,
with natural beauty and most comely ways,
and gestures that are eloquent in silence,

and something in her eyes, I know not what,
that lights the night and makes the day grow dark,
embitters honey, even sweetens wormwood.

216

All day I weep; and then at night when most
miserable mortals find repose, I find
myself in tears and all my pains redoubled;
that's how I seem to spend my life, just weeping.

I'm wearing out my eyes with this sad humor,
my heart, as well, with sorrow; I'm the most
pitiful animal, since these love arrows
keep me forever exiled from my peace.

Alas, that from one sunrise to the next,
one night upon another, I have run
already through this death which we call life!

I grieve for someone else's fault as well;
for living pity and my faithful rescue
have watched me burn in fire and won't help.

217

I wanted once to shape such just laments,
using such fervent rhymes, that I would start
a fire of pity, felt in her hard heart
that's frozen solid in midsummer's heat,

and with the wind of my inflaming words
disperse the cloud that cools it and obscures it,
or maybe make her hateful to the world
who hides the lovely eyes she melts me with.

No hate for her, no pity for myself, now;
I'm not vindictive and I'm far past pity;
it was my star, it was my rugged fate.

I'll sing her beauty, though, since it's divine,
and when I have departed from this flesh
the world will understand my death was sweet.

218

However many lovely, graceful ladies
she finds herself among, she with no equal
anywhere in this world, she does to them
what day does to the host of lesser stars.

Love seems to whisper in my ear, explaining:
"As long as she is seen here on the earth,
life will be good; after, it will be dark,
virtues will die, and with them goes my kingdom.

"If Nature took away the sun and moon,
took wind from air, took grass and leaves from earth,
took words and intellect away from man,

"fish from the sea, even the ocean's waves:
in that same way things will grow dark and empty
if Death should ever close and hide her eyes."

219

New song and weeping by the birds at daybreak
make all the valleys echo with their sound,
as do the liquid crystal murmurings
of shining, fresh, and rapid brooks and rivers.

She of the snow-white face: Aurora, goddess of dawn

She of the snow-white face and golden hair
in whose great love no flaw or lie exists
awakes me now with her own loving dance
combing her aged husband's whitened fleece.

her aged husband: Tithonus, with whom Petrarch, prematurely gray, identifies himself

Thus I awake, and thus salute the dawn,
the sun as well, still more that other sun
who dazzled me in youth and does so still.

I've seen them rise together certain days
as in a single moment he puts out
the stars, and then, in turn, she makes him vanish.

220

Out of what mine did Love extract the gold
to make those two blond tresses? From what thorns
plucked out that rose? And in what meadow found
the fresh and tender frost, the pulse and breath?

And where the pearls with which he breaks and checks
sweet words, both chaste and inconceivable?
Where did he get the many godlike beauties
that grace that forehead, brighter than the skies?

Which of the angels, from what sphere was sent
that heavenly singing, song which melts me so
that by this time there's little left to melt?

What sun provided that high, kindly light
to those great eyes that give me war and peace,
that freeze and burn my heart in ice and fire?

221

What destiny of mine, what force, what trick,
returns me to the field without a weapon
and sees me vanquished, always? If I'm saved,
I'll marvel; if I die, why, that's my loss.

Not loss at all, but gain; the sparks and lightning
endure so sweetly in my heart, still dazzling,
still tormenting, that I blaze anew, I have
been burning now for, oh, these twenty years.

I hear the messengers of death when I
can see her eyes flash lightning from afar;
and if she comes up close and turns to me

Love wounds me and anoints my wound with sweetness;
I can't recapture it, I can't express it;
my skill and tongue come nowhere near the truth.

222

"Happy and pensive, in company, alone,
you ladies who go chatting as you pass,
where is my life, who is my death as well?
Why is she not among you, as is usual?"

"We're happy at the memory of that sun,
we're sad because we lack her company now,
which jealousy and envy have removed,
who see another's good as their detraction."

"Who can curb lovers? Who can give them laws?"
"No one curbs souls. The body? Anger, sourness;
she proves this now, and so do we sometimes;

but one can read the heart upon the brow,
and thus it was we saw her beauty darkened
and all bedewed with tears her lovely eyes."

223

Sun bathes his golden chariot in the sea
and darkens all our air, and my mind too,
and I begin an anguished, bitter night
together with the stars, the moon, the sky;

and then I tell my troubles, one by one,
to one who doesn't listen, and I quarrel
with my blind fortune, with the world at large,
with Love, and with my lady, and myself.

Sleep's banished and there's no repose at all,
just sighs and lamentations until dawn,
and tears my soul sends outward to my eyes.

Dawn comes and lights the darkened air, not me;
the sun that burns my heart and yet delights it,
only that sun can make my torment sweet.

224

If faithfulness in love, a heart sincere,
a sweet devotion and a courteous longing,
chaste passions kindled in a noble fire,
long roaming lost in a blind labyrinth,

if having thoughts depicted on my brow
or barely understood in stumbling words,
or broken off by fear or simple shame,
a pallor like the violet's, tinted lovewise,

if loving someone more than my own self,
if sighing constantly and always weeping
nourished by anger, sorrow, and despair,

if burning far away and freezing near,
if these are ways that I let Love distract me,
the blame is yours, my lady, mine the loss.

225

Twelve ladies chastely resting at their ease,
or say twelve stars, and in their midst a sun,
I saw alone and happy in a boat
whose like, I think, had never plowed the waves;

nor did its like take Jason, I believe,
to find that fleece that people want to wear,
or hold that shepherd Troy's still grieving for,
the two for whom the world made such a fuss.

I saw them next in a triumphal chariot;
my Laura, with her holy, modest manner,
was seated at one side and sweetly singing:

these were not human things, no mortal vision.
Happy Automedon, and lucky Tiphys,
who got to drive and steer such graceful people!

Petrarch seems
to have witnessed
a procession
featuring Laura
and twelve ladies,
first in a boat, then
in a chariot. He
compares them
to Jason and the
Argonauts and
then to Paris taking
Helen to Troy.

Automedon:
Achilles' charioteer;
Tiphys: pilot
of the Argo

226

No sparrow on a roof was as alone
as I am now, no beast in any forest,
her lovely face withheld, when I don't know
another sun, or care for other sights.

To weep forever is my greatest joy,
while laughter's pain, all food is gall and poison,
night is hard work, a clear sky's dark to me,
and bed's a kind of rugged battlefield.

They say that sleep resembles death; it's true,
death's kindred acts to liberate the heart
from all the sweet concerns that keep it living.

Oh, fertile, happy country, you alone,
among your flowering banks and shaded meadows,
possess what I'd possess, my dearest treasure.

sparrow on a roof:
alludes to Psalm 102

happy country:
the Vaucluse

227

You breezes that surround those curling tresses,
moving among them, softly moved by them,
you scatter that sweet gold and then again
you gather it and wreathe it in fair knots:

you live in eyes from which the wasps of love
so sting me that I feel it even here
and weep and stagger, seeking for my treasure,
like any animal that shies and stumbles;

for first I think I've found her, then I learn
I'm far away; I'm solaced, then dejected,
see what I wish for, then I see the truth.

Oh, happy air, go live with that sweet ray,
and as for you, clear running stream, why can't
we trade our paths and courses, you and I?

228

Love opened my left side with his right hand,
and there within my very heart he planted
a laurel tree so green that its rich hue
exceeds the color of all emeralds.

With pen for plow, with labored sighs for wind,
with tears from my own eyes a gentle rain,
this tree has flourished so that its perfume
reaches to Heaven, feat unparalleled.

Honor and fame, virtue and great charm,
chaste beauty dressed in a celestial garb,
these are the roots of this most noble plant.

It's in my breast wherever I may go,
a happy burden, and with my chaste prayers
I worship it as one more holy thing.

229

I sang and now I weep; and from my weeping
take no less sweetness than I took from singing,
because my senses, still in love with heights,
are focused on the cause, not the effects.

Therefore I manage, in an equal measure,
mildness and harshness both, cruel gestures
and humble courtesy; I'm not weighed down,
and scorn itself can't pierce my tempered armor.

Let Love and Fortune, world and lady mine,
go right on treating me the way they do;
I don't think they can take away my joy;

whether I die or live or pine away,
there is no nobler state beneath the moon,
so sweet the plant that has this bitter root.

I sang and now I weep: compare the opening of Number 230

230

I wept and now I sing, because that sun
does not withhold her light from these my eyes
and I can see chaste Love both well and truly,
and revel in his power and sacred ways;

thus he has generated such a flood of tears
to shorten life's accustomed span that I
cannot be rescued here by wing or feather,
much less by bridge or ford, by oar or sail.

My weeping has a source so deep and wide,
the shore itself so distant from my sight,
that I can hardly compass it in thought.

Now pity sends me back, not palm or laurel,
but peaceful olive, and the weather clears
and dries my tears and bids me go on living.

flood of tears: his own tears have marooned him like Noah.

peaceful olive: suggests a gesture of friendliness by Laura

231

I lived quite well contented with my fate,
without a tear or any sort of envy;
if other lovers have a better fortune,
their thousand joys aren't worth one pain of mine.

But now those lovely eyes, for which I won't
repent my sorrows nor can wish them less,

cloud: sickness   are covered by a cloud so dark and heavy
that my life's sun is almost quenched and lost.

Oh, Nature, cruel compassionate mother,
so potent and with such conflicting urges,
why make things charming but unmake them too?

All powers come from one great living fountain;
but how can You, oh, highest Father, let

another: Death   another rob us of Your dearest gift?

232

Alexander murdered
his friend in a drunken
rage; Philip of Macedon
was his father. Pyrgoteles,
Lysippus, and Apelles were
exclusively authorized
to depict him in marble,
bronze, and paint,
respectively; Tydeus, one
of the seven against
Thebes, gnawed on the
head of his enemy as he
was dying; Sulla and
Valentinianus were said
to have died in fits of rage;
Ajax committed suicide from
anger when not awarded
the armor of Achilles.

Anger defeated victorious Alexander,
and made him thus a lesser man than Philip.
What good that Pyrgoteles and Lysippus
alone could sculpt him, or Apelles paint him?

Anger drove Tydeus to such a rage
that as he died he gnawed on Menalippus;
anger made Sulla not just bleary but
completely blind, then ultimately killed him.

Valentinianus knows that anger
leads to such punishments, and so does Ajax,
who killed a host of others, then himself.

Anger's a temporary madness, or
a long one if unchecked, that takes its subject
to certain shame and sometimes on to death.

233

What fortune was it that from those two eyes,
the loveliest that live, one sent a message,
when they were darkened and disturbed by pain,
that made my own eyes dark and very sick!

I had come back, still hungering to see
the person I care most for in this world;
Heaven and Love had grown less cruel to me
showing more kindness than they had before;

for from my lady's eye, the right one, or
from her right sun, there came to my right eye
the illness that delights and does not pain;

as if it had both intellect and wings,
it hit me like a star across the heavens,
and Nature and true Pity held their course.

Laura had an infected eye and Petrarch caught the infection. We don't know whether this account is literal or metaphorical.

234

Oh, little room that used to be a haven
from those ferocious daily storms of mine:
now you're a fountain of nocturnal tears
that I keep hidden, shamed, throughout the day.

Oh, little bed that used to be a rest
and comfort to my pain, with what sad urns
does Love come bathing you, those ivory hands
cruel just to me, and with such injustice.

I shun my refuge and my rest, and now
I even shun myself and all the thoughts
that used to take me with them in their flight;

I find I seek the crowd (who would have thought it?)
as refuge, though inimical and hateful:
it's all from fear of being with myself.

235

Oh, woe, Love takes me where I do not wish
to go, beyond the bounds of what's permitted;
that's how I come to vex her, this great monarch
who is enthroned forever in my heart.

No careful pilot ever steered a ship,
full of rich merchandise, more carefully
to keep it off the rocks, than I do this,
my leaky bark, steered clear of her harsh pride,

but tears, a lashing rain, and fierce wind-sighs
have driven it almost aground in seas
teeming with dreadful night and bitter winter

and made it thus vex others, bringing woe
and torment to itself, half-swamped by waves
drifting along without its sails or rudder.

236

Love, I do wrong and see that I do wrong
but act still like a man whose breast is burning;
my pain increases and my reason fails:
it's almost overcome by my distresses.

I used to curb my hot desire because
I didn't want to cloud her lovely face;
but now I can't: you've seized the reins from me
and in its hopelessness my soul's grown bold.

Thus if my soul exceeds her normal limit,
you're doing it, you so arouse and heat her
that she'll do anything to get salvation,

and even more, attain those heavenly gifts
my lady owns; please make my lady see
and then forgive herself for my trespasses.

237

The sea has fewer fish among its waves,
and up beyond the circle of the moon
as many stars are not seen in the night,
nor do as many birds live in the woods,
or fields have so much grass, or any meadow,
as I have cares at heart, come every evening.

From day to day I hope it's my last evening
that separates my earth from its own waves
and lets me find my rest beneath some meadow:
such woes as mine no man below the moon
has ever suffered; they know this, the woods
that I go searching through by day and night.

separates my earth:
perhaps reflecting a
theory of Augustine's
on death, based on
the separation of the
earth and waters by
God at creation

I do not think I've had a peaceful night
but I've run wild by morning and by evening
since Love made me a dweller in the woods.
Before I rest, the sea will lose its waves,
the sun will get his brightness from the moon,
and April's blooms will die in every meadow.

I wander, self-consumed, meadow to meadow,
careworn by day, and then I weep at night;
I am about as stable as the moon.
As soon as I perceive the gloom of evening,
sighs issue from my breast, from my eyes waves
that flood the grass and then uproot the woods.

I find all cities hateful, love the woods
which house my cares as I go through the meadow
and pour my thoughts out, murmuring like waves,
throughout the peaceful silence of the night:
because of this I wait all day for evening,
when sun departs and makes way for the moon.

I wish that, with the lover of the moon,
I too had gone to sleep in some green woods

the lover of the moon:
Endymion

and she who, before vespers, brings me evening
with Love and with the moon upon the meadow
might come alone to stay with me one night,
while day and sunlight stay beneath the waves!

Beside harsh waves and by the moon's pale light,
song born at night and raised amid the woods,
may you be in lush meadows by the evening.

238

This sonnet probably
commemorates the
visit of Charles of
Luxembourg to
Avignon in 1346.

A royal nature, intellect angelic,
bright soul, a ready gaze, eyes of a lynx,
a rapid foresight, elevated thoughts
well worthy of their dwelling in his breast.

A number of fine ladies had been chosen
to help adorn this high and festive day,
and his sound judgment quickly saw among them
the face most perfect in that crowd of beauties.

He used his hand to wave aside the others,
all greater in their age or in their fortune,
and kindly summoned that one to his side.

He kissed her eyes and brow with such glad kindness
that every lady there was filled with joy,
and I with envy for his strange, sweet action.

239

Sometime near dawn there rises a sweet aura,
enlivening the springtime, opening flowers,
and all the small birds then begin their verses;
I feel my thoughts come sweetly in my soul
stirred by the one who holds them in his power,
and then begin again to sound my notes.

If I could temper into such soft notes
the sighs I make, that they would sweeten Laura,
and reason with this person and her power!
Winter, I think, will be a time of flowers
before love blossoms in that noble soul
that never seems to care for rhymes or verses.

How many tears, alas, how many verses,
have I dispersed along the way, what notes
have I attempted to subdue her soul!
She stands like some harsh mountain, blocks the aura
that seems as though it moves the leaves and flowers
but cannot work against a stronger power.

Love likes to vanquish men and gods with power,
as you can read about in tales and verses,
and as I found when buds were turning flowers;
neither my lord, Sir Love, nor his good notes,
nor my own tears or prayers can teach this Laura
to free from life or torments my sad soul.

In this last need, oh, miserable soul,
summon your wit and strength and all your power,
while you still have this breath of life, this aura;
there's nothing that's beyond the reach of verses,
since they can charm a serpent with their notes
and decorate the frost with newborn flowers.

The meadows laugh right now with grass and flowers:
how could it be that her angelic soul

In this sestina,
the pun *l'aura*
(breeze)/Laura
occurs seven
times, as one
of the key
repeated words.

could fail to hear the sound of amorous notes?
Well, maybe Fortune has a greater power,
and soul and I will weep and sing our verses
like some lame ox that thinks to chase an aura.

I'm trying to net the aura, grow flowers in ice,
wooing in verses a deaf and rigid soul
indifferent to Love's power and his notes.

240

I've begged Love before, and beg him again,
to sway you to pardon me—oh, my sweet pain,
my bitter joy—when faithfulness to you
pulls me away, I know, from virtue's path.

I can't deny, my lady, and don't try,
that Reason, sovereign over each good soul,
is overmastered by Desire, who leads
headlong in strange directions I must follow.

You, with that heart that Heaven brightens,
a mind so clear, virtue as lofty as
ever rained down from a propitious star,

ought tenderly to say, and with no scorn,
"What can he do? What else? My face consumes him.
Why is he lustful? Why am I beautiful?"

241

That dreadful lord whom we can't flee or hide from,
from whom there is no adequate defense,
buried his arrow in me, burning love-bolt,
and set my mind on fire with sweet pleasure;

and then to that first blow, itself quite amply
painful and deadly, he gave another
to aggravate his work, a dart of pity
that pierced my heart as well, on both sides wounded.

One wound is burning; smoke and flames pour forth.
The other distills tears that fill my eyes
as I feel pity over your sad state.

your sad state:
Laura's illness?
Some personal
unhappiness?

But these two fountains do not act to quench
the fire that consumes me; no, my pity
is simply acting to inflame desire.

242

"Gaze on that hill, my tired, yearning heart:
just yesterday we left her there, that one
who liked us for a while, had some sympathy,
and now would make our eyes produce a lake.

"Go back there; I'm content to be alone;
see if it's time that we might find relief
for all this grief that's growing round us here,
oh, partner and foreteller of my pain."

Now you forget yourself, talk to your heart
as if he were with you, you unhappy wretch,
so full of vain and foolish sentiments!

For when you went away and left behind you
the one you want, your heart remained with her;
he hid, and hides him still, within her eyes.

243

green hill: by tradition,
Caumont, said to be
Laura's birthplace;
compare Number 242

Oh, fresh and shady, flowering green hill,
where sometimes thoughtful, sometimes singing,
she sits and gives us evidence of Heaven,
she who has robbed the world of all its fame:

my heart, who wished to leave me for her once
(and that was wise, and he should stay with her),
goes counting places now where grass is signed
by her fair foot, and watered from my eyes.

He draws in close to her and says, each step:
"Ah, could that wretch be here for just a while,
since he's exhausted by his tears and life!"

She smiles at that. But this game isn't fair:
without my heart, I'm stone; you're paradise,
oh, holy, sweet, and lucky place of hers!

244

This sonnet is a reply
to one from Giovanni
Dondi dell'Orologio;
Petrarch replicates
his correspondent's
rhyme scheme.

My ills oppress me; I'm terrified by worse,
toward which the way is broad and smooth, I fear,
and just like you I've wandered into madness
and rave together with you of hard thoughts;

so heavy is this loss, this cruel shame,
should I ask God for war or beg for peace?
But why this brooding? Aren't our destinies
already fixed, ordained at that high throne?

I don't deserve the honor you accord me,
I think you're hoodwinked by Lord Love, who often
makes us see crooked, though we've healthy eyes.

Still, I can counsel you to lift your soul
and aim toward Heaven while you spur your heart,
because the road is long, the time is short.

245

Two roses, freshly picked in Paradise
the other day, born on the first of May—
a fine gift from a lover, old and wise,
distributed between two younger ones,

along with words and such a smile as
might tame a wild man and teach him love,
so that a brilliant and a loving ray
transformed the visages of both his friends.

"The sun's not seen an equal pair of lovers,"
he offered, as he gave a smile and sighed;
then he gave hugs to them and turned away.

He portioned out the roses and the words;
my weary heart is glad and fearful still:
oh, happy eloquence, oh, joyful day!

246

The breeze that softly sighs and moves among
the laurel's leaves and through her golden hair
so transports souls with new and charming sights
that they depart their bodies and go wandering.

A white rose born among the cruel thorns;
who could discover here on earth her equal?
The glory of our time! Oh, living Jove,
make sure I die ahead of her, I pray!

That way I will not have to see the loss
and great communal blight: world without sun,
my own eyes blind, that have no other light,

my soul bereft, that thinks of nothing else,
my ears gone deaf, with nothing left to hear
when her sweet words have vanished from our midst.

The first line of the
original—"L'aura
che 'l verde lauro
et l'aureo crine"—
contains three puns
—*breeze*, *laurel*,
and *golden*—
on Laura's name.

247

Some will assume that in my praise of her,
she whom I love on earth, my style must err
in making her the noblest one of all,
holy and wise, beautiful, chaste, and charming.

I think the opposite; what's more, I fear
she'll take offense at all my humble words,
since she deserves much higher, finer ones:
who doesn't credit this, let him come see her,

and then he'll say: "What this man hopes to do
would wear out Athens, Arpinum, Mantua,
and Smyrna, one lyre and the other.

"A mortal tongue can't reach her state, it's too
divine to touch upon. Love draws and drives
this tongue: it is not choice, it's destiny."

The cities are supposedly the birthplaces of Demosthenes, Cicero, Virgil, and Homer; one lyre and the other: Latin and Greek

248

Whoever wants to see what Heaven and Nature
can bring about among us, let him come
and gaze at her, sole sun, not just for me
but for this blind world that's forgotten virtue;

let him come soon, for Death too often takes
the best ones first and leaves the bad behind:
she's much awaited in the blessèd realms;
this mortal beauty passes, it can't last.

He'll see, if he arrives in time, all virtues,
every beauty, every regal habit, joined
together in one body, fully tempered;

he'll say my rhymes are mute and that my wit
is overcome by so much brilliant light.
But if he comes too late, he'll weep forever.

249

What fear I feel when I recall that day
I left my lady looking sad and pensive,
and my heart stayed behind! And yet there's nothing
I think about more gladly or more often.

Again I see her, standing humbly there
among the lovely ladies, like a rose
among some lesser blooms, not sad, or happy,
like one who fears but feels no other ills.

Her normal ornaments were laid aside,
the gay clothes and the garlands and the pearls,
her song and laughter and her sweet, kind speech.

And so I left my life there, full of doubts;
and now sad omens, dreams, and darkest thoughts
attack me here. Pray God they may be false!

250

My lady used to visit me in sleep,
though far away, and her sight would console me,
but now she frightens and depresses me
and I've no shield against my gloom and fear;

for now I seem to see in her sweet face
true pity mixing in with heavy pain,
and I hear things that tell my heart it must
divest itself of any joy or hope.

I seem to see: in
his dream, which
proves prophetic

"Don't you recall that evening we met last,
when I ran out of time," she says, "and left
you standing there, your eyes filled up with tears?

"I couldn't and I didn't tell you then
what I must now admit is proved and true:
you must not hope to see me on this earth."

251

wretched vision:
the dream he
has just had

Oh, wretched vision, horrid likelihood!
Could it be true that now, before her time,
her good light is extinguished, that has made
my life content with hope and sorrow both?

If it were true, though, wouldn't I have heard it
through other messengers, such thunderous news,
not just from her? Let God and Nature not
permit such loss, and let my thoughts be false!

I must still hope for sight of her sweet face
whose loveliness both keeps me still alive
and gives our world what honor it possesses.

And if indeed she's left her lovely dwelling
to rise to those eternal halls forever,
I pray my own last day be not far off.

252

In doubt about my state I weep, I sing,
I hope and fear, I try to ease my pain
with sighs and rhymes. With all his might,
Love rasps upon my heart, using his file.

Now, will her lovely, holy face restore
to my eyes, ever, light that first awoke them
(alas, I have no sense of my own worth)
or will they be condemned to weep forever?

Will Heaven, claiming what belongs to it,
not care what happens to those left behind
who need her eyes for sun, are else in darkness?

I live in fear, in a perpetual war,
and am no longer what I was, like one
who walks a dangerous road, afraid and lost.

253

Oh, glances sweet and little words of wisdom,
will I see you again, and will I hear you?
Blond hair that Love has used to bind my heart
and lead it, captured, to its execution!

Oh, lovely face that shaped my own harsh fate,
face that I weep for, never to enjoy!
Oh, secretive deception, loving trick,
to bring me pleasure that turns into pain!

Even if sometimes from those gentle eyes,
where I most live and where my thoughts most dwell,
there comes to me a touch of honest sweetness,

quite promptly, Fortune, driving me away
and breaking up the goodness I might taste,
sends me to travel, on horses or on ships.

254

I listen still, and still I hear no news
of her, my sweet, beloved enemy,
and know not what to think or say of it,
since fear and hope together pierce my heart.

To be that beautiful has done much harm
to people in the past; this one's more lovely
and also much more chaste: does God perhaps
think best to make of her a star in Heaven,

or rather, a full sun? If so, my life,
my brief repose, and my long line of troubles,
are coming to an end. Oh, separation,

why have you kept me far from my harm's source?
My little story is already told,
and my life ended in its middle years.

255

To wish for evening and to hate the dawn,
that's the proclivity of happy lovers;
for me the evening compounds woes and weeping.
I like the morning better, happier hour,

when sometimes at one moment the two suns
appear, to show me two resplendent Easts,
so similar in beauty and in light
that Heaven itself might fall in love with earth,

as happened when those boughs were growing green
that have their deep roots in my heart and tell
that I must love another more than me.

If two opposing hours sway me so,
it's natural to want the one that calms me
and hate the one that brings me suffering.

256

I'd like to take revenge on her, whose gaze
and speech destroy me first, and then, as if
to make my pain the worse, who flees and hides
depriving me of eyes both sweet and cruel.

Thus bit by bit she saps and wears away
my weary spirits, she devours them,
and like a lion roars above my heart
at night when I might otherwise get rest.

My soul, which Death is happy to evict,
departs from me and uses that release
to go and visit her, who threatens it.

I'd be surprised if sometimes when my soul
speaks to her, weeps, and then embraces her,
she didn't have her sleep disturbed, and listen.

257

My eyes, intense and heavy with desire,
were fixed upon that face I sigh and yearn for,
when Love, as if to say, "What are you thinking?"
imposed my second love, her hand, between us.

My heart, still struggling like a just-hooked fish,
or like a fledgling bird entrapped by lime,
did not respond to such a lively virtue
or turn his busied senses toward the truth;

instead my sight, losing its object, found
a new means to its end, as in a dream,
the end without which it finds nothing good.

My soul, caught up between opposing glories,
experienced things I still don't understand:
celestial joy along with some sweet strangeness.

258

Bright sparks came from that pair of lovely lights
and cast a mild radiance upon me,
and then came sighing, from a most wise heart,
such gentle floods of lively eloquence

that just the memory of it here consumes me
when I recall that day and start to think
about the way my spirits swooned, responding
to this new change from her accustomed harshness.

My soul, brought up on sorrow, nursed on pain
(how great the power of established habit!),
was so much weakened by the double pleasure,

trembling and caught between its fear and hope,
that at the taste of unpredicted goodness
it seemed as though it might abandon me.

259

I've always sought a solitary life—
the stream banks, woods, and meadows all know this—
in order to avoid minds blind and deaf
that have lost sight of how to get to Heaven;

and if my wishes had to be fulfilled
far from the fragrant air I knew in Tuscany,
the Sorgue would welcome me to its dark hills
and help me to both weep and sometimes sing.

But my old fortune, ever my sworn foe,
brings me back here, where I grow filled with anger
to see my lovely treasure in the mud;

back here: Avignon?

just once, though, she was friendly to this hand
I'm writing with; and not unjustly, either.
Love saw it, as my lady knows. And I.

just once:
perhaps Laura
clasped his hand.

260

Two lovely eyes, brimming with virtue's sweetness:
I saw them under such a lucky star
that my heart scorns all other nests of love
next to those two with their amazing charm.

Whoever is most praised, in any age,
on any foreign shore, cannot compete:
not she who brought so much travail to Greece
and to poor Troy its final throes and shrieks,

she who brought . . .
travail: Helen

not that fine Roman who ripped up her breast,
both chaste and angry, with her steel, and not
Polyxena, Hypsipyle, or Argia.

that fine Roman:
Lucrece, who took
her own life after
being raped by Tarquin

If I'm not wrong, this excellence of hers
is Nature's glory, a delight to me,
new to this world and soon to disappear.

Polyxena: daughter of
Priam, beloved of Achilles;
Hypsipyle: seduced by
Jason; *Argia:* wife of
Oedipus's son Polyneices

new to this world: more
recent than the other
beauties mentioned

261

Should any lady look for lasting fame,
for wisdom, virtue, or for courtesy,
let her look deeply in my enemy's eyes,
she whom the world considers my madonna.

She can learn there how honor's won, God's loved,
how chastity can be combined with gaiety,
and which way is the straightest route to Heaven,
where she is wanted and anticipated;

and how to speak (no style can equal it),
and lovely silences and those fine ways
which human wit cannot set down on paper.

She can't learn there the endless comeliness
that dazzles all of us, for that sweet light
comes by good fortune, not by any art.

262

—"Life is most precious, so it seems to me,
and next, true virtue in a woman fair."
—"You've got the order wrong! There never were,
Mother, things dear or lovely without virtue,

Laura is the speaker here, apparently in conversation with her mother.

"and anyone who lets herself lose honor
is not a woman and is not alive;
though she may look the same, her life's a death,
or worse than that, made bitter by her sorrow.

"I never marveled at Lucrece's choice
except that she resorted to the knife
when I'd have thought her anguish would suffice."

Philosophers will come and go, and may
dispute of this forever; they'll stay below,
and she will mount toward Heaven in her flight!

263

Tree: the laurel, i.e., Laura. At this point the most authoritative manuscript, Vatican 3195, has seven blank pages, apparently acknowledging Laura's death.

Tree of victorious triumph, crowning both
poets and emperors, to their honor:
how many days you've made me sad or happy
in this my very brief and mortal life!

True Lady, focused solely on your honor,
which you can reap above all others here,
the snares and nets and birdlimes set by Love
cannot deceive you or defeat your wisdom;

nobility of blood and other things
prized by us all, like pearls, rubies, gold,
you rightly scorn as vile worldly burdens;

and your high beauty, matchless in this world,
would pain you if it didn't serve as foil
to set off your best treasure, chastity.

264

I walk in thought, and in my thoughts I am
assailed by such self-pity that it leads
to bouts and fits of weeping,
much different from the ones I used to have:
for seeing every day my end come near
I've begged that God will furnish me with wings,
the kind our reason uses
to move from mortal prisons up to Heaven.
But up to now I've found that nothing helps,
no sighs or tears or prayers that I've expressed;
and that's appropriate, I think, because
a man who's fallen down along the way
deserves to lie there on the ground if it's
quite clear he has the power to stand and walk.
Those arms are still wide open,
stretched out in mercy, ready for my trust,

but fear locks up my heart;
I see the woes of others, dread my own,
and am spurred on but fear it's much too late.

    One thought keeps speaking in my mind; it says:
"What are you yearning for? Help from what quarter?
Can you not see, poor fool,
how time runs by and lengthens your dishonor?
Make a decision now, and make it firmly,
to root up from your heart the love of pleasure
that never makes you happy
and never even gives you time to breathe.
    "If you're already wearied and disgusted
by the ephemeral sweetness which the world
holds out to you, so treacherously each time,
why would you go on hoping to attain it
since it lacks any peace or true endurance?
While your own body lives
you have the means of reining in your thoughts.
So grasp it while you can;
delay is dangerous, as you well know,
and starting now will not be premature.

    "You know quite well how much substantial sweetness
your eyes have taken from the sight of her,
she whom I wish was still
unborn, in order that we might have peace.
And you remember, you remember well,
when her bright image rushed into your heart,
there where no other flame
from any other torch could have got in.
    "She set it burning, and if that false flame
has lasted many years, awaiting still
a day that, luckily for your salvation,
will never come, then you can rouse yourself
to a more sacred hope: gaze at the heavens,
revolving overhead,
immortal and adorned; if your desire,

so happy in its sickness,
can gloat about a glance, a word, a song,
what will it feel when it's fulfilled above?"

Another thought, both sweet and sour, seated
securely in my soul, heavy but welcome,
weighs greatly on my heart,
mauling it with desire and sweet hope;
and for the sake of kind and glorious fame
it does not feel my freezing or my burning
whether I'm thin or pale;
I kill it, and it springs right back to life.
This thought's been growing in me day by day
since first they wrapped me in my baby clothes
and one grave likely will enclose us both;
for when my soul's denuded of my limbs
this lust for glory can't accompany it.
If Greek or Latin tongues
should praise me when I'm dead, that is just wind;
and since I hate acquiring
what one brief hour disperses, let me try
to leave these shadows and embrace the truth.

But that one passion that so fills me up
blocks out the others that are born beside it,
and time runs by again
and she's my subject: I forget myself,
and all the light of those clear, lovely eyes
which gently melts me with its steady heat
has hold of me, a rein
against which I can use no wit or force.
What good then does it do me to fit out
my little boat for distant voyaging
when it's tied down and jammed between the rocks?
You, dear my Lord, who free me from the knots
that bind the world in many different ways,
You who could liberate me,
why will You not remove my blush and shame?

Like someone in a dream
I see my death approaching, wish to fight,
but find myself unarmed, devoid of weapons.

   I see what I am doing, I'm not fooled
by an imperfect knowledge of the truth;
Love forces me. He makes
his poor believers leave the path of honor;
from time to time I feel it, in my heart,
a fine disdain, severe and growing harsh;
it rises in my face
and shows my hidden thoughts to other people.
   To love a mortal thing with that same faith
that should belong to God alone, is quite
forbidden if we truly wish for honor.
This fact, like some loud voice, calls back my reason,
which wandered off behind my senses, lost;
but though it hears and thinks
it should come back, bad habit rules again
and sets before my eyes
she who was born, it seems, to make me die
because she pleased me, and herself, too much.

   And I don't know what space the heavens had
in mind for me when I came new to earth
to join this bitter war
that I have waged so long against myself;
nor can I see, because my body veils it,
how soon the day will come that ends my life;
but I can see my hair
changing its color as my passions cool.
   Now that I think my time is getting near
and my departure cannot be far off,
like one who's learned from getting lost, I go
alert and wary, thinking back to when
I veered from the right hand and lost the port:
and partly I feel shame
and filled with sorrow, think of turning back;

but on the other hand,
my pleasure's an addiction grown so strong
it wants to bargain and cajole with Death.

Song, here I am, and carrying a heart
that's colder with its fear than frozen snow,
because I know, beyond all doubt, I'm dying;
while I have pondered, most of the short thread
allotted to me has been spooled away;
no weight was ever greater
than what I try to shoulder in this state,
for Death walks at my side
and while I seek wise counsel for my life,
I see what's good but hold fast to the bad.

265

A wild and hardened heart, a cruel will,
housed in a humble and angelic body;
if this keeps up, this harsh approach of hers,
she'll have me as a prize of little honor;

for when the flowers and the grass and leaves
are born and die, bright day and then dark night,
I weep at all such times. I have good cause,
given my fate, Lord Love, and then my lady.

I live on hope alone, remembering
that I have seen how water can, by trying,
wear away marble and the hardest rock:

no heart's so hard that tears and prayers and love
cannot sometimes rouse pity and affection,
no will so cold that it cannot be warmed.

266

Ah, my dear lord, each thought calls me to see
you whom I always have before me, though
my wretched fortune (could it treat me worse?)
hems me in, spins me, makes me go backward;

then all the sweet desire Love inspires
takes me toward death so gradually that I
do not perceive it; I call on my two lights
in vain, sigh everywhere, by night and day.

Devotion to my lord, love for my lady,
these are the chains I've labored to create,
and it was I, myself, who forged and bound them;

a laurel, green, a column, nobly born,
the one for eighteen years, fifteen the other,
I've carried in my breast unstintingly.

267

Alas! That lovely face, that gentle gaze.
Alas! That proud and carefree way of walking!
And oh, the talk that humbled savage minds
and made the base-born stand up and be valiant!

That smile, alas!, that also launched the dart
that meant my death, the only good I hope for!
Oh, royal soul, worthy to rule an empire,
if you had not arrived so recently:

for you I now must burn, must breathe in you,
for I am yours alone; and with you taken,
no other fortune could bereave me so;

you loaded me with hope and with desire
when I last saw you, you my living pleasure;
the wind has carried all your words away.

268

What do I do? Can you advise me, Love?
It's surely time to die,
and I've already waited much too long.
My lady's dead, she took my heart along;
if I'm to follow it,
I need to interrupt these awful years,
because I cannot hope
to see her on this side, and waiting hurts,
since every joy I had
was turned to tears the moment she was gone
and life on earth holds no more sweetness for me.

Love, you can feel this bitter, heavy loss,
so I complain to you;
I know you're grieving, taking on my grief,
or say our grief, for on the selfsame rock
we've wrecked our ships, and in
one selfsame moment has our sun gone dark.
What skill could ever put
my sorry state in words that matched its meaning?
Oh, world gone blank, you ingrate,
you have good cause to weep with me today,
for with her loss you've lost what good you held.

Your glory has collapsed and you don't see it;
you were not worthy, either,
while she was living here, to know her or
be touched and trodden by her holy feet,
since something that amazing
should be adorning Heaven with its presence.
But I, alas, who have
no life or self without her love, am left
to weep and call for her:
that's what remains of all the hopes I had,
and that alone is all that keeps me going.

Oh, God, it's now just earth, that lovely face
that spoke to us of Heaven

and of the happiness to come, above!
    Invisible, her form's in Paradise,
released from that dim veil
that shadowed here the flower of her years,
    to be reclothed with it
another time, and never take it off,
when we see her become
more beautiful and kindly than before,
eternal beauty then surpassing mortal.

    More beautiful than ever, and more graceful,
she comes into my mind
a place she knows her sight is ever welcome;
    this is one column that supports my life,
the other her bright name,
that resonates so sweetly in my heart.
    But recollecting now
that all my hope is dead, which was alive
while she was blossoming,
I am destroyed, as Love well knows, and I
hope she can see it too, from where she dwells.

    Ladies, who wondered at her beauty and
her most angelic life,
and her celestial bearing on this earth:
    grieve for me now, and let your pity fill you
for me, and not for her,
since she has peace and I am left at war,
    and if the way to follow
and be with her should be closed off for long,
Love holds me back from severing this knot.
He speaks within me, and he reasons thus:

    "Rein in the giant sorrow that transports you,
since excess of desire
will lose that Heaven that your heart so longs for,
    "where she is living, she who now seems dead,
and smiles to look upon

her beautiful remains, and sighs for you;
    "and her great fame, she asks
that you not let it die, but sing it still
in many places here,
your tongue and voice still making bright her name
all for the sake of eyes so dear to you."

    Flee the clear weather, Song,
the greenery too; don't go where there is laughter,
don't go where there is singing;
go where there's weeping, don't seek cheerful people,
disconsolate widow, you are dressed in black.

269

column: Cardinal Colonna died July 3, 1348.

The column's broken, the green laurel's down,
that gave some shade to my most weary cares;
I've lost what I can't hope to find again,
Boreas to Auster, Indian to Moorish sea.

Death, you have taken from me double treasure
that made me glad to live, and walk with pride;
land cannot replace it, empire even,
nor Oriental gems and potent gold.

But since this is the will of destiny,
what can I have except a soul that's sad,
eyes that are wet, a head forever bent?

Oh, life of ours, apparently so lovely,
how easily you lose, in just one morning,
what we spent years and great pains to obtain!

270

You seem to show me, Love, that you would like
to see me slip into the yoke again;
you'll need to pass a test,
novel and strange, if you'd subdue me, then.
Go find my much-loved treasure in the earth,
wherever it is hidden from my sight,
making me poor and wretched,
and fetch that wise, chaste heart that held my life;
    and if it's true your power is as great
as it is said to be, in Heaven and in
the Abyss (for here among us mortals each
well-born person feels
your worth, I think, and your tremendous power),
take back from Death what she has taken from us
and raise your standard in that lovely face.

    Put back in her fair eyes the living light
that was my guide, rekindle the soft flame
that still, alas, consumes me,
though it's been quenched. Didn't it burn, though?
You'll never see a thirsty doe or stag
seek out a spring or river with such zeal
as I seek those sweet means
of so much torment, still; I know myself,
    and know my yearnings, which are huge, and make
me rave from merely thinking of them, while
I race down roads that lead nowhere at all
and with my weary mind
pursue a thing I never hope to reach.
Now, when you summon me, I can ignore you,
you have no power outside your own realm.

    Make me experience that gentle aura
outside myself, the way I do within,
for it had power, singing,
to dissipate both scorn and anger here,
to clarify a stormy mind and banish

the massing clouds of darkness and of baseness,
and it refined my style,
which rose to heights it can no longer reach.
　　Give me some hope that matches my desire,
and since the soul is stronger in its rights,
give back to eyes and ears their proper object,
without which they can't function:
they grow imperfect and my life is death.
Your force is spent on me in vain, you know,
as long as earth is covering my first love.

　　Restore me to that glance that worked like sunshine
upon the ice that used to weigh me down;
I'll meet you at that pass
through which my heart crossed, never to turn back;
carry your golden arrows and your bow,
and let her speak to me the way she did,
sounding the very words
from which I learned what love was all about.
　　Revive the tongue in which were set the hooks
that caught me, always, with the very bait
I never stop desiring; hide your snares
in blond and curly hair,
for that's the thicket where my will is limed;
spread out her tresses, hand them to the wind,
for they're the chains that you can use to bind me.

　　No one will free me from that golden snare,
neglected artfully and thick with ringlets,
nor from the burning spirit
that hovered sweetly in her cruel gaze
and day and night kept my desire green
greener than any laurel, any myrtle,
when woods have donned and shed
their leaves, and meadows their long grass.
　　But since Death's had the pride to boldly shatter
the knot I never could escape, and since
you cannot find, wherever you might go,
someone to tie a second,

why bother, Love, to flourish all your tricks?
The season's past and you have lost the weapons
that made me shake, so what can you do now?

Your weapons were those eyes that shot forth arrows
blazing with unseen fire, arrows that had
nothing to fear from reason,
for humans are defenseless against gods;
the thoughtfulness and silence, smiles and laughter,
virtuous bearing and expressive speech,
and words that, understood,
were capable of making base souls noble,
the mild and humble but angelic mien
that won such praise, from this side and from that,
and then her sitting down and standing up
that left a man in doubt
which one deserved more admiration:
these were the arms you used to conquer hearts,
and now you are disarmed, and I am safe.

These souls the heavens send to your domain,
you bind them this way, now, and, then, that way,
but me you've bound in just
one knot, because the heavens willed it so.
That knot is cut, but freedom doesn't please me;
instead I weep and cry: "Oh, noble pilgrim,
what heavenly decree
first bound me up and first gave you release?
"God, who removed you early from our world,
showed us exalted virtue of your sort
only to stir and heat up our desire."
Love god, I do not fear
new wounds from you, or new hurt at your hands;
you bend your bow in vain, your shots go wild;
your power melted when her eyes were closed.

Death has released me, Love, from all your laws;
the one who was my lady is in Heaven,
leaving my life both sorrow-filled and free.

271

That burning knot which, hour after hour,
kept me tied up for twenty-one long years
has been untied by Death; never such sorrow,
and now I know I can't be killed by grief.

Not wishing to lose power yet, Sir Love
had set another snare among the grasses
and with new tinder lit another fire,
making it hard for me to get away.

And if I hadn't learned so much before
from my experience, I'd have been his prey
and burned the hotter, being drier wood.

But Death, against whom wit and strength are helpless,
has given me my freedom, since she has
shattered that knot and scattered all the fire.

272

Life runs on by and does not pause an hour,
and Death comes following with giant strides;
and past and present things make war on me,
and future things assault me here as well;

both memory and anticipation sit
upon my heart, now one side, now the other;
unless I can take pity on myself
I'll soon be free of any thoughts at all.

The times my sad heart knew a little sweetness
all come back to me now; at the same time,
I watch the storm clouds massing for my voyage:

the squall has reached the harbor, and my helmsman
lies down exhausted, masts and rigging shattered,
the lovely stars I steered by all extinguished.

273

What are you doing? Thinking? Why look still
backward to times that can return no more?
Desolate soul, why are you throwing wood
onto the very fire that's burning you?

Those tender words and those enchanting glances
that you've described and pictured, one by one,
have left the earth behind, and you well know
it's late, and foolish, to expect them here.

Oh, don't renew this deadly enterprise,
don't follow these deceptive, longing thoughts;
find one that's sure and certain, a good end;

come search for Heaven; nothing pleases here,
since beauty made us ill while it was living
and being dead it robs us of our peace.

274

Give me my peace, oh, all you cruel thoughts!
It's not enough that Love and Death and Fortune
besiege my fortress and attack my gates?
I have to have some inside foes as well?

And you, my heart, are you still what you were?
Traitor to me and me alone, you shelter
spies in our midst and you make pacts with those
who are my enemies, so swift and deadly.

Through you Love sends his secret messages,
Fortune holds court and revels in her pomp,
and Death preserves the memory of that blow

that will break up whatever's left of me;
in you my vagrant thoughts are armed with error:
I blame you, therefore, for my every ill.

275

My eyes, our sun's gone dark; or rather say
it has climbed up to Heaven, where it shines
and waits for our arrival there and mourns,
and wonders why there should be a delay.

My ears, angelic words are sounding there
where listeners exist who understand them.
My feet, your range won't take you to the place
where she is lodged, who used to make you move.

Why therefore do you all make war against me?
I'm not the reason you can't see her, hear her,
or find her living anywhere on earth.

You can blame Death; or you can praise the One
who binds and frees, opens and shuts at once,
and after grieving brings us into joy.

276

Because the bright, angelic sight of her
has, by abruptly passing, plunged my soul
into deep sorrow and the darkest horror,
I try to ease my grief a bit by speaking.

I surely have some right to lamentation
(as she well knows, and Love is quite aware)
because my heart had just a single balm
against the sorrow that this life contains;

and this one remedy you've stolen, Death.
And you, you happy earth, you get to have
that lovely face, and cover it and guard it:

and where does that leave me, blind and despairing,
because the soft and sweet and loving light
that filled my eyes is now no longer with me?

277

If Love does not come up with some new counsel
I'm going to trade my life for something else
because such fear and sorrow load my soul:
desire thrives, despite the death of hope,

and I am filled with restlessness and terror
and all my life, by day and night, is tears,
exhausted, rudderless in stormy seas,
a dangerous journey, and without an escort.

I must invent a guide because the true one
is in the earth; no, she's in Heaven, where
she shines the brighter: only to my heart,

not to my eyes, robbed of the light they need
by this dark veil of sorrow and lament
that makes my hair turn white before its time.

278

In the age of her lovely flowering,
when Love is apt to have his greatest sway,
she left her earthly vesture in the earth
and took her leave, departing, my life's aura,

and rose to Heaven, living, nude, and lovely;
from there she rules me and she drains my strength.
Oh, why can't I be rid of mortal things,
live my last day, first of a life to come,

so that my soul can follow her, as free
and light and glad as are my rising thoughts,
and let me put all these old woes behind me?

All this delay is nothing but dead loss
that makes me just a burden to myself.
How good to die, three years ago today!

three years ago:
Laura's death date,
which places this
poem in 1351

279

summer breeze:
l'aura estiva

If I hear birds lamenting, or green leaves
that summer breeze is stirring very softly,
or the faint murmur of the lucid waters
that run along beside a flowery bank

where I am sitting, lost in thought and writing,
I see her, then, whom Heaven reveals, earth hides,
I see her and I hear and understand her,
as from afar she answers to my sighing:

"Why do you waste yourself before your time?"
she asks me, full of pity. "Why pour out
this river of affliction from your eyes?

"Don't weep for me, for dying made my day
an endless one, and when I closed my eyes
I opened them to one great inner light."

This sonnet
praises the
Vaucluse.

280

I've never been where I could see more clearly
the vision that I sought and never found,
or where I felt such freedom, calling out,
my love-cries rising to the skies above;

I know no other valley that contains
so many nooks and caves where one can sigh;
I don't think Love has had such charming nests
on Cyprus or on any other shore.

The waters talk of love, the breeze, the branches;
the little birds and fish, the flowers, the grass,
all beg me always to remain in love.

But you, born lucky, call to me from Heaven,
and by the memory of your death you urge me
to scorn this world and all of its sweet hooks.

281

How many times, in flight and seeking refuge,
from others and myself, have I come here
into this sweet retreat, bathing the grass
with tears, of course, disrupting the air with sighs!

How many times, alone and full of fear,
have I sought out the shadowy dark places,
seeking in thought to find the high delight,
that Death has snatched, calling, "Death take me too!"

Now I have seen her, in the form of nymph
or other goddess, rising from the bed
of this, the river Sorgue, here on its bank

and treading its fresh grass, I swear, as if
she were a living woman, and her face
has shown me that she's truly sorry for me.

282

You soul in bliss, who often come to me
and comfort these afflicted nights of mine
with your bright eyes, which death has not extinguished
but made more beautiful than mortal eyes:

how I rejoice that you should choose to gladden
these times that are so sad, with your true sight!
Thus I begin to find your beauties present
in all those places where they used to live.   *those places:*
                                                       the Vaucluse

Where I went singing of you, years and years.
Now, as you see, I wander, full of weeping—
not tears for you but tears for my great loss.

I find but one repose in all this anguish,
and that's the fact that you return; I know you;
I know you by your walk, voice, face, and dress.

283

Oh, Death, you have stained the loveliest face
and quenched the most beautiful eyes ever seen;
you've loosed the brightest spirit, virtue-filled,
from the amazing body-knot that held it.

In one quick moment you have seized my wealth,
silenced the gentlest accents ever heard,
and filled me with such lamentations that
the things I see and hear are painful to me.

My lady does indeed come back, from pity,
to soothe my sorrow and its great excess;
I find no other solace in this life;

if I described the way she speaks and shines
I would inflame all hearts with love—indeed,
not men alone: the hearts of bears and tigers.

284

The time so short, the thought so swift that brings
my lady back to me—despite her death,
my sorrow's remedy is close at hand:
for while I see her nothing does me harm.

Love, who has tied me to a cross in torment,
quails when he sees her at my soul's shut gate,
the place whereat she kills me still, because
her sight's so sweet, her voice is truly gentle.

She's like a lady coming home again,
and with her bright brow driving out the dark
that filled my heart with sad and heavy thoughts;

and soul, who can't bear seeing such strong light,
sighs deeply, saying, "Oh, the blessed hours,
that day when your eyes opened this bright path!"

285

Never did tender mother her dear son,
or loving wife her much-beloved spouse,
with many sighs and great anxiety,
offer such heartfelt counsel in a crisis

as she gives me, who sees my heavy exile,
and from on high, from her eternal home,
revisits me with all her old affection,
her forehead creased with double obligation,

a mother's and a lover's. She shows fear,
and she shows fiery virtue, and she tells me
what to avoid and what I should pursue,

and tells the story of our lives, and urges
me not to tarry lifting up my soul.
And while she speaks I feel at peace—a truce.

286

Could I portray the gentle breeze of sighs
I hear from her who was my lady once
(she's now in Heaven, but she seems to me
to live and walk and feel and love and breathe),

oh, what hot thoughts her portrait might arouse
as I spoke out, so loving and so kind
is her demeanor toward me when she visits,
for fear I'll miss the way, backslide, or stray.

She tutors me to go straight on, and I,
who know her chaste allurements and just prayers,
with their sweet murmur, low and full of pity,

must learn to bend myself to her calm will
as I soak up the sweetness of her words,
which have the power to make a stone shed tears.

gentle breeze:
l'aura soave

287

Sennuccio del
Bene, Florentine
poet, d. 1349

Though you have left me, my Sennuccio,
alone and grieving here, I take some comfort
that you have fled the body where you were
a prisoner and a corpse, and flown away.

Now you can see the poles together, see
the wandering stars and all their twisting journeys,
and you can see how poor our seeing is,
and I can ease my woe with your new joy.

third sphere: where
the souls of the
love poets dwell

I ask you to salute, in the third sphere,
Dante and Master Cino and Guittone,
and Franceschino and the rest of them.

Say to my lady how I live here weeping
and turn into a beast, lost in the woods,
remembering her face and holy deeds.

288

I've filled the whole surrounding air with sighs,
watching from these harsh hills the gentle plain
where she was born, who held my heart in hand,
there as she budded, there as she bore fruit,

then went to Heaven, leaving me behind
and so distraught from her quick parting that
my weary eyes, that seek her far, in vain,
leave nothing dry in their vicinity.

In all these hills there's not a shrub or stone,
nor branch nor green leaf living on these slopes,
nor flower in the dale, nor blade of grass,

nor thread of water trickling from these springs,
nor savage forest beast, that doesn't know
about my sorrow and its bitterness.

289

Flame of my soul, lovely beyond all beauty,
whom Heaven greatly favored while on earth:
she's gone too early, turning toward her home,
and toward her star, most worthy of her presence.

I start to waken now, and I can see
that it was for the best she put me off
and quenched my burning juvenile desires,
turning toward me a face both sweet and angry.

I thank her now, grateful for her high counsel,
the way she used her gentle face and anger,
proposing my salvation, as I burned.

Oh, graceful arts and their condign effects:
one of us worked with words, the other glances:
I to her greater glory, she my virtue.

290

How this world goes! For what upset me once,
I'm pleased and grateful now; I understand
that I was tortured to procure salvation
and my short war was for eternal peace.

Oh, hope, and oh, desire, always false,
a hundred times more so for this world's lovers!
How much worse off we'd be if she'd consented
who now lies in the earth and lives in Heaven!

But blinded Love, along with my deaf mind,
led me so far astray that by their force
I took myself into the realms of Death;

and blessed be she who turned my course around,
and sent me toward a better shore, and curbed
my wicked will so that I might not perish!

The goddess
Aurora, dawn,
was married to the
ancient Tithonus;
more puns on
Laura's name
are built into the
rhyme scheme
of the octave.

291

When I see dawn descending from the sky
with rose complexion and with golden hair,
love overcomes me and I lose my color,
and sigh and say: "Oh, there is Laura, now.

"Happy Tithonus, you can know the hour
when you will get your blessed treasure back;
but what am I to do about my laurel?
For if I wish to see her, I must die.

"Your partings aren't so hard, since she comes back,
returning to you every night, and not
repelled, apparently, by your white hair;

"my nights are desolate, and my days dark
because the one who took away my thoughts
has left me holding nothing but her name."

292

Those eyes I spoke about so heatedly,
the arms, the hands, the feet, and, yes, the face
that had estranged me from my very self
and made me different from other people,

those curling locks of purest shining gold,
the lightning loosed by that angelic smile
that used to turn this earth into a paradise,
are all turned back to dust, aware of nothing.

And still I live, which makes me sad and angry,
abandoned by the light I loved so much,
lost in a storm, on a dismasted ship.

So let my love song have an end here now;
the vein of my accustomed wit is dry,
and all my lyre can produce is sobs.

293

If I had known that sighs turned into rhyme
would have effects so pleasing to the ear,
I would have taken early sighs in hand,
made them more frequent, polished up their style.

Now that she's dead, who moved me to speak out
and stood there at the summit of my thought,
I can't, not having any file so sweet,
turn harsh, dark rhymes to bright and graceful notes.

I'm certain that my purpose at the time
was venting my emotions in some fashion,
easing my heart, not trying to gain fame.

I simply wept, I didn't weep for honor;
now I would like to please, but that high being
calls me to join her and I'm tired, silent.

294

She sojourned in my heart, alive and fair,
like some high lady staying in a cottage;
now I've become, because she's passed away,
mortal indeed, and dead, while she's a goddess.

My soul, ransacked and stripped of all its wealth,
and Love, denuded, having lost his torch,
ought to rouse pity that would crack a stone,
but no one's here to tell or write their sorrow,

because they weep within, and every ear
is deaf but mine, and I am in such pain
that I am left with nothing but these sighs.

Undoubtedly, we're merely dust and shadow;
undoubtedly, desire is blind and greedy;
undoubtedly, our fond hopes will deceive us.

295

My thoughts would once chat softly to themselves
and talk about their object in this way:
"Soon she'll feel pity, wish she hadn't waited;
she's thinking of us now, in hope or fear."

Because the final day and fatal hour
have robbed her of the life she had among us,
she sees and hears and feels our state from Heaven:
no other hope of her is left to us.

Oh, gentle miracle, oh, happy soul,
oh, beauty high and rare, without a copy,
that soon went back to where it first existed!

She has a crown and palm there, for her deeds,
who made both bright and famous in the world
her lofty virtue and my crazy passion.

296

Once I accused myself, now I excuse,
in fact I rate myself quite highly now,
thanks to the worthy prison, the sweet blow
that I have kept concealed these many years.

Envious Fates, how soon you broke the spindle
that spun the soft, bright thread around my bonds,
and broke the golden arrow by which death
grew more attractive than it usually is!

For there was never any soul in love
with gaiety and liberty and life,
that would not change its natural tendency

and choose to groan for her instead of sing
for someone else, happy to have such wounds,
prepared to die for her or live in bondage.

297

Two great opponents were united once:
Beauty and Chastity lived in such accord
her holy soul experienced no conflict
when they moved in to sojourn with her there.

Now Death has left them separate and scattered:
one lives in Heaven, adding to its glory,
one's in the earth, which covers up those eyes
that used to shoot their amorous darts at me.

The gracious acts, the wise and humble speech,
that came from someplace lofty, the sweet gaze
that used to wound my heart (which shows it still)

have vanished, all, and since I'm slow to follow,
perhaps I'll have a chance to consecrate
her precious name with this exhausted pen.

298

When I turn round to scan those recent years
that fled away, and scattered all my thoughts,
and quenched the fire in which I froze and burned,
and ended my repose from heavy labors,

and broke the faith of amorous deceits,
and put my wealth in just two far-fetched places,
the one in Heaven, the other in the earth,
and lost the profits from my painful gains,

I rouse myself and find myself so naked
that all misfortunes seem to be attractive
compared to what I feel by way of sorrow.

Oh star of mine, oh Fortune, Fate, oh Death,
oh Day forever sweet and cruel to me,
see how you've brought me to this low estate!

299

Where is that brow that with the smallest sign
could jerk my heart around, this way and that?
Where are the lashes and the two fair stars
that shed the light that helped me find my way?

Where is the worth, the knowledge, and the wisdom?
The skillful, virtuous, sweet, and humble speech?
Where are the beauties gathered in her person
that ruled my will so long on her behalf?

Where is the noble shadow of that face
that gave refreshment to my tired soul,
the place where all my thoughts were written down?

Where is the one who held my life in hand?
How much this brokenhearted world has lost!
Just like my eyes, which never will be dry.

300

How much I envy you, you greedy earth,
who get to clasp the one who's taken from me,
and keep me from the air of her sweet face
in which I once found peace from all my war!

How much I envy Heaven, locking in
that which it greedily gathered to itself,
the spirit freed from her most lovely limbs,
that rarely will unlock itself for others!

How much I envy souls whose fortune now
is having her sweet, holy company,
the very thing I sought with so much passion!

How much I envy hard and pitiless Death,
who having quenched the life I had through her,
dwells in her eyes but will not summon me!

301

Oh, valley echoing with my laments,
and river, often swelling from my tears,
beasts of the woods, wandering birds, and fish
that live between these verdant riverbanks,

air warmed and clearing from my constant sighs,
sweet path that has become so bitter to me,
hill that I loved and now have come to hate
where Love still leads me, as he used to do:

I recognize you in your well-known forms,
but not, alas, myself, since I've become
one who was glad and now is plunged in grief.

I used to see my love, and I've returned
to see the place where, naked, she passed on
to Heaven as she shed her lovely vesture.

302

My thought transported me to where she was,
she whom I seek and do not find on earth;
I saw her there, in the third sphere's bright circle;   *third sphere:*
she was more beautiful, and seemed less proud.   see Number 287

She took me by the hand: "You'll be with me,
in this same sphere, if my desire is true;
I am the one who gave you so much war
and had my day cut off before the evening.

"No human mind can comprehend my bliss;
I wait for just two things: you, and that veil   *that veil:* Laura's
I left behind on earth and you loved so."   body, to be restored
                                                           at the Last Judgment

Ah, why did she grow silent, drop my hand?
For at the sound of words so kind and chaste
I could have stayed forever with her there.

303

You, Love, who stayed with me in happy times
along these banks so friendly to our thoughts,
you used to walk and talk with me, discoursing,
along the river, settling old accounts:

and you, you flowers, grasses, leaves, and shadows,
you caves and waves, soft breezes, hills, and valleys
that harbored all my amorous travails
and all my frequent and too violent storms:

oh, wandering denizens of these green woods,
oh, nymphs, and you who feed and shelter there
within the grassy depths of liquid crystal:

my days were bright and have become as dark
as Death, who makes them so! In this world, then,
our destiny's determined when we're born.

304

Then when my heart was eaten by love's worms
and burning steadily in amorous flames,
I combed the solitary, wild hills
for footprints of a wandering wild creature,

and I dared, singing, to complain of Love
and of the one who was so cruel to me;
but wit and rhyme were fitful at that age
because my thoughts were new and faltering.

The fire is dead; a little marble now
stands over it. But had it grown, with time,
into old age, as it has done with others,

armed with the rhymes that I no longer have,
and with a style of speaking that matured,
I could split stones and make them weep with sweetness.

305

Beautiful soul, freed from the knot that was
the loveliest thing that Nature ever knit:
from Heaven turn your thought to my dark life,
which had glad thoughts but now is turned to tears.

Your heart is free now from the false opinion
that sometimes made your sweet face harsh and cruel;
since you're released from cares, please turn your gaze
in my direction, listening to my sighs.

Look down at the great rock that births the Sorgue
and you'll see one among the grass and waters
who's nourished by your memory and by sorrow;

he wants you to abandon your old dwelling,
where love was born between us, so you won't
have to see what displeased you in your people.

306

The sun that showed me how to get to Heaven,
the glorious steps unto the highest Sun,
has shut my light and her terrestrial prison   *her terrestrial*
away from me, in some indifferent stones,   *prison:* the body

and I've become a creature of the forest
who wanders far, on tired, lonely feet,
bearing a heavy heart, eyes wet and downcast,
around a world that's like a mountain desert.

Thus I go searching places where I saw her;
Love, you're my only company; you come
to try to show me where I need to go;

and I don't find her, but I see her footprints,   *Avernian:* associated
her sacred steps along the road to Heaven,   with Avernus, entrance
far from Avernian and Stygian lakes.   to the underworld;
                                                        Stygian lakes: formed
                                                        by the mythological
                                                        underworld river Styx

307

I thought I had the skill to soar in flight
(not my own power, but his who spreads my wings)
and sing a song that's worthy of that knot
with which Love binds me and which Death will loosen.

I found myself too slow and just as frail
as some thin branch that bears a heavy burden;
I said: "He flies to fall who mounts too high,
nor can a man perform what heavens deny him."

No clever feather ever flew so high
(let alone one with heavy tongue or style)
as Nature did when she made my sweet hindrance;

Love followed suit, and took such special care
adorning her that I was quite unworthy
even to see her; that was just good luck.

308

The one for whom I traded Sorgue for Arno
and honest poverty for slavish riches
turned holy sweetness into bitterness
and left me scrawny, dying of starvation.

Since then I've often tried in vain to capture
her lofty beauty, for succeeding ages,
that they may cherish her and love her too,
but style can't incarnate that face of hers.

Still, now and then, I dare to shadow forth
some of the praises that were always hers,
as many as are stars across the sky;

but when I reach the fact of her divineness,
a bright, brief sun that shone upon this world,
my wit and art and daring all collapse.

309

The high, new miracle that in our time
came to the world but did not wish to stay,
whom Heaven merely showed us, then took back
in order to adorn its starry cloisters:

Lord Love, who first set free my tongue, wants me
to show her to whoever didn't see her,
and to that end a thousand times he's worked
my wits, my time, my papers, pens, and inks.

But poetry has not attained its peak,
I know that well, and so does anyone
who's ever tried to write or speak of Love;

let thoughtful people love the silent truth
that passes anything in language, sighing:
"Blessed be the eyes that saw her while she lived!"

310

Now Zephyrus returns, bringing fine weather
and his sweet family of grass and flowers,
chattering Procne, weeping Philomena,
and Spring, decked out in white and in vermilion;

the meadows laugh, the sky grows clear again,
great Jove delights in looking at his daughter,
the earth and air and water fill with love,
and every animal obeys love's call.

To me, alas, the sighs that come are heavy;
she draws them upward from my deepest heart
she who has carried off its keys, to Heaven,

and all the birdsong, all the flowering meadows,
the soft and gentle gestures of fair ladies,
are like a wilderness of savage beasts.

Zephyrus: the west wind

Procne: the swallow; *Philomena:* the nightingale

Jove . . . daughter: Venus

311

That nightingale who weeps so tenderly,
lamenting for his children or his mate,
fills all the sky and fields with dulcet sweetness
in many notes and trills, grieving and skillful,

and through the night he keeps me company
and helps me to recall my bitter fate;
for I have no one but myself to blame
for not believing Death could rule a goddess.

How easy to deceive one who's too sanguine!
That pair of lights was brighter than the sun;
who ever thought to see them dark on earth?

I start to understand what my harsh fate
is trying to teach me, as I live in tears:
nothing on earth that pleases can endure.

This echoes a
famous sonnet
by Cavalcanti.

312

Not lovely stars that wander through clear skies,
nor well-caulked ships traversing tranquil seas,
nor armored knights crossing the countryside,
nor quick and happy creatures in the woods,

nor timely news of an awaited joy,
nor poems of love in high and courtly style,
nor, by clear fountains and lush meadowlands,
fair ladies singing sweetly, full of virtue,

nor any other thing can touch my heart:
she who is buried with it, she alone,
was all the light and mirror of my eyes.

Living is pain, so heavy and so long,
that I call for my end and long to see her,
the one I never should have seen at all.

313

The time is gone, alas, when I could live
refreshed amid the fire; the one I wept for
passed away, the one I wrote about,
but left me with my pen and all these tears.

Her face is gone, so sanctified and charming,
and as it went, her eyes speared through my heart,
that heart, once mine, which left to follow her,
as if enveloped in her lovely mantle.

She took it with her down into the grave
and then to Heaven, where she triumphs now,
adorned with laurel for her chastity.

And would that I were with them there, alas,
freed from the mortal veil that chains me here,
beyond these sighs, amid those blessèd souls!

314

Mind, you foresaw your pains and injuries,
pensive and sad even when times were good,
seeking intently, in her lovely sight,
some consolation for impending troubles:

her gestures and her words, her garments, face,
the pity newly mixing with her woe,
had you but understood, you might have said:
"This is the final day of years of sweetness."

Such sweetness, then, oh, miserable soul,
the way we burned together in the moment,
seeing those eyes I would not see again,

and leaving in their keeping, as I would
with friends I trust completely, my best treasure:
my loving thoughts and my most loving heart.

315

My flowering green age was passing by,
the bonfire in my heart was cooling down,
and I was coming to that place in life
where one has turned to face the downward slope;

and bit by bit my precious enemy
was starting to gain confidence, lose fears,
and her sweet honesty was starting to
convert my bitter pains into new joys;

the time was coming near when Love could be
good friends with Chastity, and lovers might
sit down together and talk naturally.

Then Death felt envy at my happy state,
or else my hope, and Death attacked it there
and fell upon it in the middle way.

316

It was the time to find a peace or truce
from so much war, and that was maybe happening,
except that those glad steps were stopped by one
who evens out all inequalities;

for as a cloud dissolves itself in wind,
her life was gone, too quickly, and I lost
her two enchanting eyes to guide my way,
which now I have to follow with my thoughts.

She might have waited, since my hair, gone gray,
and years, gone past, were all transforming me,
and she need have no fear of what I'd say;

I would have talked to her, with virtuous sighs,
about my lengthy labors; now, from Heaven,
she sees, I'm sure, and she regrets them too.

317

Love helped me sail into a tranquil harbor
after the long, tumultuous times of storm,
into the years of chaste maturity
that rids itself of vice and takes on virtue;

my heart and my great loyalty were clear
and not displeasing to her lovely eyes.
Oh, vicious Death, how quick you are to spoil
the fruit of years in something like an hour!

If she had lived, we were approaching this:
I could have spoken and in those chaste ears
set down my ancient burden of sweet thoughts,

and she'd have answered me, perhaps, in kind,
sighing a little, using holy words,
our hair and faces showing how we'd changed.

318

That time a tree had fallen, seemingly
uprooted by an ax or by the wind,
its noble foliage scattered on the earth,
its wretched roots exposed and pale in sunlight,

I saw another tree, Love's object in me,
the subject of Euterpe and Calliope;
it twined and grew around my heart as ivy
will make its home along a trunk or wall.

That living laurel where my best high thoughts
had made their nest, and where my burning sighs
had never managed to disturb the branches,

transferred to Heaven, though it left its roots
in that first faithful dwelling; from that place
someone calls mournfully and hears no answer.

This sonnet is an allegory of Laura's death, physical and spiritual, as two trees, one dead and one—her soul, still rooted in his heart—surviving.

Euterpe and Calliope: Muses of music and poetry, respectively

319

Swifter than any deer my days have fled
like shadows, and what good I've seen has been
less than an eye blink, just a few clear hours
kept sweet and bitter in my memory.

Oh, world of misery, unstable and severe,
whoever trusts you must be wholly blind;
in you my heart was lost; the one who holds it
has turned from flesh and blood to empty dust.

And yet her better form is still alive
and will live, always, in the highest Heaven;
it makes me love her beauty more and more,

and as I go around with graying hair
all I can think about is what she's like
and what it meant to see her lovely veil.

320

I feel the ancient aura, and I see
the gracious hills wherein the light was born
that kept my eyes alive with joy and passion
while it pleased Heaven, eyes now sad and wet.

Oh, transitory hopes, oh, crazy thoughts!
The grass is grieving and the waters troubled,
the nest is cold and empty where she lay,
where I have wished to lie, alive or dead,

nest: Laura's birthplace;
Petrarch imagines being
buried there and having
her walk across his grave.

hoping to take some comfort from her steps
across my grave, and from the glance that burned
my heart, some rest from all my drudgery.

I served a master who was cruel and stingy,
was warmed as long as I could feel my fire,
and now I weep among its scattered ashes.

321

And is this it, the nest in which my phoenix
put on her golden and her purple feathers,
and where she kept my heart beneath her wings
and still draws forth from it both words and sighs?

Oh, root and origin of my sweet harms,
where is the lovely face that gave off light
and kept me glad, though burning in the fire?
Unique on earth, and happy now in Heaven,

you have abandoned me in lonely pain
that brings me back here, loaded down with grief,
a place I bless and honor for your sake,

to watch the night come on among the hills
from which you took your final flight to Heaven
and where your eyes once used to make it day.

nest: see Number 320
her golden and her
purple feathers:
hair and complexion

322

I'm never going to look with tranquil mind
or with dry eyes at those ingenious verses
in which Love sparkles brightly, and which Kindness
seems to have fashioned with a skillful hand.

Oh, spirit earthly mourning could not vanquish,
and who pours down from Heaven now such sweetness
that you've restored my vagrant rhymes and lines
to something like their style before Death struck:

I thought to show you something else I'd done
when I was young and gained the laurel leaves;
what spiteful planet struck you, my high treasure?

Who hides you, takes you from me much too early,
you whom I praise with tongue and hold at heart?
In you, sweet sigh, my soul is calm again.

This sonnet refers to
one written twenty-
five years earlier by
Giacomo Colonna;
Petrarch replicates
the rhyme scheme
and mourns the
writer, who had died
that same year.

This poem offers
six allegorical
renderings of the
death of Laura,
using familiar
symbols of her
to reiterate the
mystery of her loss.

323

One day as I stood gazing from my window
I saw outside it such disturbing sights
that I was getting tired just from watching;
    I saw a wild creature to my right
whose human face would stir great Jove to love,
pursued by hounds, a black one and a white one,
    who tore this noble creature
    on one side and the other so intensely
that in no time at all they drove it forward,
    trapped in a stony pass,
where all that beauty then succumbed to death
and made me sigh with sorrow for its fate.

Then on the ocean's deeps I saw a ship
with silken tackle and great sails of gold,
fashioned from ebony and finest ivory;
    the sea was calm, the breeze was blowing gently,
and there was not a cloud to veil the sky.
The ship was clearly full of precious cargo.
    And then a sudden tempest
approaching from the east struck air and water
and drove the ship against a ragged rock.
    Oh, what a heavy grief!
Crushed in a moment! Now a small space hides
those riches that were surely unsurpassed!

Within a youthful grove of trees there flowered
a sacred laurel, young and straight and slender;
it could have been a tree that grew in Eden;
    and from its shade there issued such sweet sounds
of diverse birds and other such delights
that it had rapt me from the mundane world.
    Yet as I gazed upon it
the sky around was changed, the air grew black
and lightning struck the tree; the hidden roots
    of that most happy plant
were torn, exposed; whereby my life grew sad,
because such shade can never be regained.

Within that very wood a limpid fountain
came bubbling from a stone, and its fresh waters
ran forth and spread with a delightful murmur.
    To that secluded spot, shaded and cool,
no shepherds came, or other country folk,
but only nymphs and muses joined that music.
    There I was seated, quite
transported by that harmony, and soothed
by taking in that sight: a chasm opened
and took it all away,
the fountain and the place, to leave me grieving
so that the memory fills me still with fear.

    I saw a wondrous phoenix in the forest,
both wings were crimson and the head was gold,
and in the wood it lived, alone and proud;
    I took it first to be a thing immortal
until it came to the uprooted laurel
and to the fountain that the earth had swallowed.
    All things fly toward their end:
for when it saw the scattered laurel leaves,
the broken trunk, the living water dry,
it turned its beak against
itself, as if in scorn, and vanished then,
burning my heart with pity and with love.

    And last, I saw a lady, walking pensive
among the grass and flowers, fair and happy;
it makes me burn and tremble to recall her;
    humble herself, but haughty against Love,
she wore a gown of white so subtly woven
that it resembled snow and gold at once,
    and yet her head and neck
were shrouded in a mist of darkened shadow.
Stung on the heel then, by a little adder,
she withered like a flower,
but she died confident and clearly happy:
ah, nothing but our tears live on this earth!

Song, you've a right to say:
"These visions, six of them, have given
a sweet desire for death to him, my maker."

a ballata

324

Ah, Love, when hope for recompense
for all my faithfulness was blossoming,
the one who could show mercy was removed.

Oh, Death, who feels no pity! Oh, cruel Life!
One leaves me drowned in grief
and kills my hopes before they can mature;
the other keeps me here against my will,
and I can't follow one I love
to where she's gone, for Death will not allow me.
    But she is always present,
my madonna, enthroned here in my heart,
and what my life's become, she can inspect.

This poem is an
allegory of Laura's
life and death, as
recounted to the
poet by Fortune,
who foresees Laura's
early death during
her lifetime.

325

I can't be silent, yet I fear my tongue
will not reflect what's really in my heart,
which simply wants to honor
the lady who is listening from Heaven.
How can I, if you do not teach me, Love,
find mortal words to match divinity
and works which are concealed
by high humility, so self-contained?
    Her noble soul had not been dwelling long
in that fair prison which it's now gone free from
when I at first became aware of her
and then ran speedily
(for it was April, both the year's and mine)

to gather flowers from surrounding meadows,
hoping, thus garlanded, to please her eyes.

The walls were alabaster, roof of gold;
an ivory entrance, under sapphire windows,
was where the first sigh issued
to reach my heart, the way the last one will;
and then the messengers of Love came forth
armed with their darts and with their fire
and crowned, alas, with laurel;
just thinking of them now can make me shiver.
Inside there could be seen a lofty throne
fashioned from diamond, square and clearly flawless,   *throne . . .*
where sat a lovely lady all alone;   *diamond:*
before her was a column   her chastity
crystal and so transparent that all thoughts
inscribed within it grew so evident
that often, in my sighing, I was happy.

I saw that I had come to those bright weapons
that shine and pierce and burn, to that green flag   *green flag:*
that would defeat Apollo, Jove,   the laurel
great Mars, and Polyphemus in a battle,
where weeping is forever fresh and green,
I saw all this and could not get away;
I let myself be captured
and now I can't escape by any means.
But as a man who's weeping and departs,
will sometimes see things that delight his heart,
it happened that the one for whom I'm prisoner
stood on a balcony,
and was the one thing perfect in her time,
and I began to gaze with such desire
that I forgot myself and all my pain.

I was on earth, my heart in Paradise,
sweetly forgetting every other care;
I felt my living form

grow still as marble, filling up with wonder,
and then a lady confident and swift,
ancient in years though youthful in her face,
seeing me so intent
by the expression of my face and brow:
    "Come and consult with me" was what she said,
"for I have far more power than you think
and in one moment I can gladden, sadden;
I'm lighter than the wind;
I rule and spin all things you see on earth.
Keep looking, like an eagle, at the sun
and all the while listen to my words.

    "The day that she was born, the stars that make
the happiest effects among you were
in high and noble places,
turned toward each other with a mutual love.
And Venus and her father, quite benignly,
were dominant in Heaven, while those stars
that might do evil here
were off in other places, all dispersed.
    "The sun had never shone on such a day
with air and earth all joyful, and the waters
that fill the seas and rivers were at peace.
Among such friendly lights

one distant cloud appeared, unsettling me,
for I'm afraid that it will burn and weep
if Pity doesn't change the heavens' course.

    "When she came down to this low world and life
(which, speaking frankly, isn't worthy of her),
a wondrous thing to see,
already sweet and holy, though unripe,
she was a pearl set in finest gold.
She crawled at first, then took her early steps,
and she made trees, and stones,
and earth, and water, soft and green and sweet,
    "and with her hands and feet she made the grass

grow fresh and proud; her glance made flowers bloom,
and winds grew calm and storms were quieted
just by her voice, although
her tongue was hardly weaned from mother's milk:
and thus the world, though deaf and blind, could tell
how much the light of Heaven shone in her.

    "Then as she grew, in years as well as virtue,
she reached her third stage, age of blossoming,   *third stage:*
and so much charm and beauty   adolescence
the sun had never seen, I well believe:
her eyes so full of happiness and virtue,
her speech so full of sweetness and of health.
All tongues are dumb to tell
the things about her only you have learned:
    "her face shines bright with such celestial light
that your eyes cannot look directly at it,
and for the beauty of her earthly prison
your heart is filled with fire
so much that nothing ever burned more sweetly;
and yet I think that her abrupt departure
is going to make your life taste very bitter."

    That said, she turned back to her fickle wheel,
the one that whirls around and spins our thread,
this sad and certain prophet of my losses;
after not many years
my song, the one whose loss has made me long
for death, was taken early by cruel Death,
who could not find a body half so lovely.

326

Now you have done the worst you can accomplish,
oh, cruel Death, you have impoverished
the very realm of Love, quenched beauty's light,
destroyed its flower, encased it in a grave;

and now you have despoiled our life and ripped
its ornaments away, its sovereign honor;
but fame and courage, these things are immortal,
and not within your power: keep naked bones,

for Heaven has the rest and in its brightness
glories and basks as in a brighter sun;
good people will remember her forever.

In such a victory, oh, novice angel,
may pity for me overtake your heart
the way your beauty vanquished mine on earth.

327

The aura and the fragrance and the coolness,
the laurel's shade, the sight of it in bloom,
the light and solace of my weary life:
she ... who   she took them all, who empties out the world.
empties: Death

The way the sun wanes when his sister moon
eclipses him, that's how my light is gone;
I ask for Death as remedy for Death,
because Love fills me with the darkest thoughts.

You've slept, my lovely lady, one short sleep,
and now you've wakened among blessèd spirits,
there where the soul becomes one with its Maker;

and if my rhymes have any force at all,
your name will live with noble intellects
and in eternal memory be sacred.

328

The last, alas, of all my happy days
(of which I've seen but few in this short life)
had come and turned my heart to melting snow,
perhaps to forecast these days, dark and sad.

Like someone who can tell a fever's coming
because his muscles, pulse, and thoughts grow weak
is how I felt, although I could not know
how swiftly my imperfect wealth would end.

Her lovely eyes, now bright with joy in Heaven,
and happy in the light that rains salvation,
took leave of mine, left wretched here, and poor,

and spoke to them by means of chaste, strange glow:
"Peace be with you, dear friends. Not here, no, never;
but we will see each other elsewhere, soon."

329

Oh day, oh hour, oh, the final moment,
oh stars configured to impoverish me!
Oh faithful glance, what were you trying to say
as, never to be happy, I departed?

I know my losses now; I have awakened,
for I believed (oh vain and groundless faith!)
that I was losing part, not all, in leaving:
how many hopes are scattered by the wind!

For something contrary was set in Heaven—
to douse the brilliant light by which I lived—
and that was figured in her sharp, sweet sight;

but I had put a veil before my eyes
that helped me fail to see what I was seeing,
and in an instant made my life a ruin.

330

That yearning, sweet, dear, virtuous gaze of hers
seemed to be saying: "Take what you can from me,
for you will never see me here again
once your unwilling foot has moved away."

Oh, intellect, so panther-swift, but slow
to recognize approaching sorrow, why
could you not see, in her eyes, what would come:
knowledge that burns me and destroys my hope?

Silent, but sparkling, brighter far than usual,
they said to yours: "Oh, friendly lights, that made
sweet mirrors of us for a long time now,

Heaven expects us; it seems soon to you,
but He who bound us now dissolves our knot
while yours will last, to your continued grief."

331

I used to leave the fountain of my life,
go far away, and search through lands and seas,
guided not by my will but by my star,
      and always went (for Love gave me such help)
into that exile, bitter beyond belief,
feeding my heart on memory and hope.
      And now, alas, I throw down arms, surrender
to my cruel fate, the violent destiny
that has deprived me of so sweet a hope;
now all I have is memory,
the only thing that feeds my great desire,
and so my soul is withering and starving.

      The way a runner, needing food, will tire
and go more slowly, losing all the strength
that made him swift along his given course:
      so, as my life lacks that dear nourishment

that was devoured by the one who leaves
the whole world naked and my own heart sad,
    sweetness grows bitter to me, pleasure pain,
from day to day; and thus this journey will,
however brief, I hope and fear, soon end.
A cloud, or dust in wind,
I flee from this, the pilgrimage of life,
and may that flight become my destiny.

    I never cared much for this mortal life
(the love god knows this, and I've told him, often)
except for her, who was his light and mine;
    since she has died on earth and been reborn
in Heaven, that spirit for whom I lived and breathed,
my only wish is to go join her there.
    But I will always grieve instead, because
I lacked the skill to diagnose my illness,
though Love was showing me beneath that brow
another sort of counsel:
many have died in sorrow, unreprieved,
who might have died in joy by dying sooner.

    In her eyes where my heart so loved to dwell
(until my bitter fate fell prey to envy
and banished it from having such rich quarters)
    Love had inscribed, with his own hand, the letters
that told, with pity, what would soon become
of all my lengthy journey of desire.
    Lovely and sweet if I'd died then, when dying
would not have meant my life died with me too
but rather that my best part would live on;
and now Death scatters hope;
a little earth conceals my former wealth
and I live on, to think of it and shudder.

    If my small intellect had been with me
when I most needed it, not off somewhere
distracted by another kind of hunger,

I might have read upon my lady's brow:
"You've reached the very end of all your sweetness,
and now you're at the threshold of your bitterness."
    If I had understood that, sweetly free
of my own mortal coil, in her presence,
this cumbersome and heavy flesh of mine,
I could have gone before her,
to see the throne prepared for her in Heaven;
instead I'll follow later, silver-haired.

    Song, if you find one peacefully in love,
say, "While you're happy, die;
for timely death's not grief, it is a refuge,
and he who can die well should not delay."

332

This is a double
sestina; when the
poet "doubles up
his grief," he also
commits himself to a
difficult duplication
of the form.

My fortune kindly and my life so joyful,
unclouded days and coolly tranquil nights,
the gentle sighing and the sweet new style
that used to resonate in verse and rhymes,
changed in a moment into grief and weeping,
to make me hate this life and yearn for death.

Oh, cruel, harsh, inexorable Death,
you give me reason never to be joyful,
but rather to spend all my time in weeping
through days of darkness and lamenting nights;
my heavy sighs will not turn into rhymes
and my harsh torment will not yield to style.

Where has it led me, my old loving style,
except to speak of sorrow and of death?
Where are the verses now, where are the rhymes
that used to make a good heart thoughtful, joyful?
Where are the times I talked of love all night?
When I speak now, I only think of weeping.

It once meant sweet desire, all that weeping,
and thus the sweetness smoothed the bitter style
and made me stay awake through many nights;
but now the tears are bitterness like death
because I'll never see that look, so joyful,
the noble subject of my humble rhymes.

Love set a vivid target for my rhymes
in those clear eyes, and now it ends in weeping,
reminding me of all that was so joyful,
and as I change my thoughts I change my style
and find myself entreating you, pale Death,
to rescue me from all these painful nights.

For sleep no longer visits my cruel nights,
and there's no more sonority in rhymes,
since all they seem to speak about is death,
and all my singing has transformed to weeping.
Love has no room for such a transformed style
that turns to sorrow all that once was joyful.

There never was a man who was more joyful
and then transformed to sorrow, days and nights,
and doubles up his grief in doubled style,
extracting from his heart such tearful rhymes.
I lived on hope, and now I live on weeping
and all I want from Death is just my death.

For Death has dealt me death, and only Death
could show me once again that face, so joyful,
that made me able to enjoy my weeping,
that aura, sweet, that rain that filled my nights
when I could turn my noble thoughts to rhymes
because the love god strengthened my weak style.

I wish I'd had so sorrowful a style
that I could win my Laura back from Death
as Orpheus did Eurydice, sans rhymes,

for then I would be marvelously joyful!
And if I can't I beg that soon, some night,
my life will end, and close these fountains weeping.

Think of it, Love, these many years of weeping
for what I lost, my heavy, grieving style,
my sense that they won't stop, these cruel nights;
no wonder I have turned to begging Death
to take me from this place, to make me joyful:
bring me to her for whom I make my rhymes.

If they can go so high, my tired rhymes,
and reach the one who dwells beyond all weeping,
whose beauty even now makes Heaven joyful,
she'll surely recognize my altered style
which may have pleased her some, until her death
brought her bright days, that made for me dark nights.

And all of you who sigh for better nights,
who hear of Love or write of it in rhymes,
please beg her to give in to me, grim Death,
and bring me to the port of pain and weeping;
ask her, for once, to change her ancient style
that deals out sorrow: she can make me joyful.

She'll make me joyful in one night, ere long,
and thus in this harsh style, with anguished rhymes,
I pray that Death will come relieve my weeping.

333

Go, doleful rhymes, and visit the hard stone
that hides my dearest treasure in the earth;
call on her there, who will respond from Heaven
although her mortal part lies dark and buried.

Tell her that I'm already sick of living,
of sailing through these rough and heaving seas;
tell her I gather up her scattered leaves
and follow where she went, step after step,

and speak of her alone, alive and dead,
(or rather, still alive, and now immortal),
so that this world may understand and love her.

Ask her to pay attention to my death day,
which can't be far away, so she can meet me,
and summon me to where she is, in Heaven.

334

If virtuous love is worthy, still, of mercy,
and pity still retains her former power,
I shall find mercy, since my faith remains
bright as the sun, to her and to the world.

She used to fear me; now she knows, for certain,
the thing I want is what I always wanted,
and where she once heard words and saw my face
she now can read my very mind and heart.

And so I hope there will be grief in Heaven
for all my sighs; indeed, it seems it's happening,
for she returns to me, evincing pity;

which makes me hope that when I shed this husk
she will come fetch me, with our people helping,
she, the true friend of virtue and of Christ.

335

I saw, among a thousand ladies, one
of such a worth that love and fear assailed me,
for I could tell, without exaggeration,
that she resembled a celestial spirit.

She had no trace of earth or death about her
and cared for Heaven only, nothing else;
my soul, that pined and burned to be with her,
opened its wings in yearning, trying to fly;

but she was much too high for my gross weight,
and in a while she vanished out of sight;
and thinking of that freezes me in numbness.

windows: Laura's eyes   Oh, high and lovely windows, clear with light,
she who makes . . .   where she who makes so many of us sad
us sad: Death   found entrance to so beautiful a body!

336

She comes to mind (or rather say that she
stays in my mind, for Lethe can't erase her)
just as I saw her in her youthful flowering,
glowing with all the radiance of her star;

I see her as at first, so chaste and lovely,
so self-contained, so inward-turned and shy,
and I cry out: "It's she, she's still alive!"
and beg her for the gift of her sweet speech.

Sometime she answers, sometimes she is mute;
and I, like one who's wrong and then corrected,
say to myself: "Oh yes, you are deceived.

"You know, in thirteen forty-eight, upon
the sixth of April, as the day began,
her blessed soul departed from her body."

337

Something that, both in color and in fragrance,
surpassed the odoriferous, bright East,
and flowers, fruits, and grass by which the West
is known for rarities and excellence:

my sweetest laurel, tree in which there lived
every beauty, all the ardent virtues,
and seated in its shadow, resting chastely,
my noble lord and my supremest goddess.

I made a nest of all my truest thoughts
in that rich tree, and though in ice and fire,
freezing and burning, I was truly happy.

Her perfect qualities had filled the world
when God, in order to adorn His Heaven,
recalled her to Himself, as worthy of His presence.

338

Death, you have left this poor world cold and dark
without its sun, with Love disarmed and blind,
Graciousness naked, Beauty weak and sick,
me desolate, a burden to myself,

Courtesy exiled, Chastity degraded.
I grieve alone, though all have cause to grieve,
since you've dug up the brightest seed of virtue:
and once the best is dead, what will be second?

Earth, air, and sea should weep together, for
the human lineage, once she's gone, becomes
a meadow stripped of flowers, a gemless ring.

The world, while it possessed her, didn't know her;
I knew her, and I'm left behind to weep,
while Heaven gathers beauty from my weeping.

339

The poet's human
limits allowed him
to see Laura's
physical beauty
but not her soul.

I knew (since Heaven cleared my eyes so much
while Love and eagerness helped spread my wings)
things new and light and graceful, but still mortal,
which all the stars had showered on one subject.

Those many other high celestial forms,
so strange and wondrous and immortal, I
could not endure with my weak vision then
because my intellect was not attuned.

And thus the things I said or wrote of her,
who now repays my praises with her prayers,
were like a drop of water in an ocean;

because our pens cannot outreach our wits,
and even if your eyes fix on the sun,
the brighter shines its light, the less you see.

340

My sweet and dear and greatly cherished pledge
whom Nature took from me, and Heaven keeps,
how is it that your pity is so tardy,
oh, you, the one sustainer of my life?

At least you used to feel my sleep was worthy
to have some sight of you. Now you let me burn
without relief; and why delay its coming?
Anger and scorn are surely absent there,

the kind that can make even tender hearts
down here enjoy another person's torment,
and even banish Love from his own realm.

Since you can see inside me, know my pain,
and are the only one who can relieve it,
send down your shade to quiet my laments.

341

What pity, ah, what angel was so swift
to carry my heart-sorrow through the heavens?
For once again I feel, as in the past,
my lady's presence and her sweet, chaste ways,

that pacify my sad and wretched heart;
such great humility, such lack of pride,
that now I pull myself away from death
and living is no longer painful to me.

Blessèd indeed is she who can make others
blest by the sight of her or by her words,
words that for both of us have special meaning:

"My dear and faithful one, I grieve for you,
but I was cruel to you for our own good,"
she says, and more, and makes the sun stand still.

342

With food my lord always provides profusely—
tears and great sorrow—I feed my weary heart,
and often I both tremble and grow pale
when I consider that the wound's so deep.

But she, whom no one bettered, or came close to,
when she was living, visits my sickbed,
so lovely that I scarcely dare to look,
and full of pity sits there on its edge.

She strokes and dries my eyes with that same hand
for which I used to feel so much desire,
while she speaks words that make me drown in sweetness:

"What good," she asks, "is knowledge to despair?
Please stop this weeping, isn't it enough?
Would you were as alive as I'm not dead!"

343

When I think back upon that gentle glance
which Heaven honors now, tilt of her head,
her golden hair, the modest angel voice
that sweetened life for me, it breaks my heart

and makes me marvel that I'm still alive;
I wouldn't be if she who made you doubt
which was the greater, her beauty or her truth,
was not so quick to help me as day dawns.

Oh, how she greets me, sweet and chaste and kind,
and how she listens, taking note, intently,
to all my history of sufferings!

When day's full brightness seems to touch her image
she turns away, takes herself back to Heaven,
the way she knows, her cheeks still wet with tears.

344

There may have been a time when love was sweet
(although I don't recall); it's bitter now,
and nothing rivals it; whoever's learned
as I have, through great grief, knows this is true.

She who gave truth and honor to our world
and now makes Heaven bright and lovely too,
made my rest brief and rare when she was here

left me void:
Petrarch will
retract this
accusation in
the next sonnet.

and now has left me void of all repose.

Cruel Death has stripped me of my every treasure,
nor does her bliss there temper the distress
of having lost that lovely soul of hers.

I wept and sang; I cannot change my style;
thus day and night the grief my soul has gathered
pours forth both from my eyes and from my tongue.

345

Sorrow and love propelled this tongue of mine,
prone to complaint, to say what it should not:
to say of her for whom I sang and burned
something that would be wrong if it were true;

it ought to be enough to quiet me,
and give my heart sufficient consolation,
that her condition's blest, that she's with Him
who while she lived was always in her heart.

And yes, I do grow calm, console myself,
nor would I wish her back inside this hell,
I'd rather die or live on here alone;

for I can watch her with internal sight,
rising with flocks of angels, soaring high,
up to the feet of our eternal Lord.

346

The chosen angels and the blessèd souls,
all citizens of Heaven, that first day
my lady passed across, surrounded her
and marveled at her, full of reverence.

"What light is this and what amazing beauty?"
they said to one another. "Such a soul,
lovely as this one, never has arrived
up from that erring world to this high realm."

And happy to have changed her dwelling place
and equal to the most perfected souls,
yet she looks back, from time to time, to see

if I am following, and seems to wait,
and so I bend my thoughts and needs toward Heaven,
and seem to hear her praying that I hurry.

347

Lady, now living in our Maker's presence,
joyous reward for a deserving life,
seated upon a high and glorious throne
adorned with other things than pearls or purple,

oh, wonder among ladies, high and rare:
now, in the face of He who sees all things,
you see my love, you witness that pure faith
for which I spilled such tears and so much ink,

and now you know my heart was yours on earth
as it is yours in Heaven, that I wanted
nothing except the sunlight of your eyes.

I therefore make amends for that long war
in which I spurned the world and loved you only,
and pray that soon I may come join you there.

348

From the most lovely eyes, the brightest face
that ever shone, from that resplendent hair
which made the sun and gold seem less attractive,
from sweetest speech and from the sweetest smile,

from hands and arms that could have vanquished all
Love's greatest rebels, without even moving,
from feet too beautiful, so small and slender,
and from a body made in Paradise,

my spirits woke to life; now Heaven's King
and all His wingèd courtiers enjoy them
and I am left alone here, naked, blind.

I hope just one thing in this misery:
that she who can see all my thoughts quite plainly
will win me grace and let me join her there.

349

I seem to hear, each hour, in my ear
the messenger my lady sends to call me,
and thus it is I've changed, inside and out,
and in a few years I have shrunk so much

that I can hardly recognize myself:
all my accustomed life has now been banished.
To know the day precisely would be good,
but certainly it cannot be far off.

Oh, happy day when I escape at last
this earthly prison, leaving wrecked and scattered
the frail yet heavy garment that I wear,

and put behind me all these thick, dark shadows
and fly so far into the clear, bright sky
that I may see my Lord and see my lady!

350

This frail and brittle goodness that we cherish,
made out of wind and shadows, known as beauty,
never existed wholly in one body
except just once, in our time, to my sorrow;

for Nature does not wish, nor is it fitting,
to make one rich and leave the other poor;
and yet she poured all riches into one
(excuse me, if you're beautiful, or think so).

There never was such beauty, old or new,
nor will there ever be again, I think;
yet it was hidden, and the world ignored it.

She vanished soon, and so I'm glad to trade
the sight I briefly had of her with Heaven,
if I may be more pleasing in her sight.

351

A toughness that was sweet, and calm rejections,
full of chaste love and sympathetic pity,
and charming anger that I now can see
acted to check my vain and burning passions,

a well-bred speaking through which always shone
the highest forms of courtesy and chasteness,
virtue in blossom, fountainhead of beauty,
that rooted all the base thoughts from my heart,

a gaze divine enough to make man blest,
now fierce, to rein my daring mind from thoughts
of passions that have rightly been forbidden,

now swift, to offer comfort to my sorrow:
this lovely alteration was the root
of my salvation, else I had been lost.

352

Oh, happy spirit that so sweetly governed
those eyes which blazed far brighter than the sun,
and formed the sighs, and all the lovely words
that echo still within my memory:

I saw you once, aglow with virtue's fire,
walking among the grass and violets,
more as an angel than a lady might;
those feet will walk within my mind forever.

The body that you then, joining your Maker,
left in the earth, was cloaked with that soft veil
allotted to you by high destiny.

And your departure meant that Love and Courtesy
had vanished too; the sun fell from the sky;
and that was when Death started to taste sweet.

353

Wandering bird that can continue singing
while weeping for the past, and bear sweet witness
to night, to winter all around you, to
the happy months that you have left behind:

Wandering bird:
the nightingale

if in addition to your own sad griefs
you knew of my condition, like to yours,
you probably would fly straight to my bosom
to share its sorrows and its many groans.

I do not know if we'd be just alike,
since she you weep for may be still alive,
while Death and Heaven have been stingy to me;

but both this hour, and this forbidding season,
with memories of sweet and bitter years,
invite me to converse with you in pity.

354

Ah, reach your hand out to my weary mind,
Lord Love, and to my fragile, tired style,
and help me speak of her who is immortal
and now a citizen of Heaven's realm;

allow, my lord, my words to reach their goal,
true praise of her—they can't soar on their own,
because that kind of virtue and that beauty
were never in this world, which was unworthy.

He answers me: "All Heaven can do, or I,
along with wise advice and chaste existence,
all this was in her whom Death took from us;

there hasn't been a form to equal hers
since Adam's eyes first opened; that's the truth:
in tears I say it and in tears you write it."

355

Oh, time, oh, fickle heavens, wheeling past,
that leave us mortals miserable and blind;
oh, days that are more swift than wind or arrows!
Now I have learned to comprehend your frauds.

But I excuse you, and reproach myself;
for Nature gave you wings, and gave me eyes,
which I then used to gaze on things that hurt me,
and made myself ashamed and full of sorrow;

and it is time, and even well past time,
to turn them in a sensible direction,
and put an end to all my endless woes.

It's not Love's yoke my soul is casting off,
it's all my faults, and he knows with what effort;
virtue comes not from luck; it is an art.

356

aura: the breeze-
Laura-*aura* pun
once more

My sacred *aura* breathes so often, in
my weary sleeping, that it makes me bold
to tell her all the ills I've felt, and feel,
something I could not dare were she alive.

I tell of that first love-inspiring glance
that was the start of such a lengthy torment,
and then I speak of being sad and happy
as every day and hour Love gnawed at me.

She's silent, but her face is grave with pity;
she looks at me intently, and she sighs,
and sometimes tears run down her virtuous face;

and then my soul is overcome with sorrow,
and weeps, and brims with anger at itself,
which shakes it out of sleep, back to my day.

357

Each day seems longer than a thousand years
until I follow my dear, faithful guide
who led me in this world and leads me now
along a better path to carefree life;

and now the world's deceits can't hold me back
because I know them well, and so much light
shines in my heart, come all the way from Heaven,
that I can reckon both my time and losses.

Nor do I fear the threatening of death,
since my King suffered worse, to help me be
both strong and firm in following Him home,

and death invaded, a short time ago,
each vein of hers, who was my destiny,
yet did not trouble her clear face or brow.

358

Death has no way to make her sweet face bitter,
though her sweet face can sweeten Death itself;
why would I need another guide to help?
She is the one who teaches me all goodness,

and He who was not sparing with his blood,
who kicked apart the deep Tartarean gates,
and from His death, I find, I take new strength.
Come, therefore, Death, you are most dear to me,

Tartarean gates:
Christ's harrowing
of Hell

and don't delay; the time is surely ripe,
and has been so, from that first moment when
my true madonna parted from this life.

I haven't really lived a day since then;
I lived in her, with her I reached the end,
my day was done when she took her last steps.

359

My soft and gentle comforter arrives
to bring repose to this, my weary life,
and when she comes, sits on the bed's left side,
conversing in that sweet and skillful way;
    all pale with fear and anguish, I inquire,
"Where do you come from, oh, contented soul?"
She draws a palm branch, then
another one of laurel, from her bosom,
and says: "From the serene
and cloudless empyrean, holy Heaven,
I come, and I come only to console you."

I thank her humbly with my words and gestures
and then I ask her softly how it is
she knows about the state I'm in, and she:
"The waves of tears that never seem to stop,
    joined with the breeze created by your sighs,
travel to Heaven to disturb my peace.
Does it displease you so
that I have left this misery behind,
and found a better life?
It ought to please you if you loved me then
the way you showed by all your words and looks."

I answer, "I don't weep for anything
except myself, left here in pain and darkness,
for I have been as certain you're in Heaven
as one can be of something close at hand.
How could both God and Nature have created
a youthful heart with so much virtue if
Heaven and your salvation
were not intended to reward your deeds?
You're one of those rare souls
who live unblemished in our midst and then
mount instantly to Heaven when life ends.

"What else is there for me to do but weep,
both wretched and alone, nothing without you!

I wish I could have perished in the cradle
in order to avoid love's temperings."
    And she: "Why weep and so distemper who you are?
Much better if you tried to spread your wings
and cast off mortal things
and ceased your sweet, vain, elevated chatter,
to make a just account
and follow me (since you are so devoted),
to gather, at the end, one of these branches."

    "I meant to ask about that," I then answer,
"just what it is those leaves and branches mean."
And she: "Why, you can see that for yourself,
since you have honored one of them by writing.
    "The palm is victory and says that I
conquered the world and overcame myself;
the laurel stands for triumph,
of which I'm worthy through the strength of God.
Now you, if you're beset,
return to Him and ask Him for His help
so we may be united when you die."

    "Is this the same blond hair and golden knot
that bound me then," I ask, "and those same eyes
that were my sun?" "Don't run around with fools,
or talk and think the way they do," she says.
    "I am a naked spirit and rejoice
in Heaven; what you sought is dust, long since.
To help you in your troubles
I am allowed to seem the way I was
and shall seem so again,
more lovely and more loving to you too
who once was harsh for your sake and my own."

    I weep, and with her hands
she dries my face, and then she sighs so sweetly,
and scolds me gently too,
with words that could have broken stones apart;
and then she leaves, and then my sleep does too.

360

the queen: Reason

I make my plaint before the queen who rules
that part of us that can be called divine
and sits upon its summit;
and call my sweet, cruel master to account,
the ancient one; like gold refined in fire,
surrounded by my horror, fear, and pain,
like one in fear of death
who comes before a court to beg for justice.
    Thus I begin: "Lady, when I was young

my left foot: the
side of desire
and irrationality;
see Numbers
88 and 214

I set my left foot squarely in his kingdom;
much pain and anger followed,
and I have suffered such peculiar torments,
so many and so strange,
that finally my patience has been lost
and I have come at last to hate my life.

    "Thus all my time till now has been consumed
by fire and pain; how many useful paths
of virtue I disdained,
how many joys, to follow this cruel tempter!
I haven't words or genius to describe
the sheer unhappiness he's put me through,
or utter my complaints
about the grave injustice of this ingrate.
    "So little honey, so much vinegar,
aloes, and bitterness, brought to fill my life,
his sweetness proving false,
that drew me to the flock of bleating lovers!
For if I'm not deceived,
I had a nature with a high potential;
he took my peace and traded it for war.

    "He's made me love my God less than I should
and made me lose all care for my own self;
and this was for a lady
for whom I put aside all other thoughts.
In this respect he's been my only counselor,

whetting my young desire on his stone,
and giving me no peace,
when I had hopes of rest from his fierce yoke.
    "Oh, wretched man! Why did high Heaven bestow
such gifts of dear, high intellect, and wit?
My hair is turning white
and still I cannot break my stubborn will.
This cruel one I accuse
has robbed me of my freedom and has turned
a bitter life into a sweet addiction.

    "He made me search around the wilderness,
rough beasts, rapacious thieves, and wiry brambles,
hard people, harder customs,
and all the woes that can beset a traveler;
as mountains, valleys, marshes, seas, and rivers,
a thousand snares spread out in all directions,
and winter at strange times,
with danger always present, and fatigue:
    "neither did he, nor that old enemy
from whom I fled, leave me alone a minute;
and if I haven't come
long since, before my time, to early death,
well, that was Heaven's care
for my salvation, not this tyrant here
who feeds upon my sorrow and my loss.

    "Since I've been his, I've had no peaceful hour,
nor do I hope for one, and all my nights
have banished sleep and can't
make it come back with medicine or charms;
by treachery and force he's made himself
the master of my spirits, and since then
no bell has rung, in any
town I've been in, that hasn't reached my ear.
He knows in saying this I speak the truth,
    "for worms have never gnawed old wood the way
he gnaws upon my heart, making his nest

and threatening me with death.
And that's the source of all my tears and sufferings,
my words and all my sighs,
with which I wear myself and tire others.
Judge us, I beg, oh, you who know us both."

      My adversary has his sharp reproaches,
beginning thus: "Oh, hear the other side,
Lady, for it shall tell
the naked truth this ingrate has omitted.
From early years this fellow peddled lies
and threw his words around quite recklessly;
nor does he seem ashamed
(although I swapped him boredom for delight)
      "to rail at me, who kept him pure and clean
of foul desire seeking its own harm,
which now he grieves about,
and gave him that sweet life he now calls wretched,
and also gave him fame,
raising his intellect and mind to heights
they never could have managed on their own.

Atrides:
Agamemnon

*one who . . . was
brightest and
most fortunate:*
Scipio Africanus

      "He knows that great Atrides, high Achilles,
and Hannibal, so bitter to your country,
and one who in his virtue
was brightest and most fortunate of all:
I let them fall in love, as stars ordained,
in basest love with women who were slaves,
whereas for this man I
chose one among a thousand as his love,
      "such that her like will never be repeated,
no, not if Rome regained its lost Lucretia;
and I gave her such sweet
expressions in her speech and such sweet song
that low and heavy thoughts
could not survive in her vicinity.
And that's what he describes as my deception,

Lucretia: her rape,
which she responded
to with exposure of
the perpetrator,
Tarquin, and her
own suicide,
brought about
Rome's change
from a tyranny
to a republic.

"that is the wormwood and the scorn and anger,
sweeter than any woman ever seen!
Good seed has borne bad fruit,
my rich reward for helping such an ingrate.
I sheltered him so well beneath my wing
that all his words delighted knights and ladies;
I helped him rise so high
that there among a thousand brilliant wits
        "his name shines bright, and many people make
collections of his poems; otherwise
he would have been a hoarse
and mumbling courtier, lost among the mob!
I raised him up to fame
by helping him to learn, in my own school,
and from that one who has no parallel.

        "And, to tell finally my greatest service,
I've kept him from a thousand vicious acts,
for low and vile things
could never serve to give him satisfaction
(a young man shy and modest in his acts
and thoughts) once he'd become her slave and vassal;
she made so deep a mark
upon his heart, that he must emulate her.
        "All that's admired or noble in him comes
from her and thus from me, whom he complains of.
Nocturnal phantoms never
were so filled up with error as this man,
for since he's known us both,
he's had the grace of God, and of the people:
and that's the kind of thing that he complains of!

        "Again, and this is what I'll finish with,
I gave him wings to fly beyond the skies
by means of mortal things,
which make a ladder to our Maker, rightly used:
for if he could have steadily observed
the many virtues in that hope of his,

from one thing to the next
he could have risen up to the First Cause—
    "as he himself has mentioned in his rhymes.
Now he's forgotten me, and her, his lady,
whom I made the support
of his frail life." At this I raise a shout
and answer through my tears:
"He gave her to me, then He took her back."
And he: "Not me, but One who loved her most."

    And then, both turning to the seat of justice,
I shaking, he with cruel, high-pitched voice,
each one concludes his case:
"Oh, noble lady, we await your sentence."
And then she smiles and says:
"With pleasure I have listened to your pleadings;
to judge this suit will take a long, long time."

361

My faithful mirror tells me very often,
as do my tired spirit, changing skin,
diminished strength, and slow agility:
"Don't hide it from yourself now; you are old;

Nature must be obeyed, since time removes
our power to oppose her or resist her."
Immediately, as water douses fire,
I waken from a long and heavy sleep,

and I see clearly that our lives fly past,
that we have life just once, and then it's gone;
and in my heart there sounds a word of her,

the one who's loosened from her lovely knot,
who in her day was such a rarity
that no one else will ever touch her fame.

362

I fly so often on the wings of thought
to Heaven, that I almost feel I am
one of those souls who have their treasure there,
leaving their ripped-up veils behind on earth.

Sometimes my heart will shiver with a sweet
chill when I hear the one who makes me pale
say to me: "Friend, I love and honor you
because you've changed your habits and your hair."

She leads me to her Lord; I kneel down there,
begging that He will let me stay this time
and look upon them both, on their two faces.

He says, "Your destiny is firm and fixed,
and a delay of twenty years, or thirty,
seems like a lot to you but will be little."

363

Death has put out the sun that dazzled me;
my eyes, though whole and sound, see only darkness;
and she is dust who gave me heat and chills.
My laurels, faded, become oaks and elms

in which I see my good but still feel pain.
No one's alive to make my thoughts grow bold,
to freeze them or to scorch them, nor to make
them fill with hope or overflow with sorrow.

Out of the hands of him who stabs and heals,
who put me through a long and endless torture,
I find myself in sweet and bitter freedom;

and to the Lord whom I adore and thank,
who rules the heavens truly with His brow,
I turn in weariness; I've had enough.

oaks and elms:
trees that lose
their leaves,
signifying the
poet's mortality,
which he accepts
painfully

364

Twenty-one years
... ten more: 1358

Twenty-one years Love held me in the fire,
joyfully burning, full of hope and sorrow;
then ten more years of weeping since my lady
rose into Heaven and my heart went with her.

Now I am weary, and I blame my life
for so much error, which almost extinguished
the seed of virtue. And I dedicate
its final moments, my high God, to You,

penitent, sorry for my misspent years
which should have gone to better purposes,
to seeking peace and turning from my troubles.

Lord, You who put me in this prison cell:
bring me out safe, clear of eternal harm,
for I repent and do not make excuses.

365

I go around in tears about my past
which I spent loving something mortal, earthly,
and did not soar in flight, though I had wings
to make myself a less than base example.

You who can see my wickedness and suffering,
invisible, immortal King of Heaven:
help my frail soul that has been lost and strayed
and with your grace fill up her emptiness,

so that although I've lived in war and storm,
I yet may die in peace and in safe harbor,
my sojourn vain but my departure just.

Upon the little life that's left to me,
and on my death, I pray You'll put Your hand:
You know full well I look to no one else.

366

Beautiful Virgin, dressed in glorious sunlight,
crowned with the stars, who pleased the highest Sun
so greatly that He hid His light in you:
love drives me to address you, speaking praise,
but I cannot begin without your help
and His who loved and placed Himself in you.
    I call on her who always has replied
to those who called in faith.
Virgin, if mercy turns
to human things when misery is extreme
and sees their sufferings, bend to my prayer,
give succor to my war
though I am earth and you   are queen of Heaven.

    Wisest Virgin, numbered and praised among
the virgins who are blessèd and most wise,
and first among them, with the brightest lamp,
oh, steady shield to the afflicted people
against the blows of Death and fickle Fortune,
through whom they can escape and even triumph,
    oh, refuge and relief from those blind passions
that burn us foolish mortals:
Virgin, your lovely eyes
that gaze in sorrow on the frightful wounds
that have been opened in your Son's dear limbs,
turn to my doubtful state.
I come disconsolate   to you for counsel.

    Purest Virgin, whole in every part,
Daughter and mother both, of your great offspring,
you who bring light to this earth and to Heaven:
through you your Son, Son of the highest Father
(oh, glowing window in the lofty Heaven),
came down to save us in the latter days;
    you were elected, among earthly dwellings,
you were the chosen one.
Oh, blessed Virgin, then,

you who convert the tears of Eve to joy,
make me, for you can, worthy of His love,
you who are endlessly blessed,
you who sit crowned above   in the high kingdom.

Holy Virgin, full of every grace,
who through your true and high humility
mounted to Heaven, where you hear my prayers:
you who gave birth to Pity's Fountain,
and to the Sun of Justice, who brings light
into a world that's dark and full of error.
You've gathered three sweet names unto yourself:
mother, bride, and daughter,
Vergine gloriosa,
Lady unto that King who loosed our bonds
and made the world felicitous and free,
upon whose holy wounds,
I pray, quiet my heart   bringer of joy.

Matchless Virgin, unique in all the world,
who made high Heaven love you for your beauty,
which no one has surpassed, or even neared:
your holy thoughts, your mercy and chaste actions,
made you a sacred and a living temple
which God could visit in its ripe virginity.
Through you my life can come to proper joy
if at your prayers, oh, Mary,
Virgin sweet and pious,
grace comes abundant where sin thrived before.
I kneel before you on my mind's bent knees,
beg you to be my guide,
make straight my twisted path   to a good end.

Bright Virgin, stable for eternity,
the star that shines above this stormy sea,
the guide that faithful helmsmen come to know:
see what a dreadful storm I'm captured by,
sailing along alone, without a tiller,
close to the final shouts with which I'll drown.

But still my soul looks up to you for help,
sinful though it may be,
Virgin, I don't deny it,
I beg your enemy may not deride me.
Remember that our sins made God adopt
the flesh of human life   in your pure cloister.

Virgin, how many tears I've scattered here,
how many pleadings, how many prayers in vain,
and naught to show for them but pain and loss!
Since I was born, upon the Arno's bank,
searching now one way, and now another,
my life has only been a heap of troubles:
    mortal beauty, mortal acts and words
have burdened all my soul.
Virgin, do not delay,
holy and life-giving one, I'm near the end;
swifter than arrows my days have gone away
in wretchedness and sin,
and all that lies ahead   is Death, expectant.

Virgin, there's one who's dust, who makes my soul
grieve greatly, one who kept it, one who knew
nothing about my thousand sufferings;
and if she had, I don't think anything
would have been any different, since desire
would have been death to me, to her dishonor.
    Now you, the Queen of Heaven, you our goddess
(if that's appropriate),
Virgin of greatest sense:
there's nothing you don't see, and what another
would find impossible is well within your power:
close down my sorrows, since
that would bring honor to you   me, salvation.

Virgin, in whom my hopes all now reside
that you both can and will address my need:
do not abandon me at this last pass,
think not of me but of the one who made me,

not my own worth but His great likeness in me,
may that move you to care for one so low.
    Medusa and my sin have made me stone
dripping a little moisture.
Virgin, fill up my heart
with tears of holiness and true repentance;
at least my weeping should become devout
and free of earthly mud
as I was at the first   when not insane.

    Virgin so kind, the enemy of pride,
let love of our joint origin inflame you:
have pity on a bowed and humbled heart.
If I can love with such a glowing faith
a bit of mortal and corrupted dust,
how greatly will I love a noble thing?
    If from this state, so wretched and so vile,
I rise up by your hands,
Virgin, to your name then
I consecrate my thoughts and wit and style,
my tongue and my poor heart, my tears and sighs.
Show me the way to cross
as you gaze kindly on   my changed desires.

    The day draws near, it cannot be far off,
time speeds along and flies,
Virgin unique, alone,
conscience and death are stabbing at my heart:
commend me to your Son, who is the true
man and the true God,
may He accept   my last and peaceful breath.

Index of First Lines

Beautiful soul, freed from the knot that was, 216
Beautiful Virgin, dressed in glorious sunlight, 260
Because our life is brief, 57
Because she bore Love's ensign in her face, 47
Because the bright, angelic sight of her, 201
Below the foothills where she first put on, 6
Between two lovers once I saw a lady, 89
Bitter tears come raining down my face, 11
Blessed in sleep and languishing, contented, 158
Both Love and I are full of sheer amazement, 129
Bright sparks came from that pair of lovely lights, 184
But now that her sweet smile, soft and humble, 36
By the Tyrrhenian Sea, on its left bank, 54

Caesar and Jove were never so much moved, 126
Casting your eyes upon my strange new pallor, 51
Charlemagne's inheritor, who wears, 21
Clear waters, fresh and sweet, 100
Could I portray the gentle breeze of sighs, 206
Cruel star (if heavens have indeed the power, 136

Death has no way to make her sweet face bitter, 250
Death has put out the sun that dazzled me;, 258
Death, you have left this poor world cold and dark, 240
Desire spurs me on, Love guides and escorts, 158
Diana's form did not delight her lover, 43

Each day seems longer than a thousand years, 250

Father of Heaven, after days now lost, 51
Flame of my soul, lovely beyond all beauty, 208
For any animal who dwells on earth, 13
For seventeen long years the heavens have rolled, 96
Fountain of sorrow, dwelling place of anger, 117
From ice that's clear, alive, and smooth and shining, 150
From the most lovely eyes, the brightest face, 245
From thought to thought, from peak to mountain peak, 108
From time to time it seems her form and smile, 123

From wicked Babylon, that's lost all shame, 89
Full of one longing thought that sends me far, 133
Full of that sweet ineffable delight, 90

"Gaze on that hill, my tired, yearning heart:, 176
Gentle, my lady, I can see, 60
Geri, when my sweet enemy gets angry, 138
Give me my peace, oh, all you cruel thoughts!, 200
Glorious Column, raising up our hope, 7
Go, doleful rhymes, and visit the hard stone, 238
Go forth, hot sighs, and reach to her cold heart, 125
"Go on and weep, my eyes: accompany, 72
Gorging and sleep and lounging on pillows, 6
Graces that bounteous Heaven grants to few, 159
Green garments, blood red, black, or purple, 25

Hannibal won but later did not know, 81
"Happy and pensive, in company, alone, 164
Here where I half exist, my dear Sennuccio, 88
Her golden hair was loosened to the breeze, 75
Her lovely paleness made a cloud of love, 96
He who decides to entrust his life, 69
He who showed endless providence and art, 4
However many lovely, graceful ladies, 162
How many times, in flight and seeking refuge, 204
How many times Love has instructed me:, 76
How many times, using my faithful guides, 134
How much I envy you, you greedy earth, 213
How this world goes! For what upset me once, 208

I am so weary from my ancient bundle, 70
I can't be silent, yet I fear my tongue, 227
I'd like to take revenge on her, whose gaze, 183
I do not tire, Lady, of my love, 71
I don't see anymore how to escape;, 85
I'd sing of Love in such a novel fashion, 111
I fear their fierce attack, those lovely eyes, 35
I feed my mind upon a food so noble, 145

I feel the ancient aura, and I see, 223
If fair desire's still alive, Apollo, 29
If faithfulness in love, a heart sincere, 165
If fire never puts a fire out, 39
If Homer and then Virgil had but seen, 142
If I could get my thoughts down in these verses, 77
If I could hope by death to free myself, 30
If I do not deceive myself too much, 48
If I'd remained within that selfsame cave, 132
If I had known that sighs turned into rhyme, 210
If I hear birds lamenting, or green leaves, 203
I find no peace, and yet I am not warlike;, 112
If I said that, then may the one whose love, 152
If it's not love, what is it then I feel?, 111
I fled the prison in which Love had held me, 74
If Love and Death don't manage to cut short, 35
If Love does not come up with some new counsel, 202
I fly so often on the wings of thought, 258
If my life can withstand this bitter torment, 8
If that much-honored branch that shelters us, 19
If that sweet glance of hers can murder me, 140
If the rock mainly shuts this valley, 90
If the thoughts that hurt me, 97
If virtuous love is worthy, still, of mercy, 238
If you got free by any strange behavior—, 52
I go around in tears about my past, 259
I knew (since Heaven cleared my eyes so much, 241
I know quite well that natural advice, 55
I listen still, and still I hear no news, 182
I lived quite well contented with my fate, 169
I'll always hate the window from which Love, 73
I make my plaint before the queen who rules, 253
I'm never going to look with tranquil mind, 224
I'm so defeated by this endless wait, 78
I'm weary now of thinking how my thoughts, 66
In doubt about my state I weep, I sing, 181
I never saw the sun come up so fair, 121
I never wish to sing   the way I used to, 82
In just a single day I have been shown, 137

In noble blood a quiet, humble life, 161
Inside my heart I felt my spirits dying, 39
In that direction where I'm spurred by Love, 102
In the age of her lovely flowering, 202
In the sweet season of my early youth, 14
I sang and now I weep; and from my weeping, 168
I saw a maiden underneath a laurel, 26
I saw, among a thousand ladies, one, 239
I saw on earth angelic attributes, 127
I seem to hear, each hour, in my ear, 246
Italy, my Italy, though speech cannot, 105
I thought by now perhaps that I could live, 153
I thought I had the skill to soar in flight, 217
It is so weak, the thread by which it hangs, 31
It was the day the sun himself grew pale, 4
It was the time to find a peace or truce, 221
I used to leave the fountain of my life, 233
I've always loved, I go on loving still, 72
I've always sought a solitary life—, 185
I've begged Love before, and beg him again, 175
I've filled the whole surrounding air with sighs, 207
I've never been where I could see more clearly, 203
I've never seen you put aside your veil, 8
I've now passed through my sixteenth year of sighs, 91
I walk in thought, and in my thoughts I am, 187
I wanted once to shape such just laments, 162
I wept and now I sing, because that sun, 168

Just as eternal life means seeing God, 144

Lady, now living in our Maker's presence, 245
Latona's son had looked nine times already, 37
Life-giving sun, you loved that branch at first, 143
—"Life is most precious, so it seems to me, 186
Life runs on by and does not pause an hour, 199
Love, Fortune, and my mind—which now avoids, 97
Love fires up my heart with ardent zeal, 140
Love helped me sail into a tranquil harbor, 222
Love, I do wrong and see that I do wrong, 171

Love, let us pause to contemplate our glory, 145
Love opened my left side with his right hand, 167
Love sends me that sweet thought, the one which is, 133
Love sets me up, a target for his arrows, 112
Love spreads out in the grass a graceful net, 139
Love spurs me on and reins me in at once, 138
Love's put me in the grasp of fair, cruel arms, 134
Love that lives and reigns in all my thoughts, 118
Love took me in with all his promises, 67
Love used to cry, and I would cry with him, 20
Love, you who can see clearly all my thoughts, 130
Lucky, happy flowers, and well-born grass, 130

Maybe Love makes her drop her lovely eyes, 132
May fire from Heaven rain down on your tresses, 116
Mind, you foresaw your pains and injuries, 220
More fortunate than any other earth, 86
My enemy, in whom you watch your eyes, 38
My eyes, intense and heavy with desire, 184
My eyes, our sun's gone dark; or rather say, 201
My face and hair are changing, day by day, 146
My faithful mirror tells me very often, 257
My flowering green age was passing by, 221
My fortune kindly and my life so joyful, 235
My fourteenth year of sighs: if its beginning, 68
My galley, loaded with forgetfulness, 143
My good luck is both late and very sluggish;, 48
My ills oppress me; I'm terrified by worse, 177
My lady used to visit me in sleep, 180
My luck, along with Love, had blessed me so, 149
My mad desire has gone so far astray, 5
My sacred *aura* breathes so often, in, 249
My soft and gentle comforter arrives, 251
My sweet and dear and greatly cherished pledge, 241
My thoughts would once chat softly to themselves, 211
My thought transported me to where she was, 214
My weary eyes, when I direct you toward, 9

Nature, and Love, and that sweet, humble soul, 141
Never did tender mother her dear son, 206
New song and weeping by the birds at daybreak, 163
Noble spirit, you who rule those limbs, 43
No matter where I turn my weary eyes, 128
No ship that ever landed, weather-racked, 20
No sparrow on a roof was as alone, 166
Not from the Spanish river Ebro to, 157
No tired helmsman ever fled to port, 124
Not just that single naked hand, 149
Not lovely stars that wander through clear skies, 219
Not Tesin, Po, Varo, Arno, Adige, Tiber, 123
Now look at this, Love: how a youthful woman, 95
Now that the heavens, earth, and winds are silent, 131
Now when I listen to you speak, so sweetly, 120
Now you have done the worst you can accomplish, 231
Now Zephyrus returns, bringing fine weather, 218

Oh, blessed and lovely soul, which Heaven waits for, 21
Oh day, oh hour, oh, the final moment, 232
Oh, Death, you have stained the loveliest face, 205
Oh, Envy, you old enemy of virtue, 135
Oh, fresh and shady, flowering green hill, 177
Oh, glances sweet and little words of wisdom, 182
Oh, happy spirit that so sweetly governed, 247
Oh, little room that used to be a haven, 170
Oh, lovely hand that grasps my heart, enclosing, 148
Oh, noble spirit warm with burning virtue, 122
Oh, put me where the sun kills flowers and grass, 121
Oh, scattered steps, oh, ardent, craving thoughts, 129
Oh, time, oh, fickle heavens, wheeling past, 249
Oh, valley echoing with my laments, 214
Oh, woe, Love takes me where I do not wish, 171
Oh, wretched vision, horrid likelihood!, 181
Once I accused myself, now I excuse, 211
One day as I stood gazing from my window, 225
Out of what mine did Love extract the gold, 163

The closer that I come to the last day, 28
The column's broken, the green laurel's down, 195
The day, the month, the year, oh, bless them all, 50
The golden feathers that surround her white, 141
The gold, the pearls, the flowers red and white, 38
The gracious lady whom you loved so much, 75
The heavenly breeze that sighs in that green laurel, 147
The high, new miracle that in our time, 218
The lady whom my heart is always watching, 87
The last, alas, of all my happy days, 232
The longed-for virtue that was flowering in you, 82
The man whose hands were ready to turn Thessaly, 37
The more I spread my wings, filled with desire, 117
The noble tree I've loved so many years, 50
Then when my heart was eaten by love's worms, 215
The one for whom I traded Sorgue for Arno, 217
There may have been a time when love was sweet, 243
There never was a lake or river, Orso, 34
The sacred prospect of your city makes, 55
The sea has fewer fish among its waves, 172
The soft breeze spreads and vibrates in the sunlight, 148
The star of love was flaming in the East, 29
The stars, the heavens, and the elements, 126
The sun that showed me how to get to Heaven, 216
The sweet hill country where I left myself, 157
The time is gone, alas, when I could live, 220
The time so short, the thought so swift that brings, 205
The tranquil breeze that passes, murmuring, 147
The way a simple butterfly, in summer, 118
This frail and brittle goodness that we cherish, 246
This humble wild thing, with tiger's heart, or bear's, 125
This noble breeze that clears the hills again, 146
This noble soul that starts to move away, 28
Those eyes I spoke about so heatedly, 209
Those lovely eyes that hurt me are the only, 66
Those verses full of pity where I saw, 95
Though you have left me, my Sennuccio, 207
To make a graceful one his sweet vendetta, 3

White-haired and pale, the old man takes his leave, 10
Whoever wants to see what Heaven and Nature, 179
With food my lord always provides profusely—, 242

You breezes that surround those curling tresses, 167
You, Love, who stayed with me in happy times, 215
Your charger, Orso, can be given reins, 79
You seem to show me, Love, that you would like, 196
You soul in bliss, who often come to me, 204
You, Soul, who see so many different things, 151